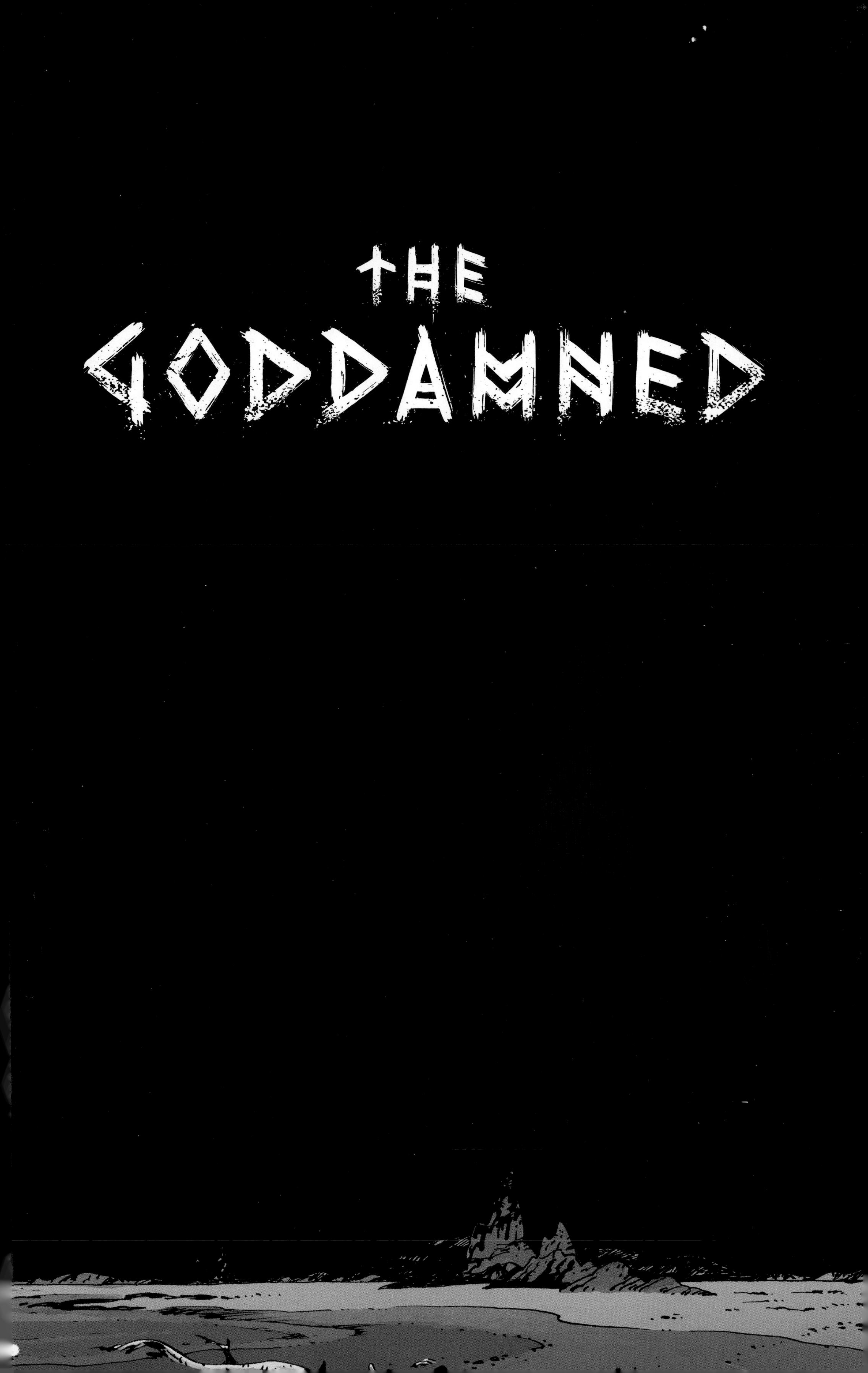
THE GODDAMNED

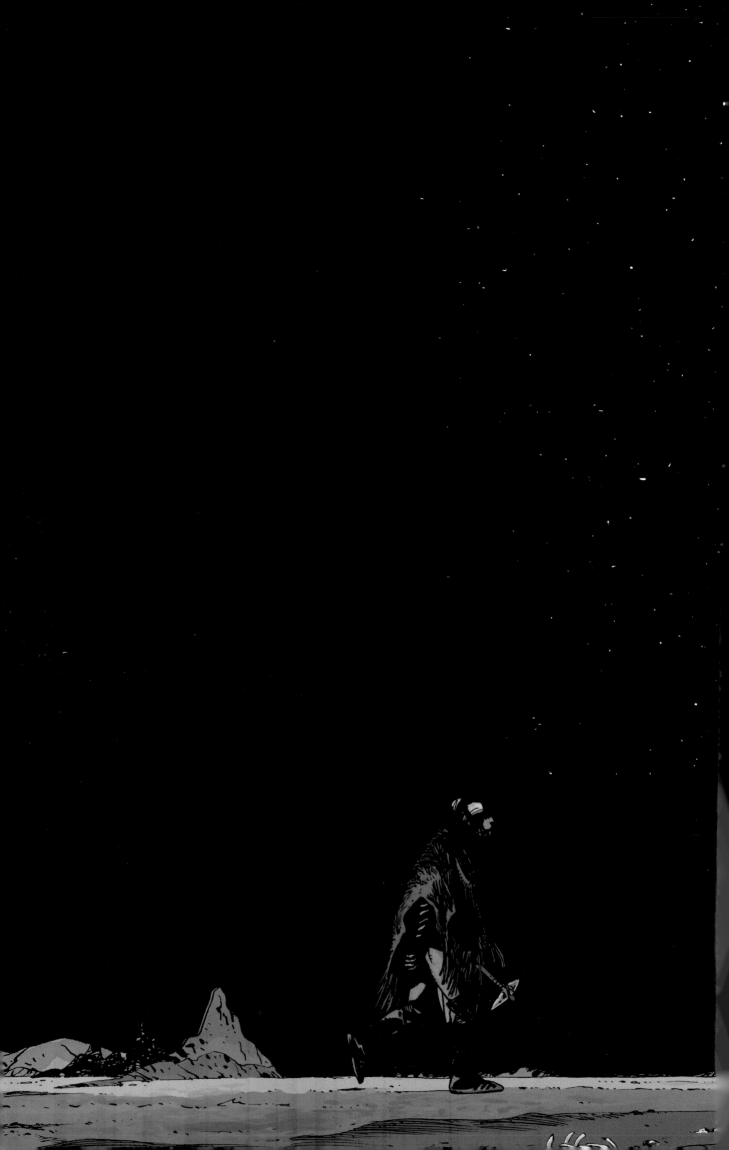

THE GODDAMNED

Book One

BEFORE THE FLOOD

written by

Jason Aaron

illustrated by

R.M. Guéra

colors by **Giulia Brusco**

letters + design **Jared K. Fletcher**

editor **Sebastian Girner**

The Goddamned *created by* Aaron & Guéra

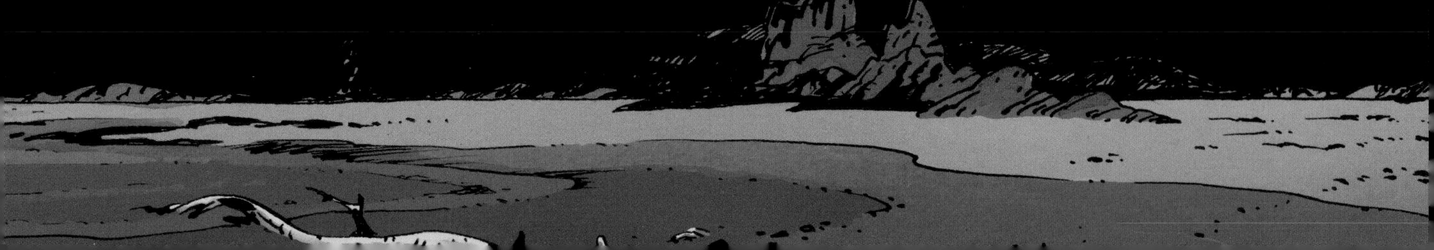

THE GODDAMNED OVERSIZED "BEFORE THE FLOOD" HC,
October 2017. First Printing. Published by Image Comics Inc.
Office of publication: 2701 NW Vaughn St., Suite 780, Portland,
OR 97210. Copyright © 2017 Golgonooza, Inc. and rmGuéra. All
rights reserved. Contains material originally published in single
magazine form as THE GODDAMNED #1-5. "The Goddamned,"
the The Goddamned logo, and all characters herein and the
likenesses thereof are trademarks of Golgonooza, Inc. and
rmGuéra, unless expressly indicated. "Image" and the Image
Comics logos are registered trademarks of Image Comics, Inc. No
part of this publication may be reproduced or transmitted in any
form or by any means (except for short excerpts for journalistic
or review purposes) without the express written permission of
Golgonooza, Inc., rmGuéra, or Image Comics, Inc. All names,
characters, events, and locales herein are entirely fictional. Any
resemblance to actual persons (living or dead), events, or places,
without satiric intent, is coincidental. Printed in the USA.

ISBN: 978-1-5343-0318-8

Representation: Law Offices of Harris M. Miller II, P.C. (rights.
inquiries@gmail.com).

chapter one

The Mark of Cain

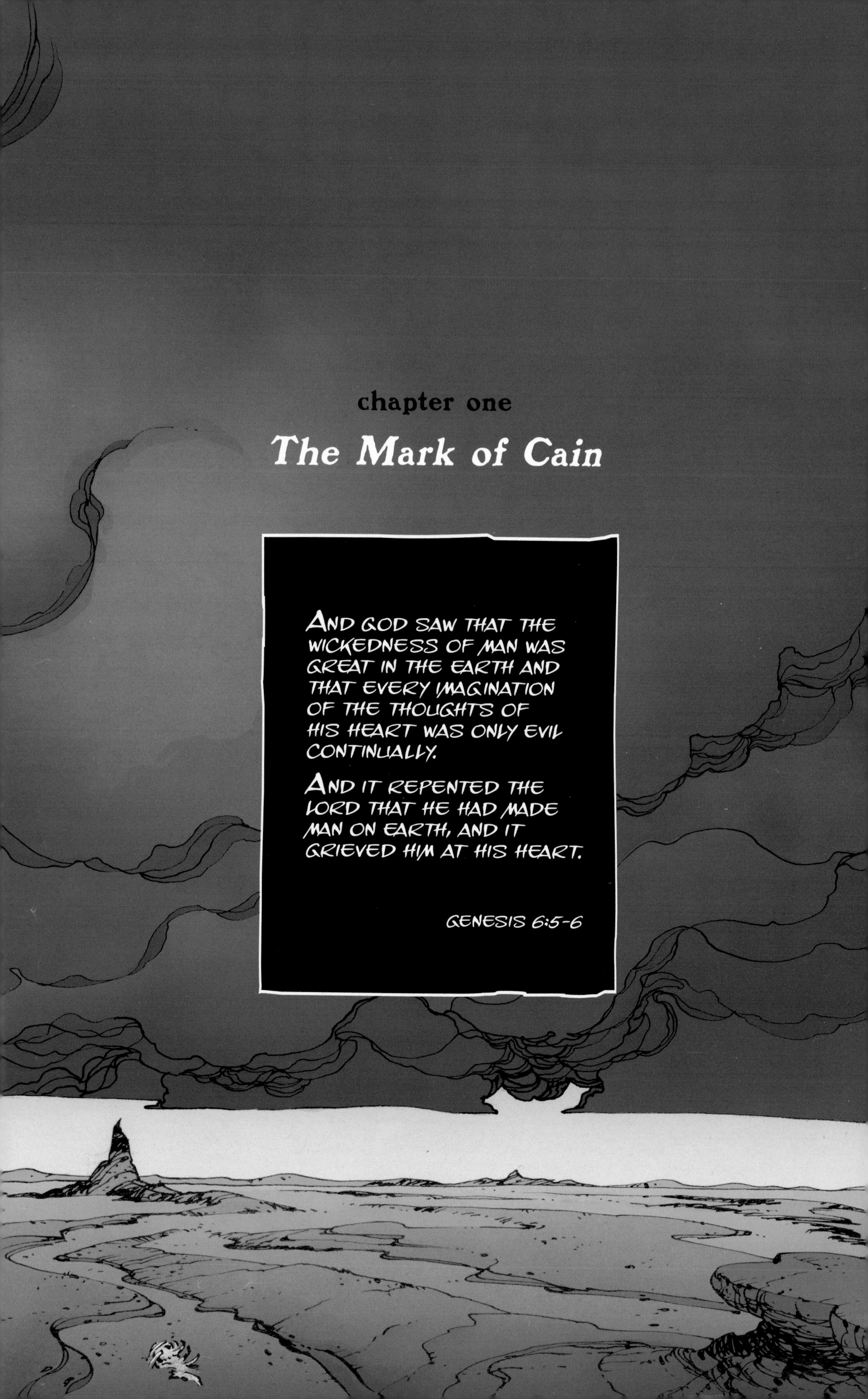
AND GOD SAW THAT THE WICKEDNESS OF MAN WAS GREAT IN THE EARTH AND THAT EVERY IMAGINATION OF THE THOUGHTS OF HIS HEART WAS ONLY EVIL CONTINUALLY.
AND IT REPENTED THE LORD THAT HE HAD MADE MAN ON EARTH, AND IT GRIEVED HIM AT HIS HEART.
GENESIS 6:5-6

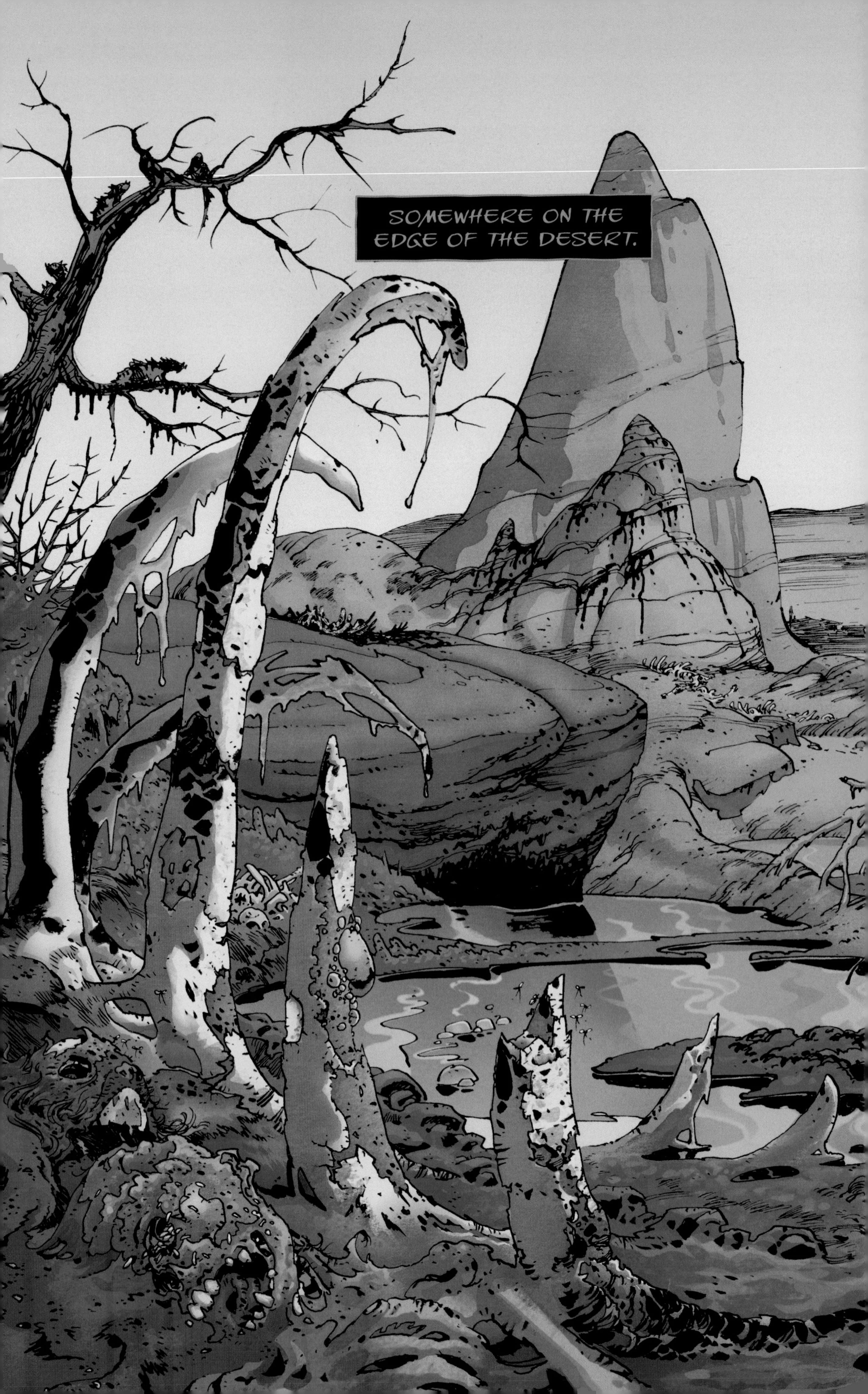
SOMEWHERE ON THE EDGE OF THE DESERT.

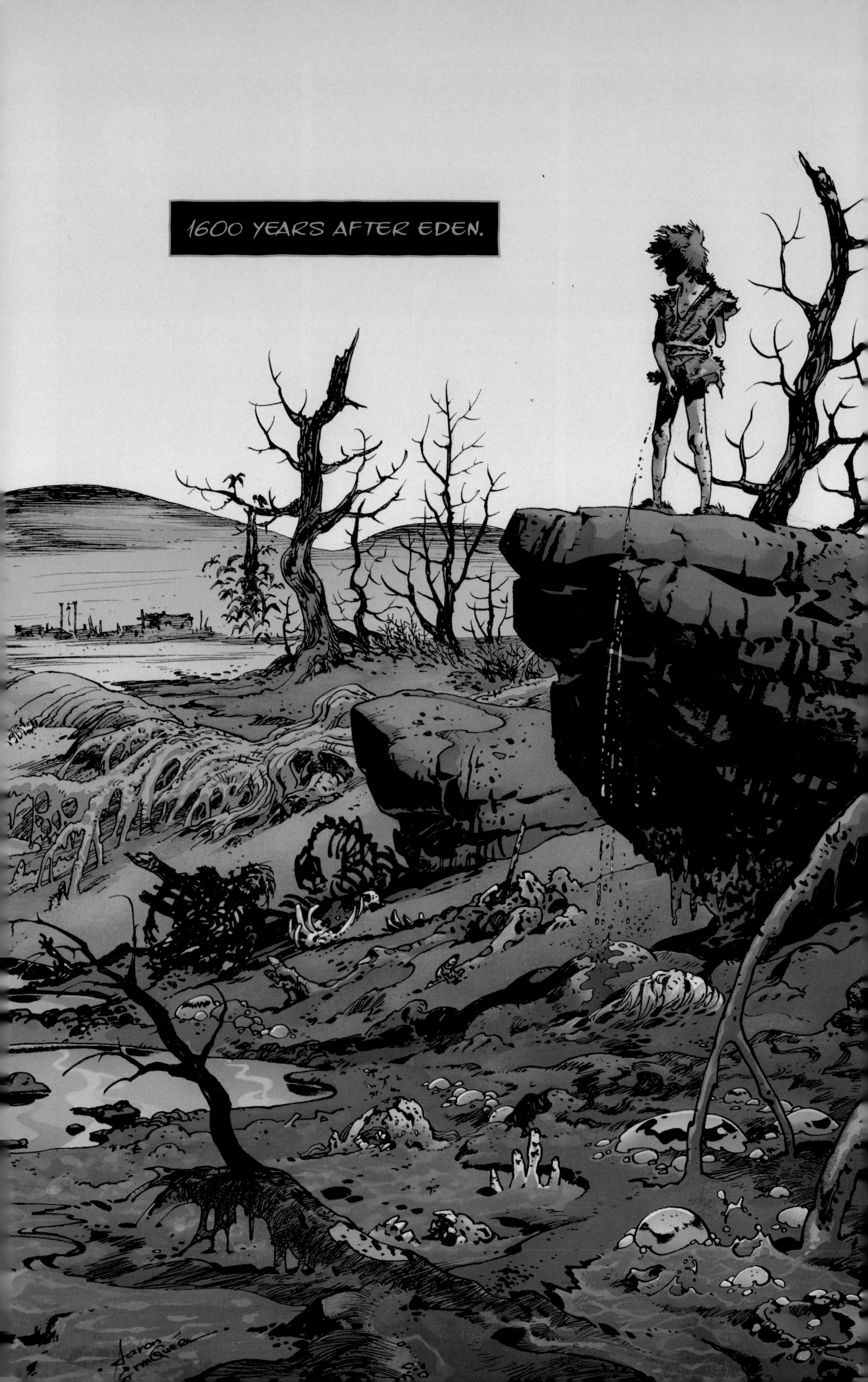
1600 YEARS AFTER EDEN.

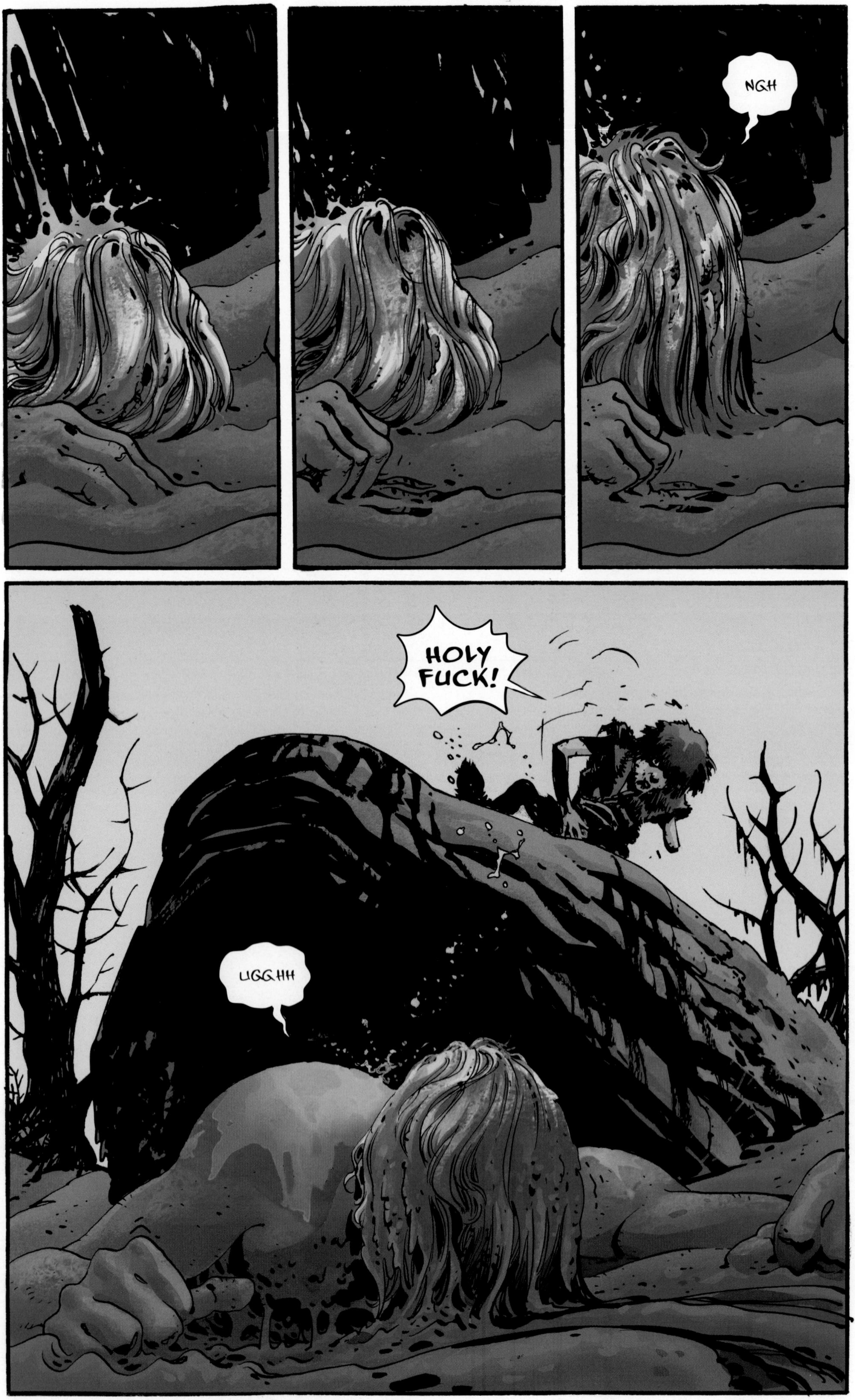
NGH
HOLY FUCK!
UGGHH

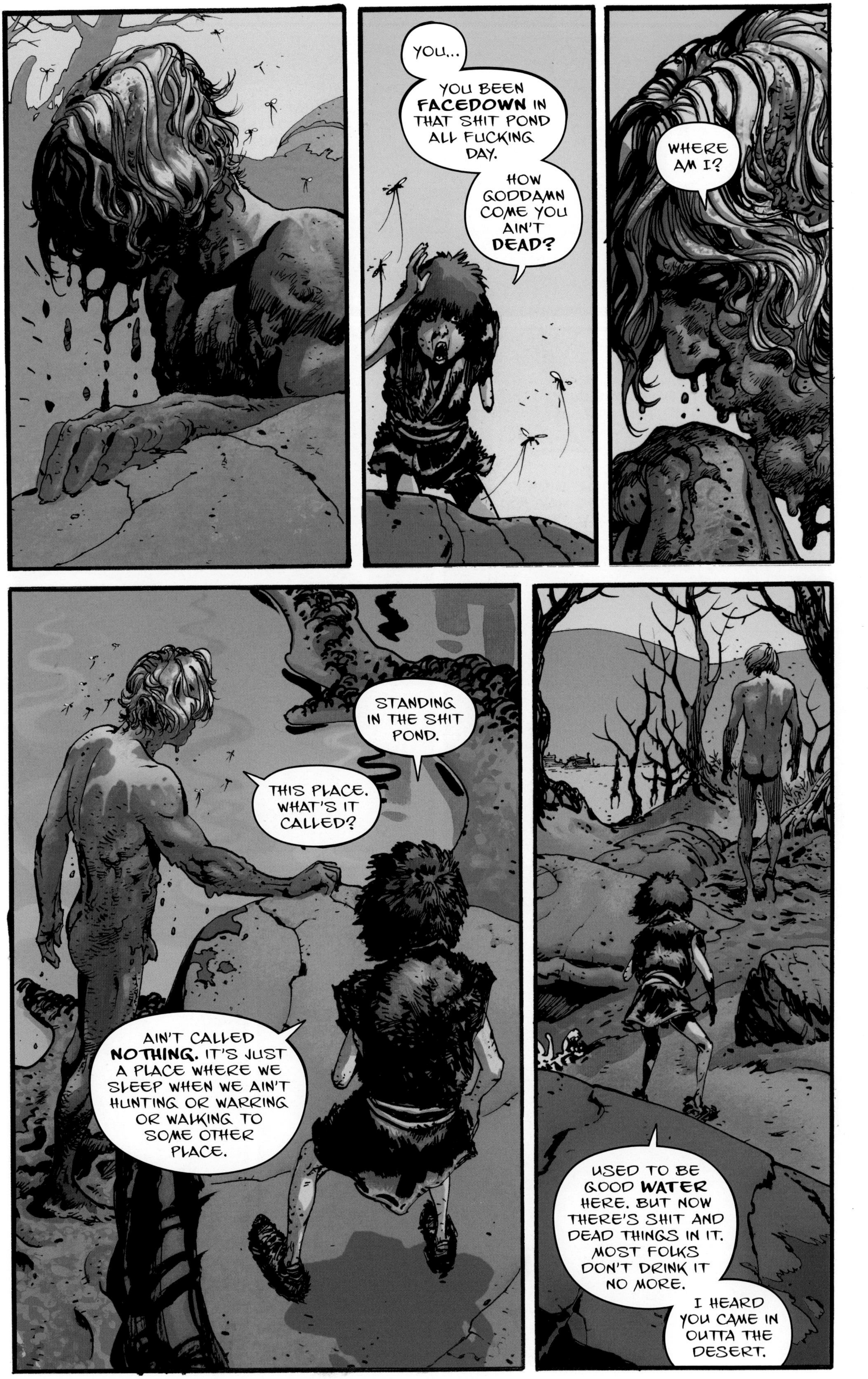
YOU...
YOU BEEN FACEDOWN IN THAT SHIT POND ALL FUCKING DAY.
HOW GODDAMN COME YOU AIN'T DEAD?
WHERE AM I?
STANDING IN THE SHIT POND.
THIS PLACE. WHAT'S IT CALLED?
AIN'T CALLED NOTHING. IT'S JUST A PLACE WHERE WE SLEEP WHEN WE AIN'T HUNTING OR WARRING OR WALKING TO SOME OTHER PLACE.
USED TO BE GOOD WATER HERE. BUT NOW THERE'S SHIT AND DEAD THINGS IN IT. MOST FOLKS DON'T DRINK IT NO MORE.
I HEARD YOU CAME IN OUTTA THE DESERT.

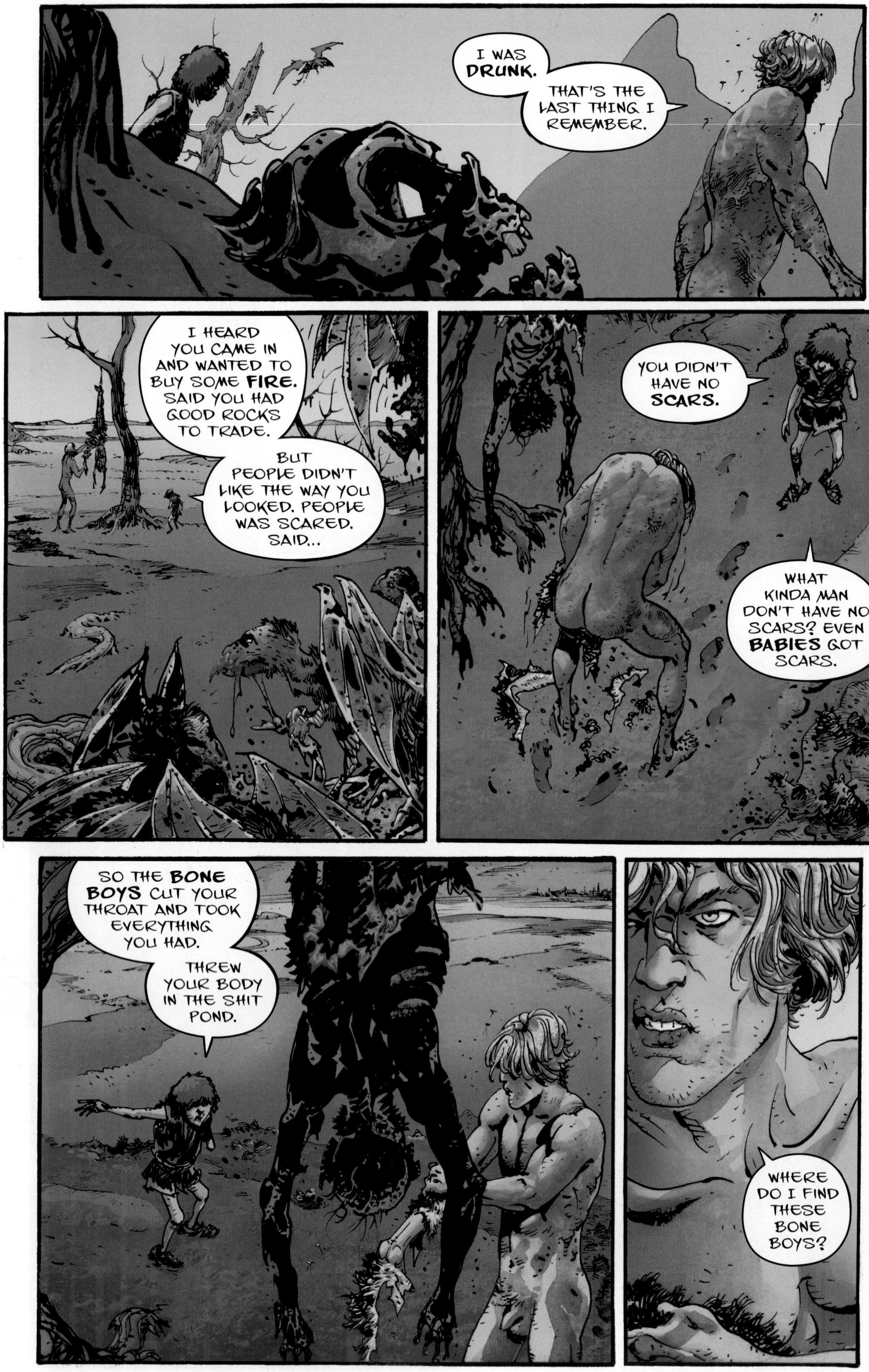
I WAS DRUNK.
THAT'S THE LAST THING I REMEMBER.
I HEARD YOU CAME IN AND WANTED TO BUY SOME FIRE. SAID YOU HAD GOOD ROCKS TO TRADE.
BUT PEOPLE DIDN'T LIKE THE WAY YOU LOOKED. PEOPLE WAS SCARED. SAID...
YOU DIDN'T HAVE NO SCARS.
WHAT KINDA MAN DON'T HAVE NO SCARS? EVEN BABIES GOT SCARS.
SO THE BONE BOYS CUT YOUR THROAT AND TOOK EVERYTHING YOU HAD.
THREW YOUR BODY IN THE SHIT POND.
WHERE DO I FIND THESE BONE BOYS?

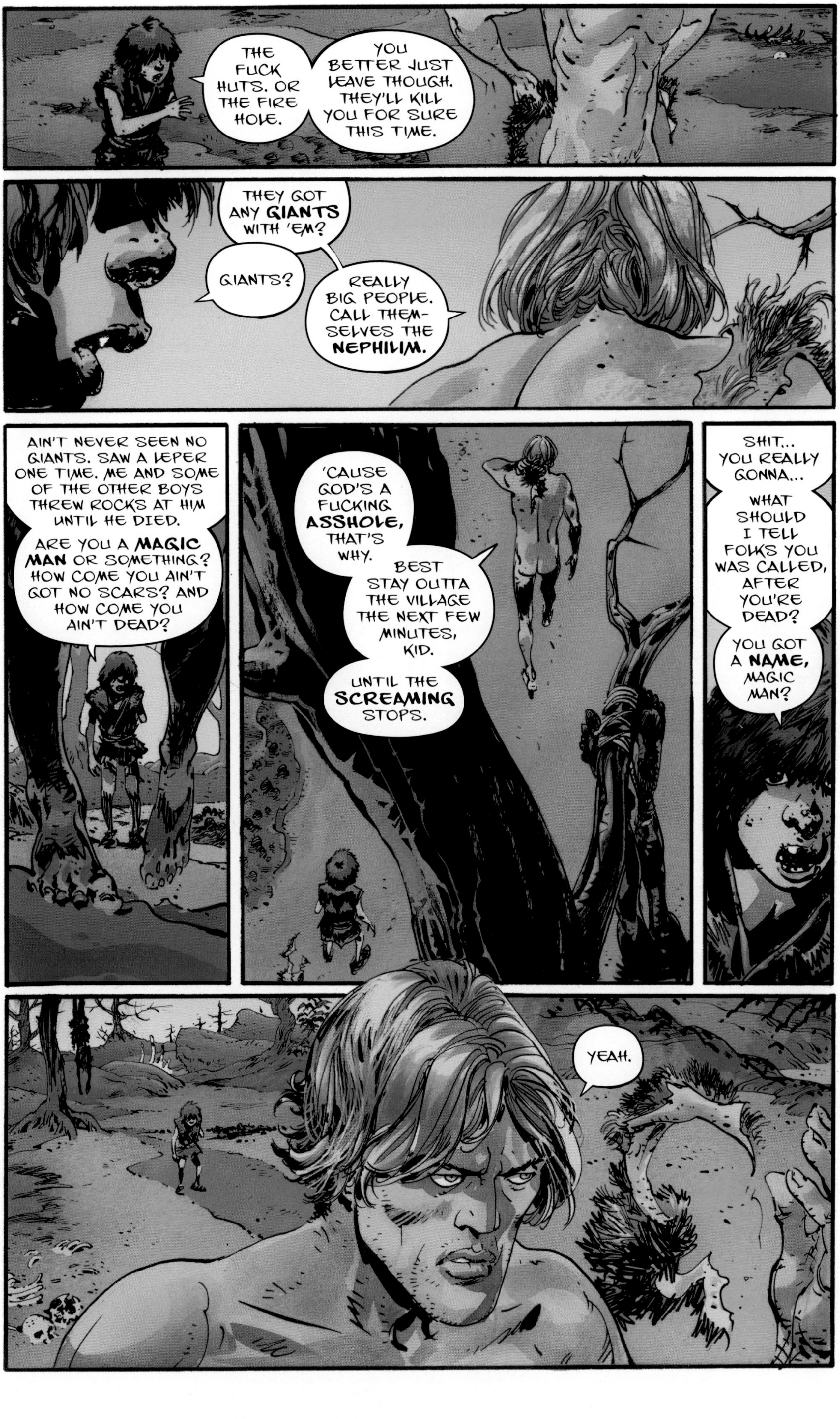
THE FUCK HUTS. OR THE FIRE HOLE.
YOU BETTER JUST LEAVE THOUGH. THEY'LL KILL YOU FOR SURE THIS TIME.
THEY GOT ANY **GIANTS** WITH 'EM?
GIANTS?
REALLY BIG PEOPLE. CALL THEMSELVES THE **NEPHILIM.**
AIN'T NEVER SEEN NO GIANTS. SAW A LEPER ONE TIME. ME AND SOME OF THE OTHER BOYS THREW ROCKS AT HIM UNTIL HE DIED.
ARE YOU A **MAGIC MAN** OR SOMETHING? HOW COME YOU AIN'T GOT NO SCARS? AND HOW COME YOU AIN'T DEAD?
'CAUSE GOD'S A FUCKING **ASSHOLE,** THAT'S WHY.
BEST STAY OUTTA THE VILLAGE THE NEXT FEW MINUTES, KID.
UNTIL THE **SCREAMING** STOPS.
SHIT... YOU REALLY GONNA...
WHAT SHOULD I TELL FOLKS YOU WAS CALLED, AFTER YOU'RE DEAD?
YOU GOT A **NAME,** MAGIC MAN?
YEAH.

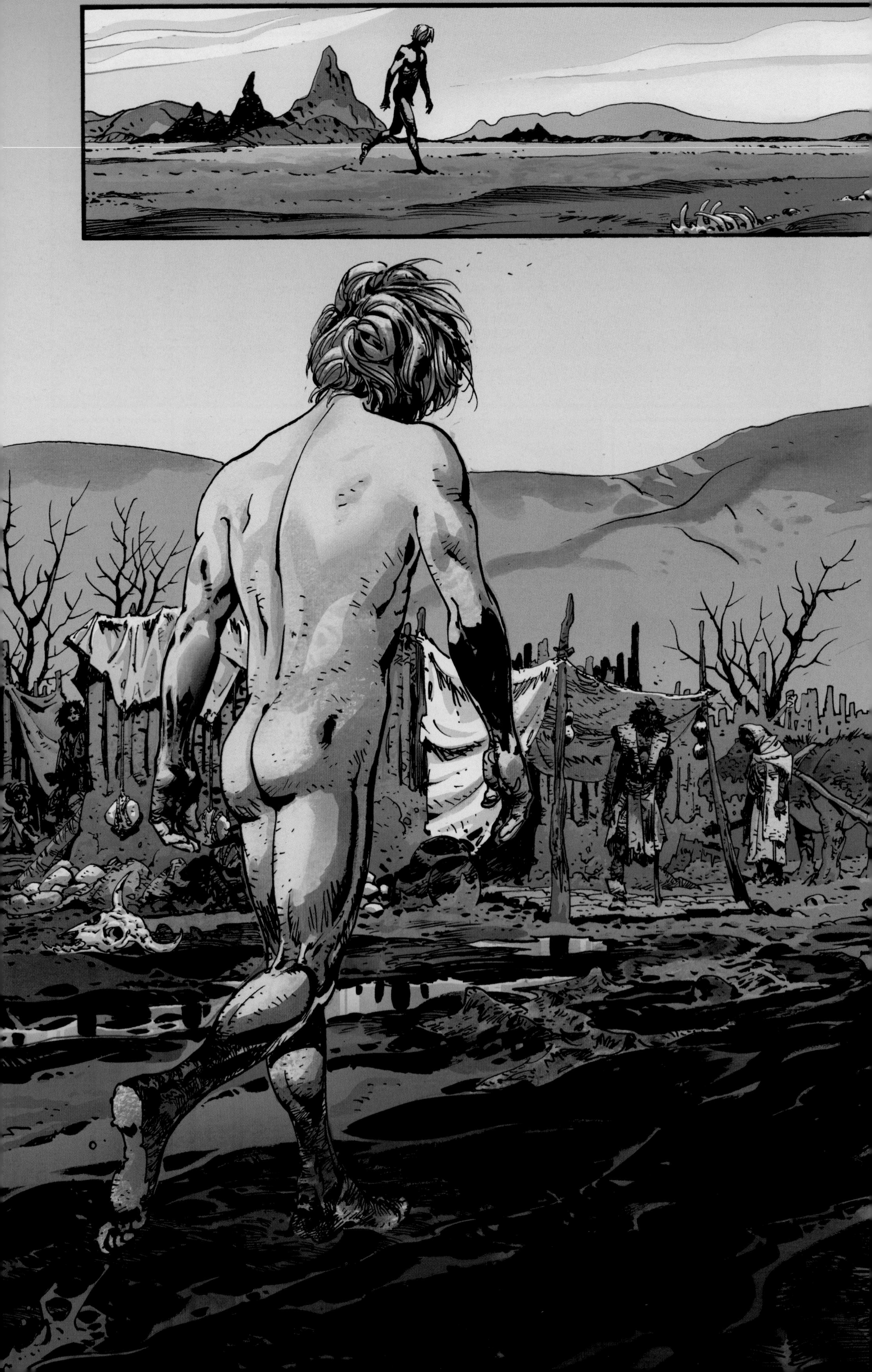

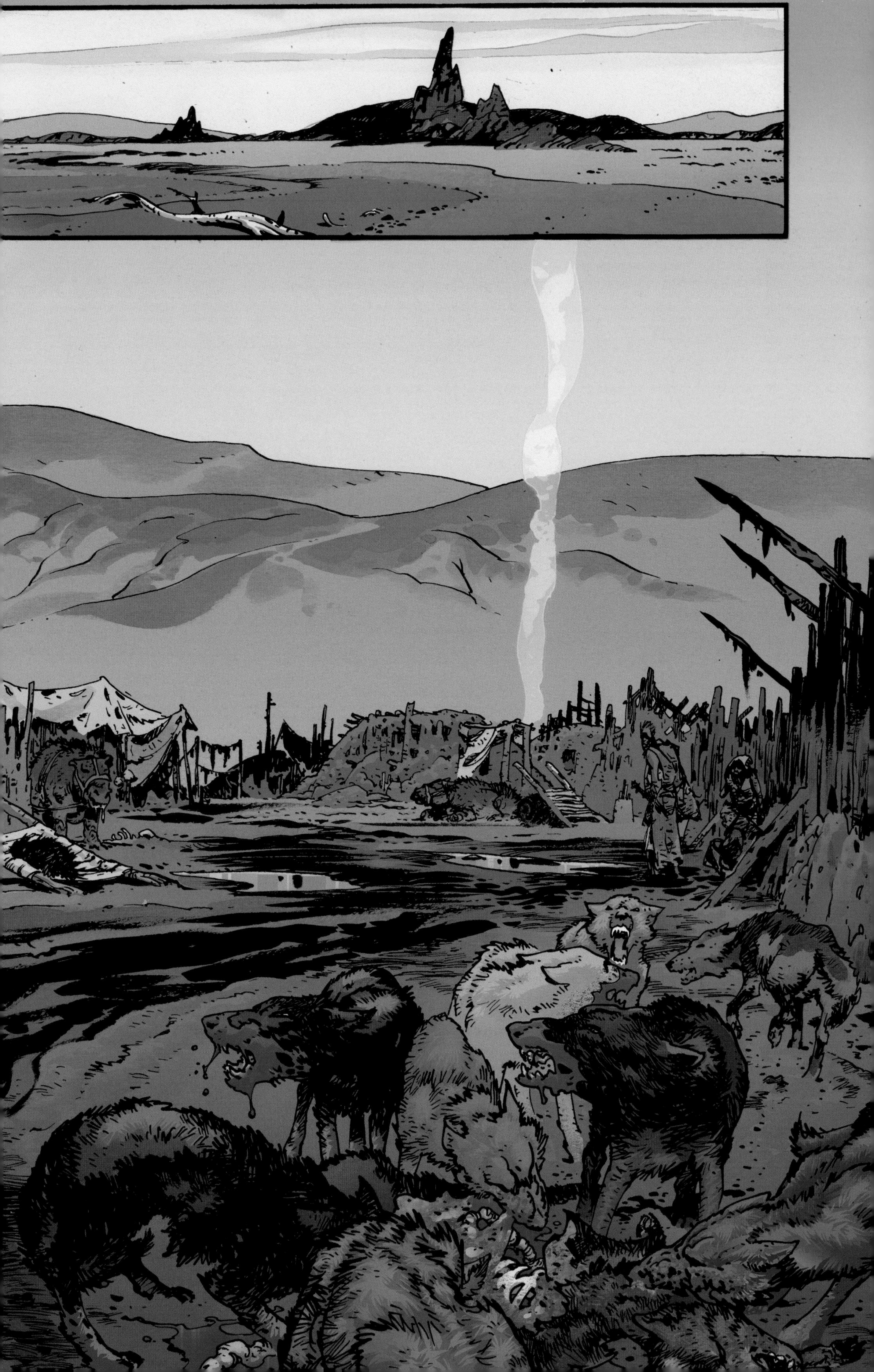

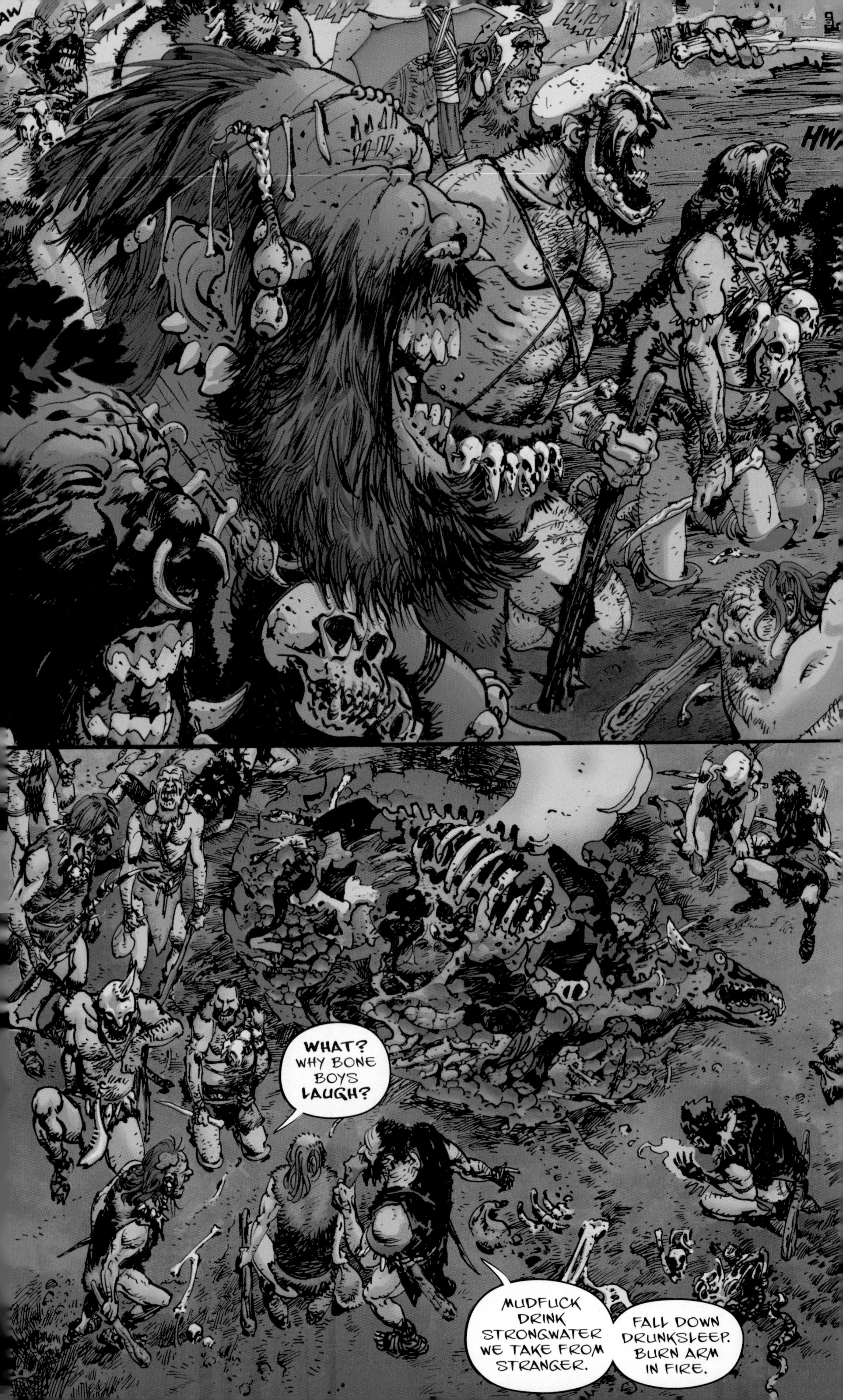
WHAT? WHY BONE BOYS LAUGH?
MUDFUCK DRINK STRONGWATER WE TAKE FROM STRANGER.
FALL DOWN DRUNKSLEEP. BURN ARM IN FIRE.

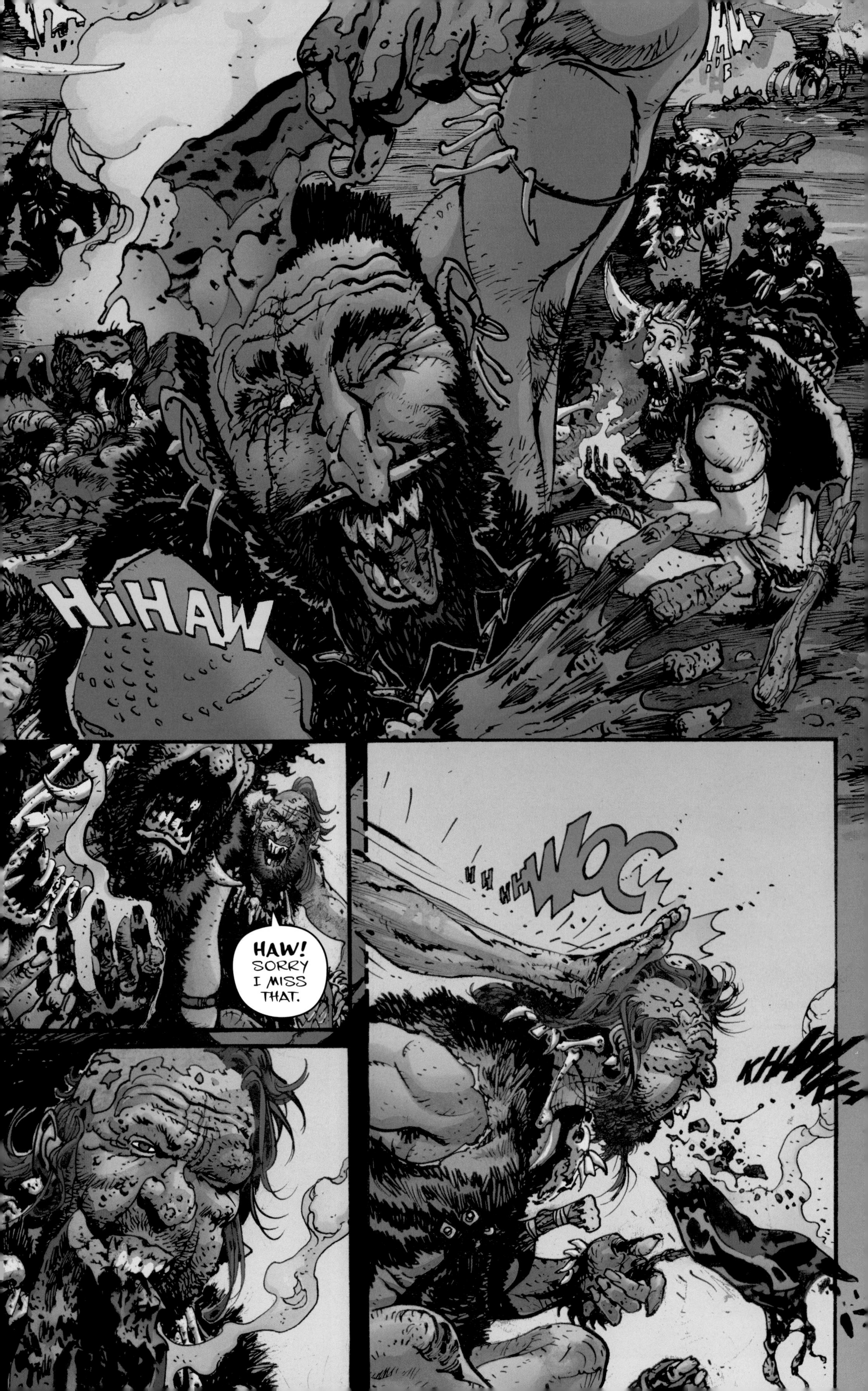
HiHAW
HAW! SORRY I MISS THAT.
WOC

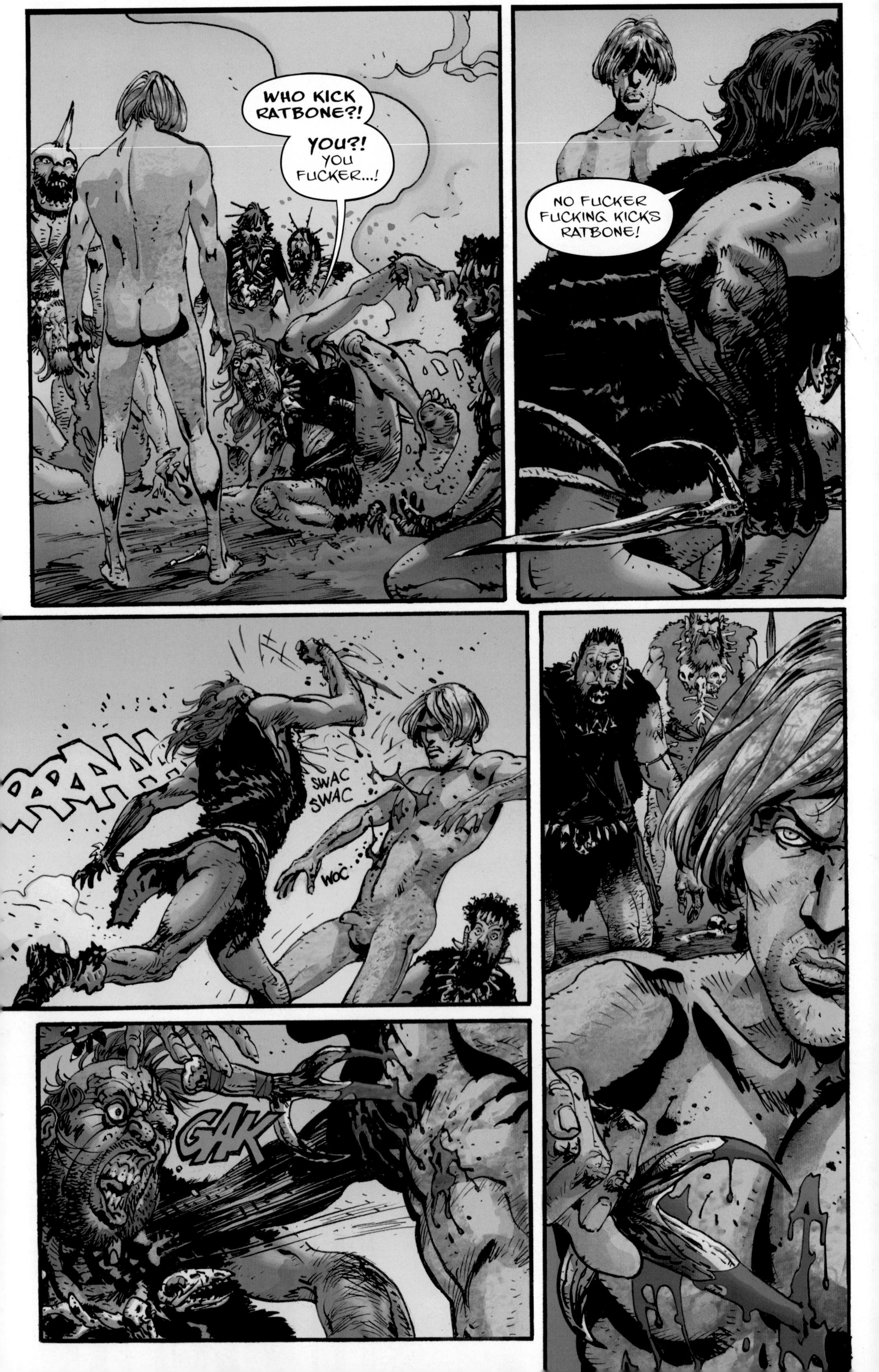
WHO KICK RATBONE?!
YOU?! YOU FUCKER...!
NO FUCKER FUCKING KICKS RATBONE!
SWAC SWAC
WOC
GAK

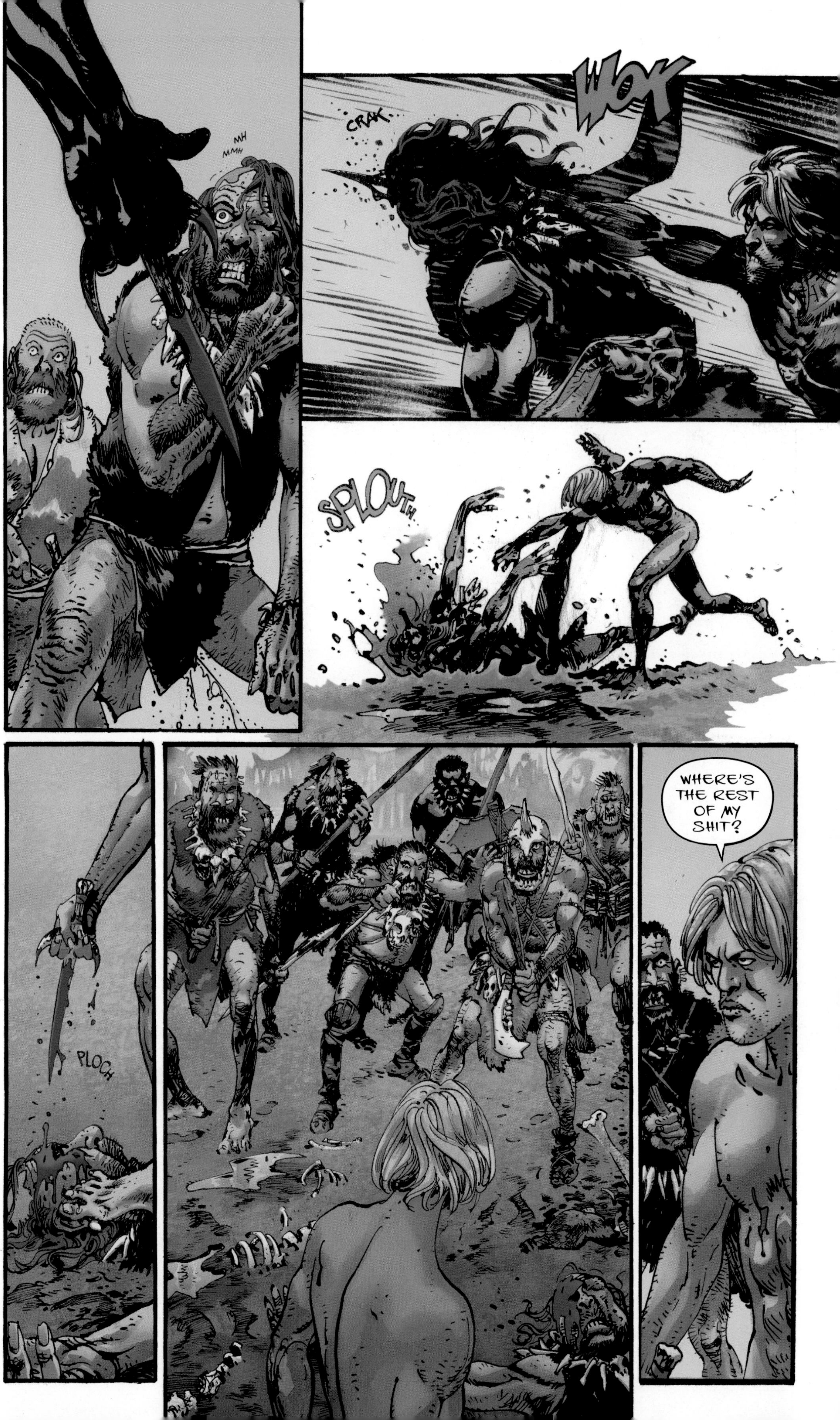
MH
MMH
CRAK
WOK
SPLOUTH
PLOCH
WHERE'S THE REST OF MY SHIT?

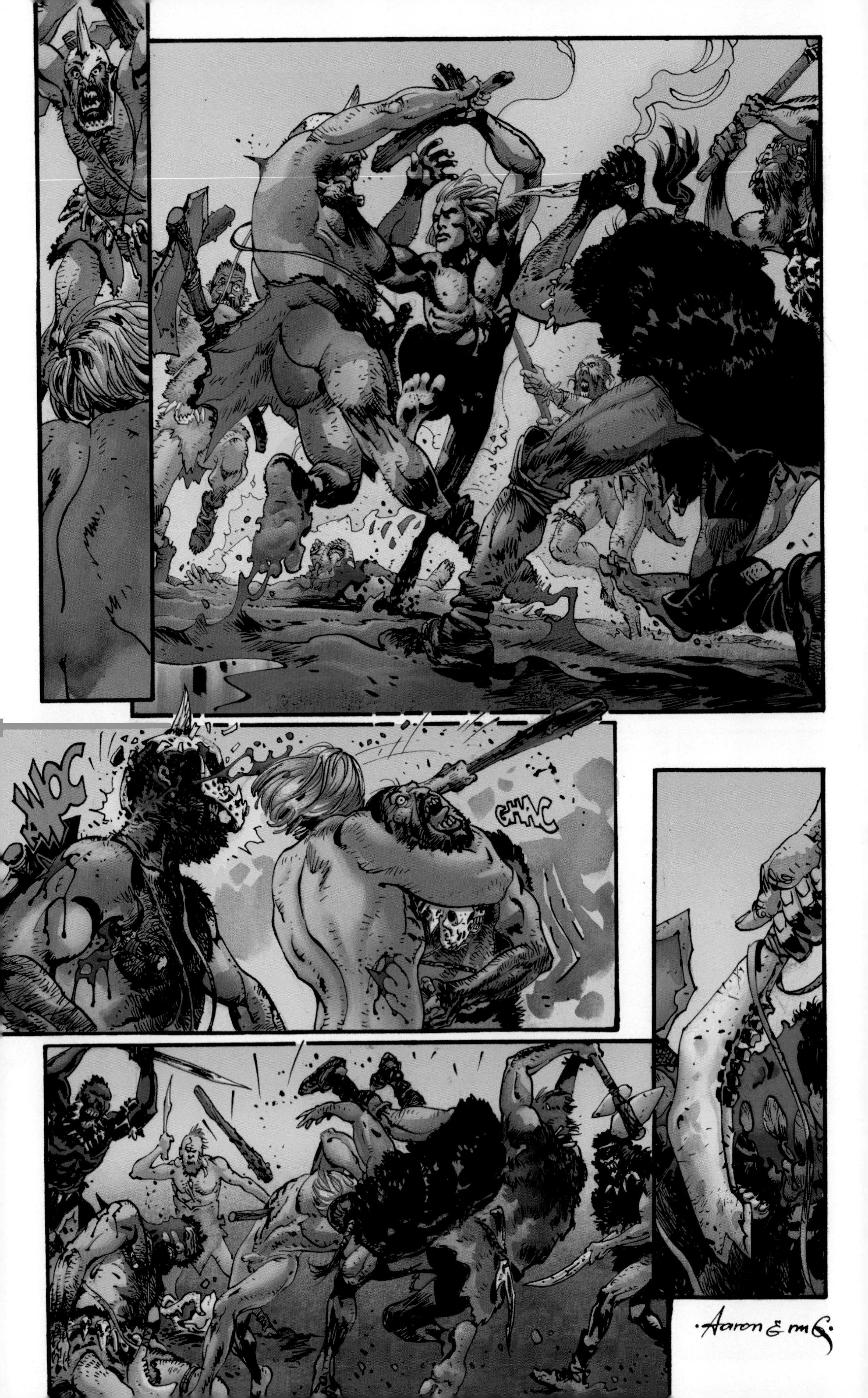
WOC
GHAC

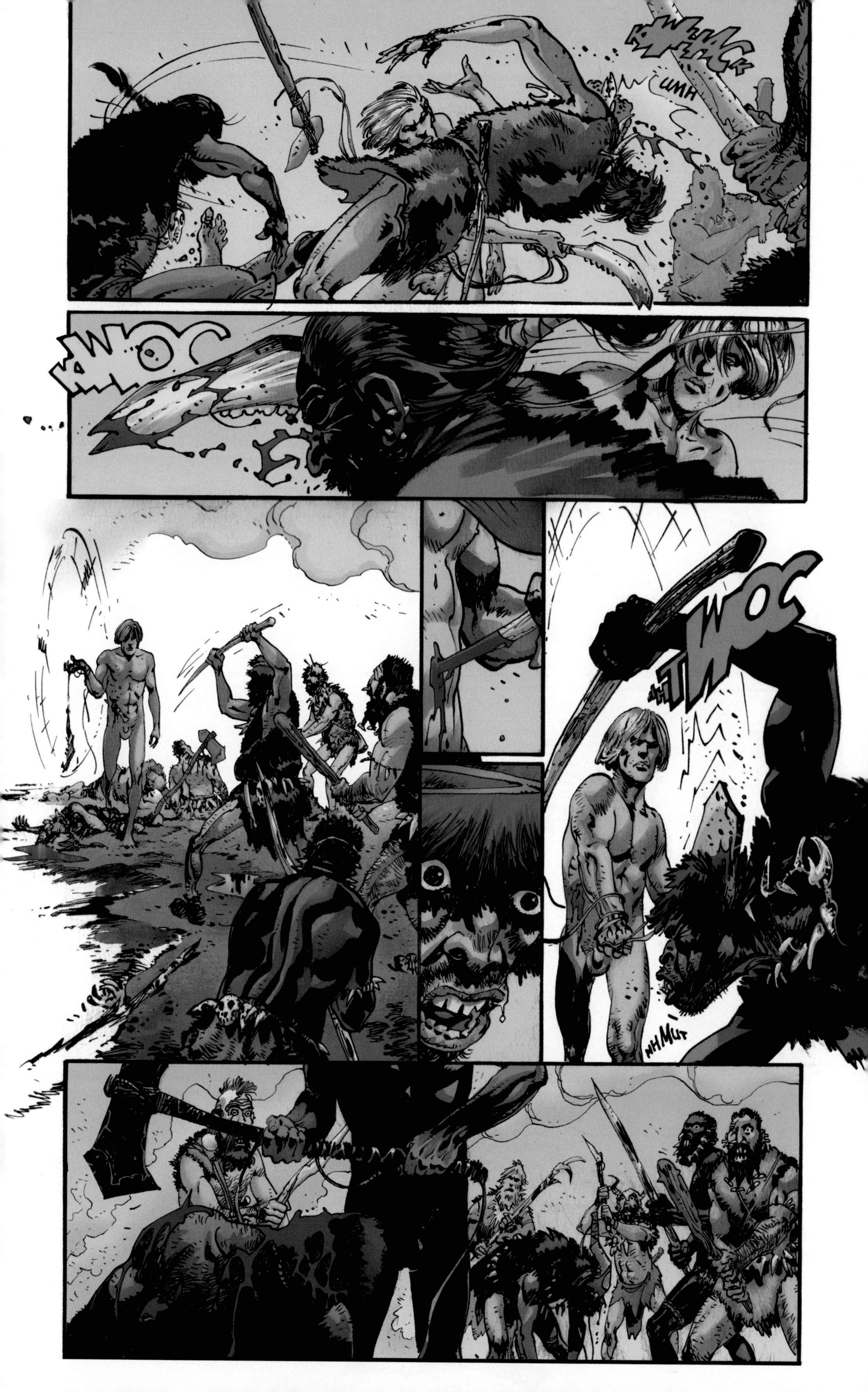

KWHACK
UMH
WOC
TWOC
NHMUT

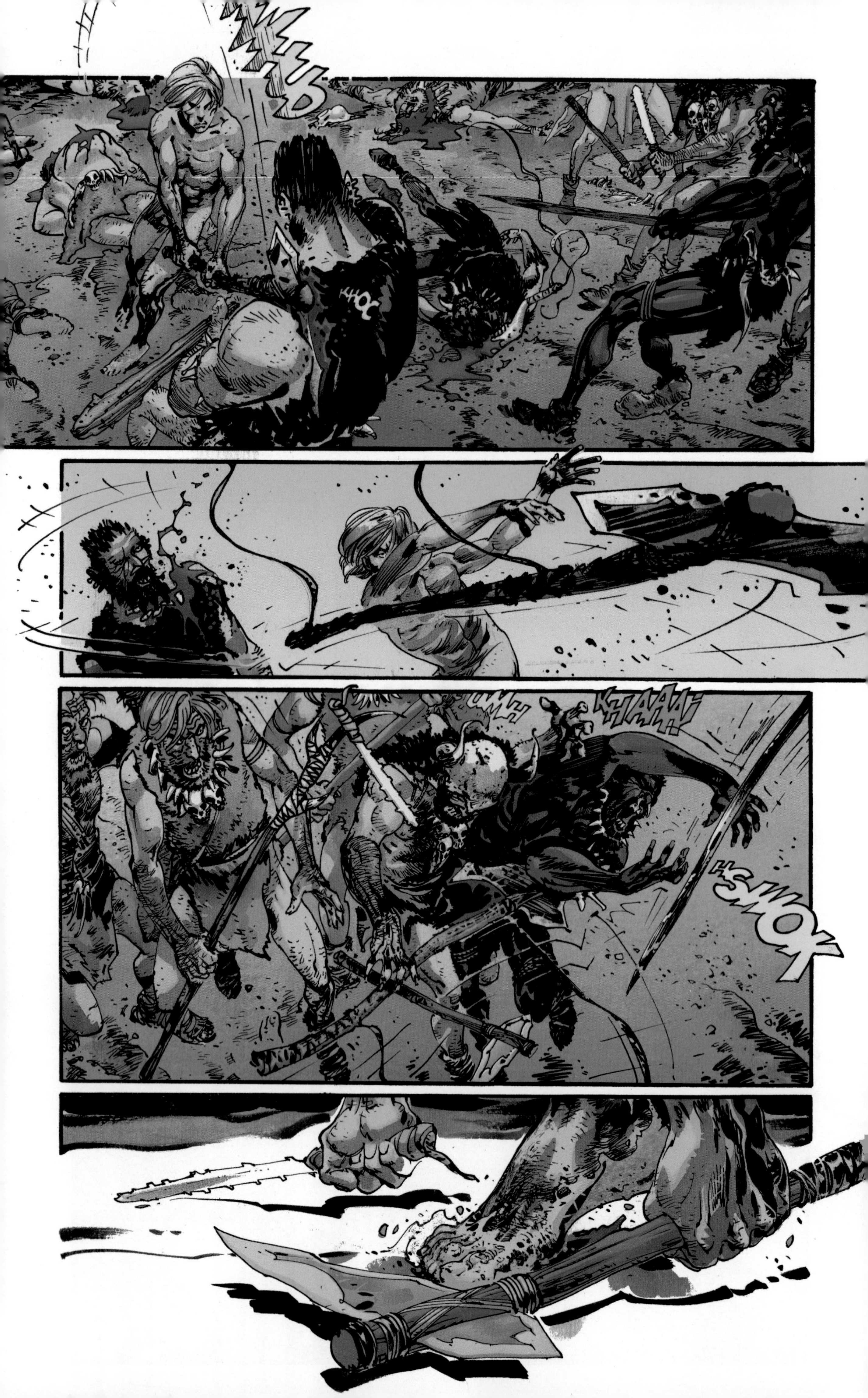
KHAAAA!

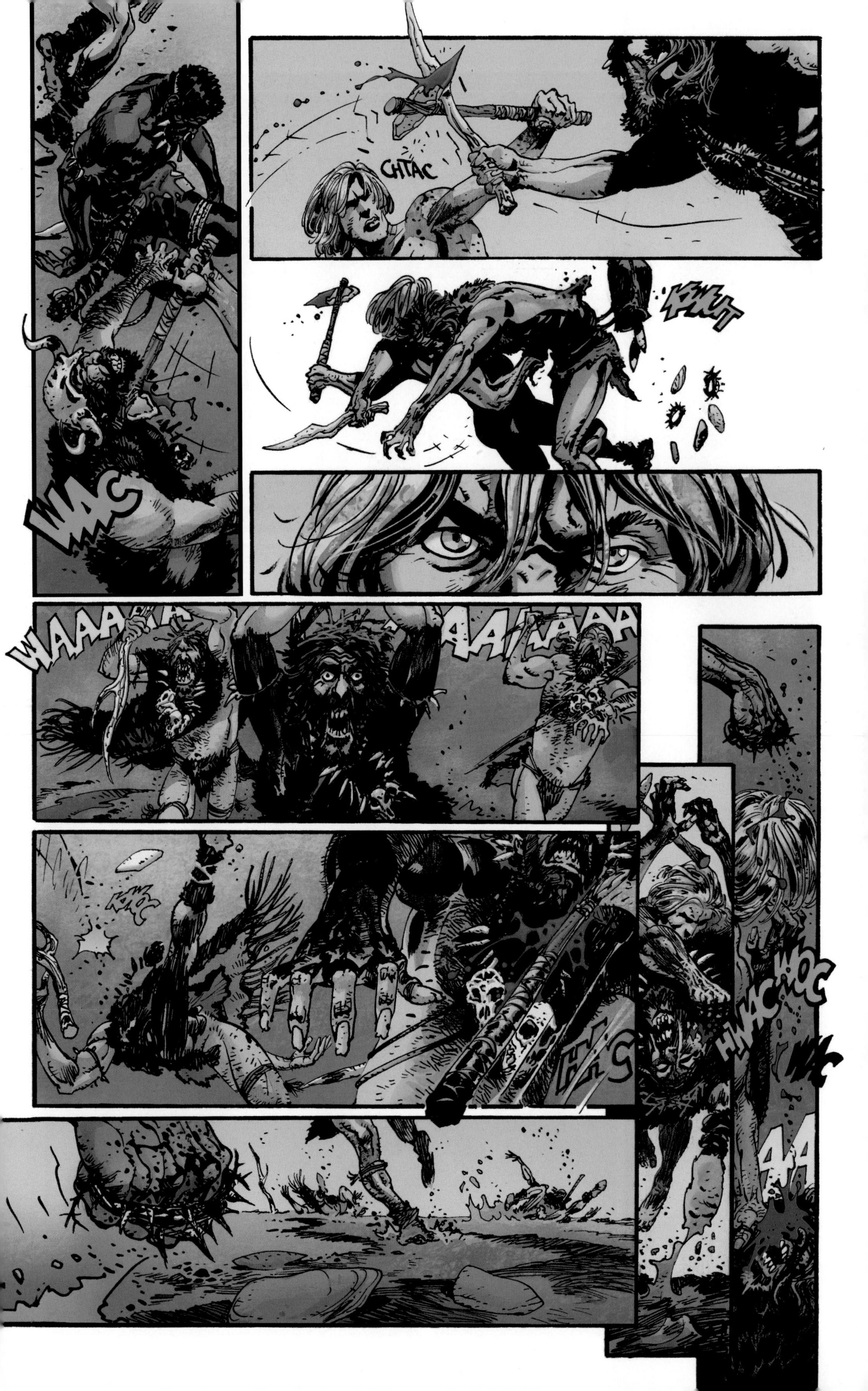
CHTAC
KWUT
WAC
HWAC
WOC
WAC

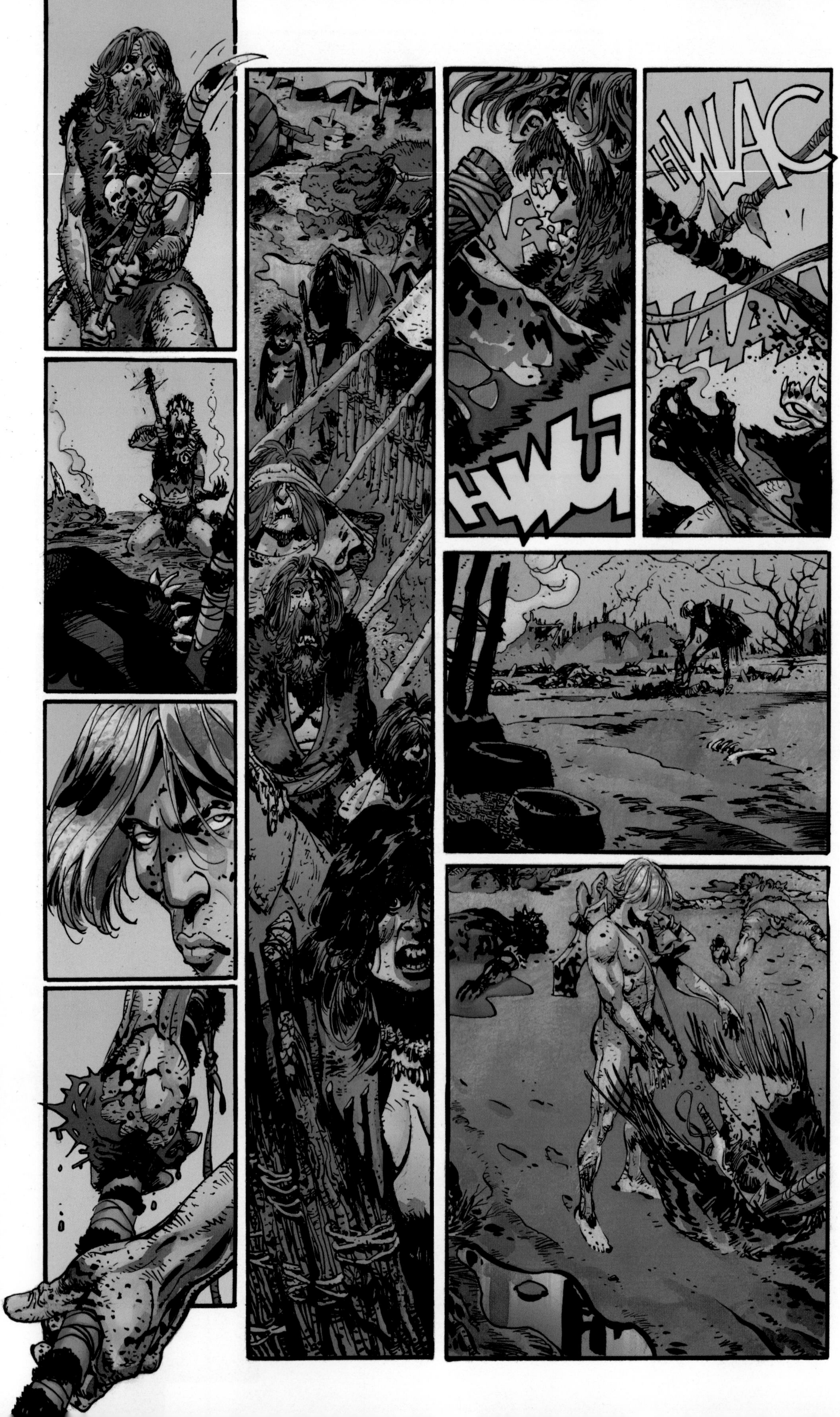
HWAC
HWUT

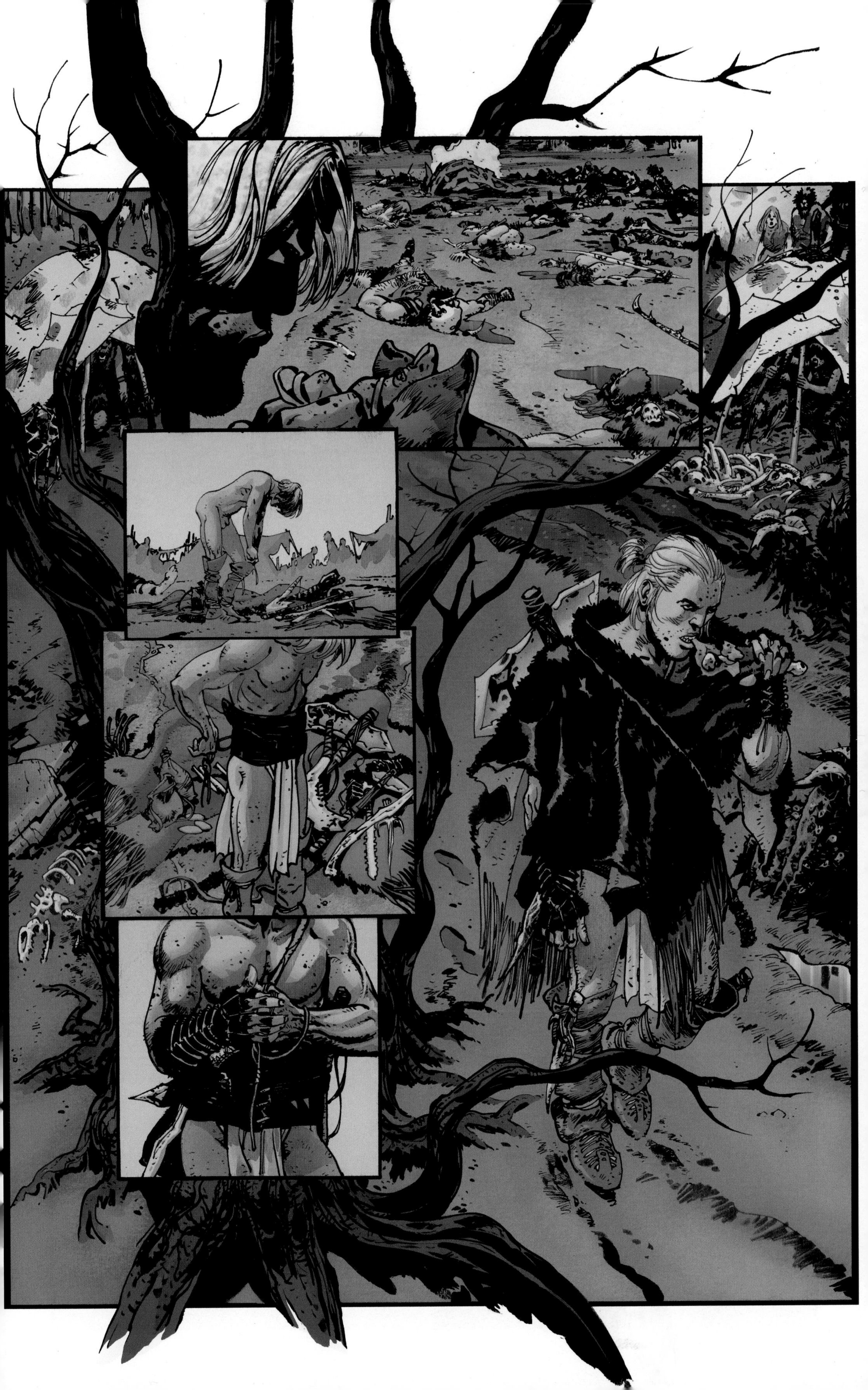

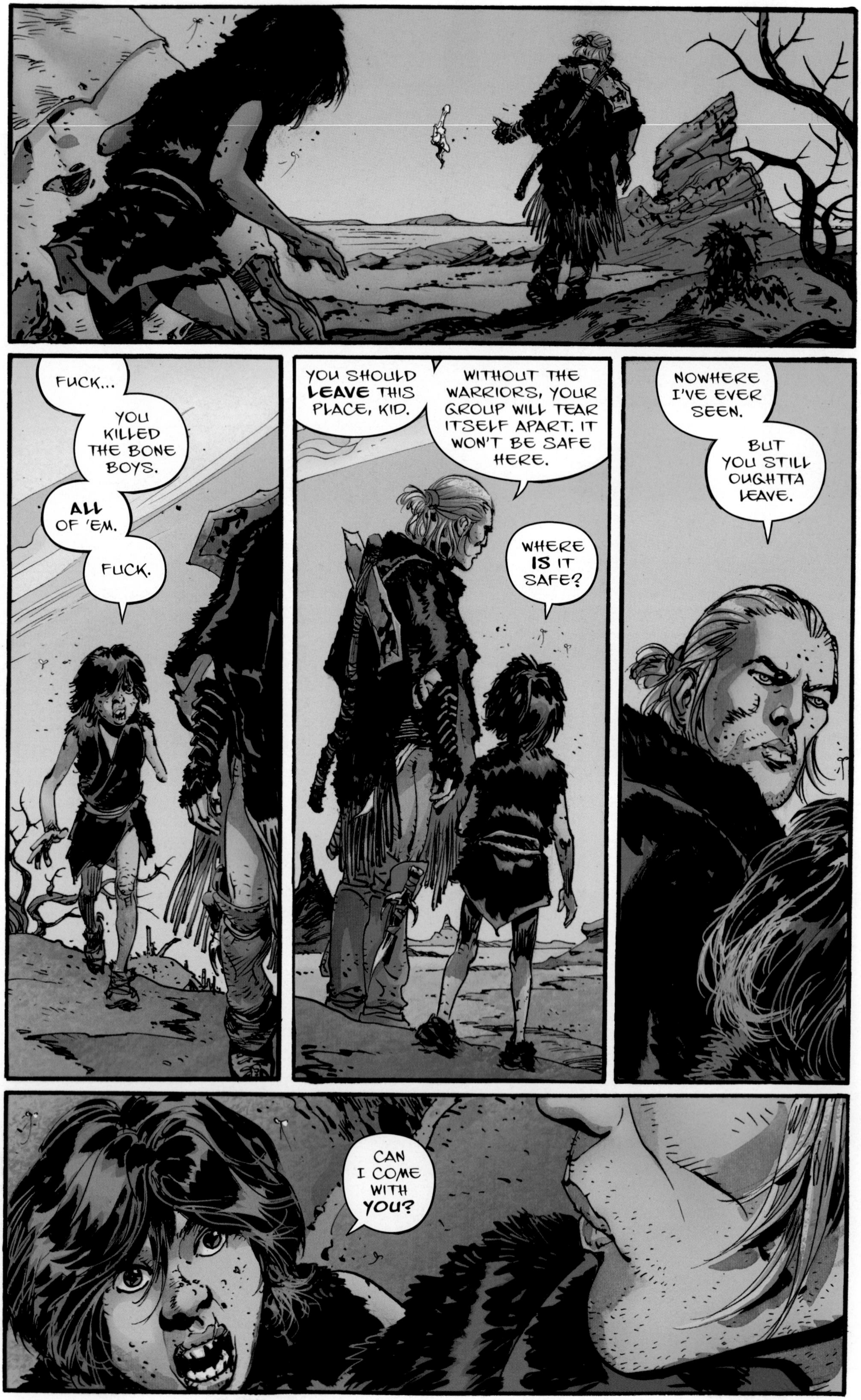
FUCK...
YOU KILLED THE BONE BOYS.
ALL OF 'EM.
FUCK.
YOU SHOULD LEAVE THIS PLACE, KID.
WITHOUT THE WARRIORS, YOUR GROUP WILL TEAR ITSELF APART. IT WON'T BE SAFE HERE.
WHERE IS IT SAFE?
NOWHERE I'VE EVER SEEN.
BUT YOU STILL OUGHTTA LEAVE.
CAN I COME WITH YOU?

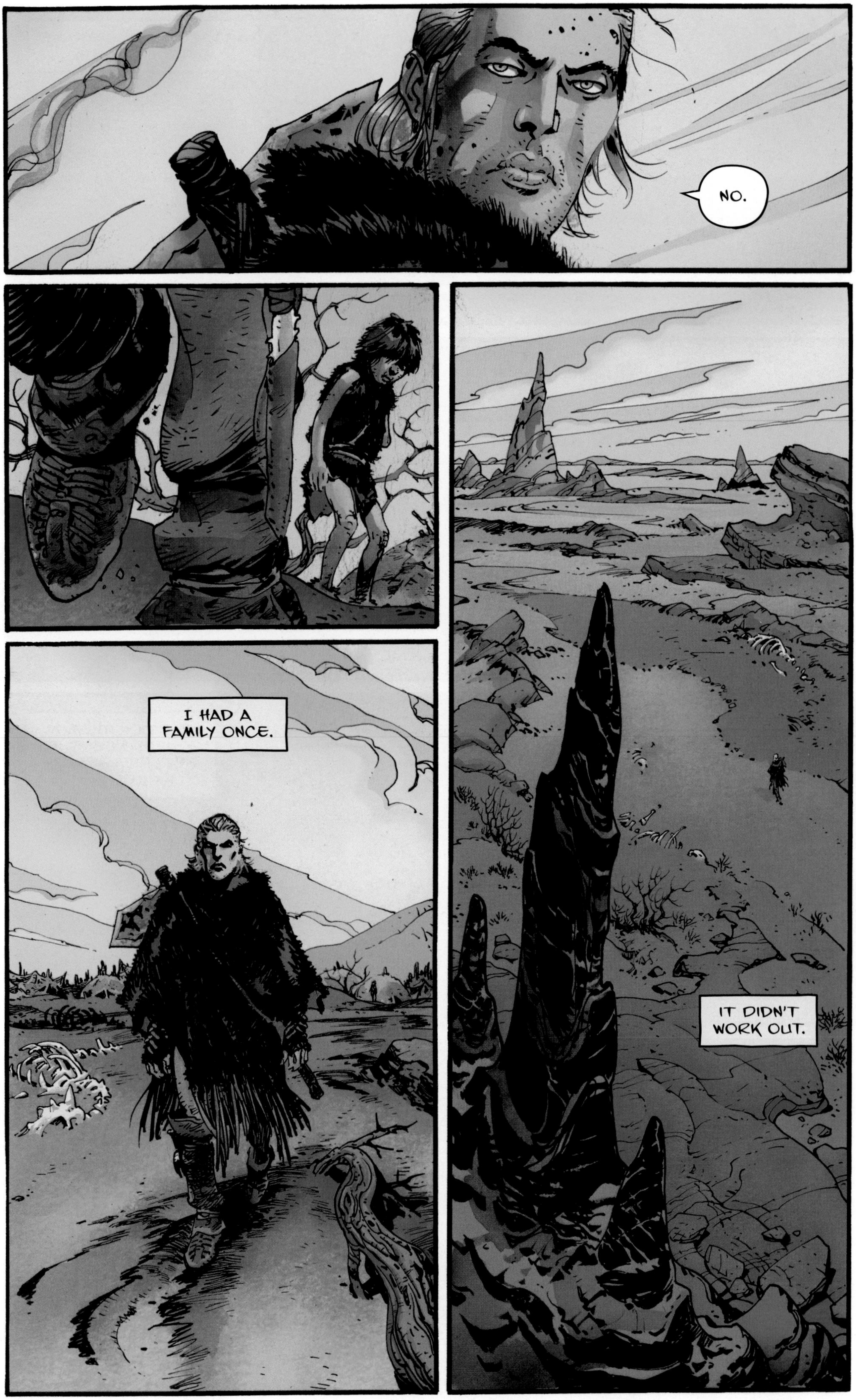
NO.
I HAD A FAMILY ONCE.
IT DIDN'T WORK OUT.

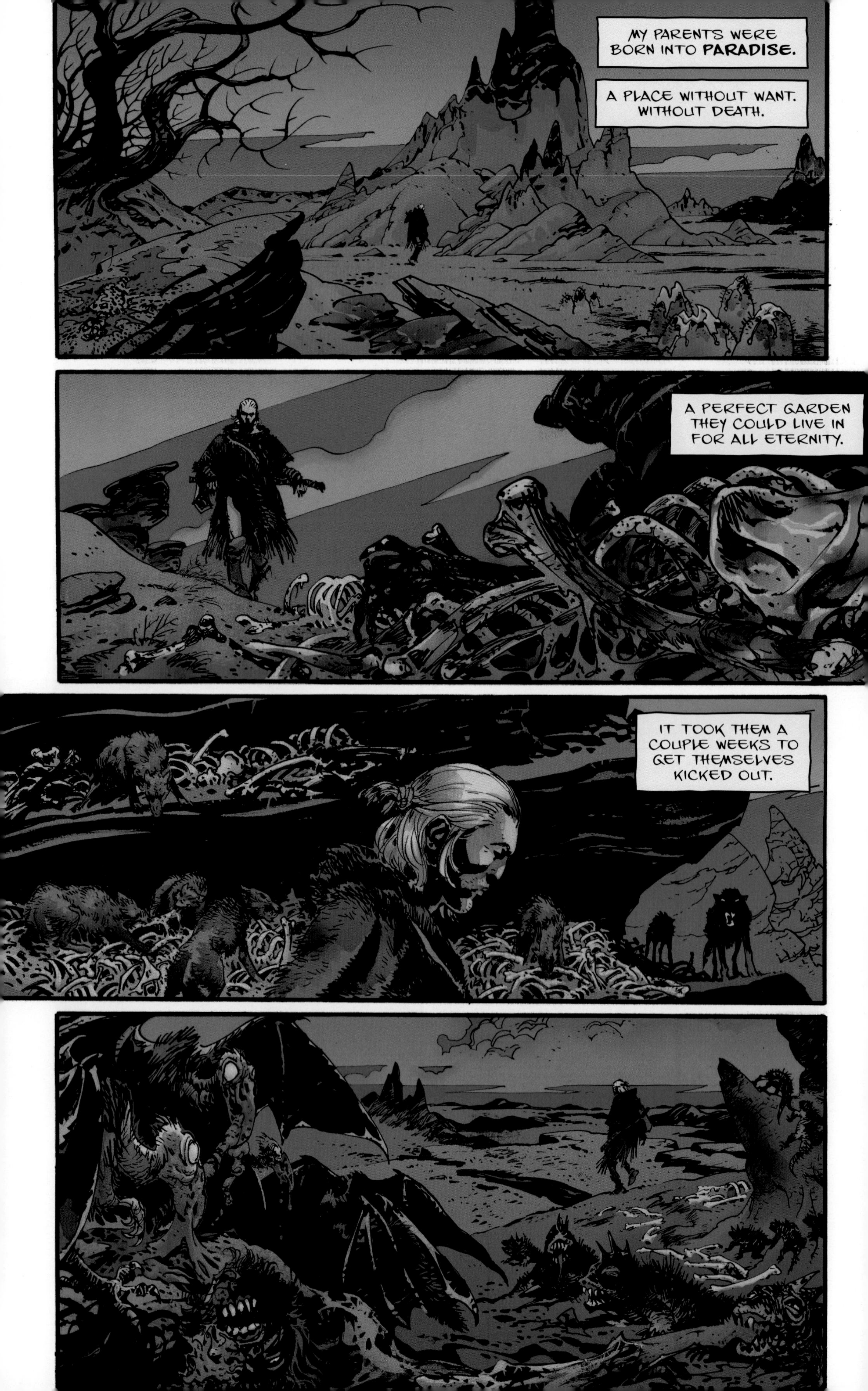
MY PARENTS WERE BORN INTO **PARADISE.**
A PLACE WITHOUT WANT. WITHOUT DEATH.
A PERFECT GARDEN THEY COULD LIVE IN FOR ALL ETERNITY.
IT TOOK THEM A COUPLE WEEKS TO GET THEMSELVES KICKED OUT.

THAT'S ABOUT WHEN MY **BROTHER** **AND** I CAME ALONG.

LIFE WAS HARD IN THOSE DAYS, BUT THE WORLD WAS STILL A TRANQUIL PLACE.

BOUNTIFUL.

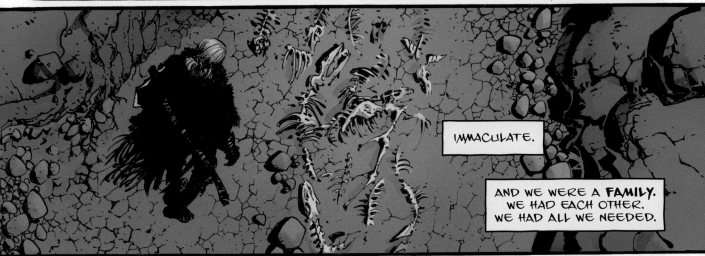

IMMACULATE.

AND WE WERE A **FAMILY.** WE HAD EACH OTHER. WE HAD ALL WE NEEDED.

IF ONLY I COULD'VE BEEN CONTENT WITH THAT.

IF ONLY I HADN'T GOTTEN SO GODDAMN **ANGRY.**

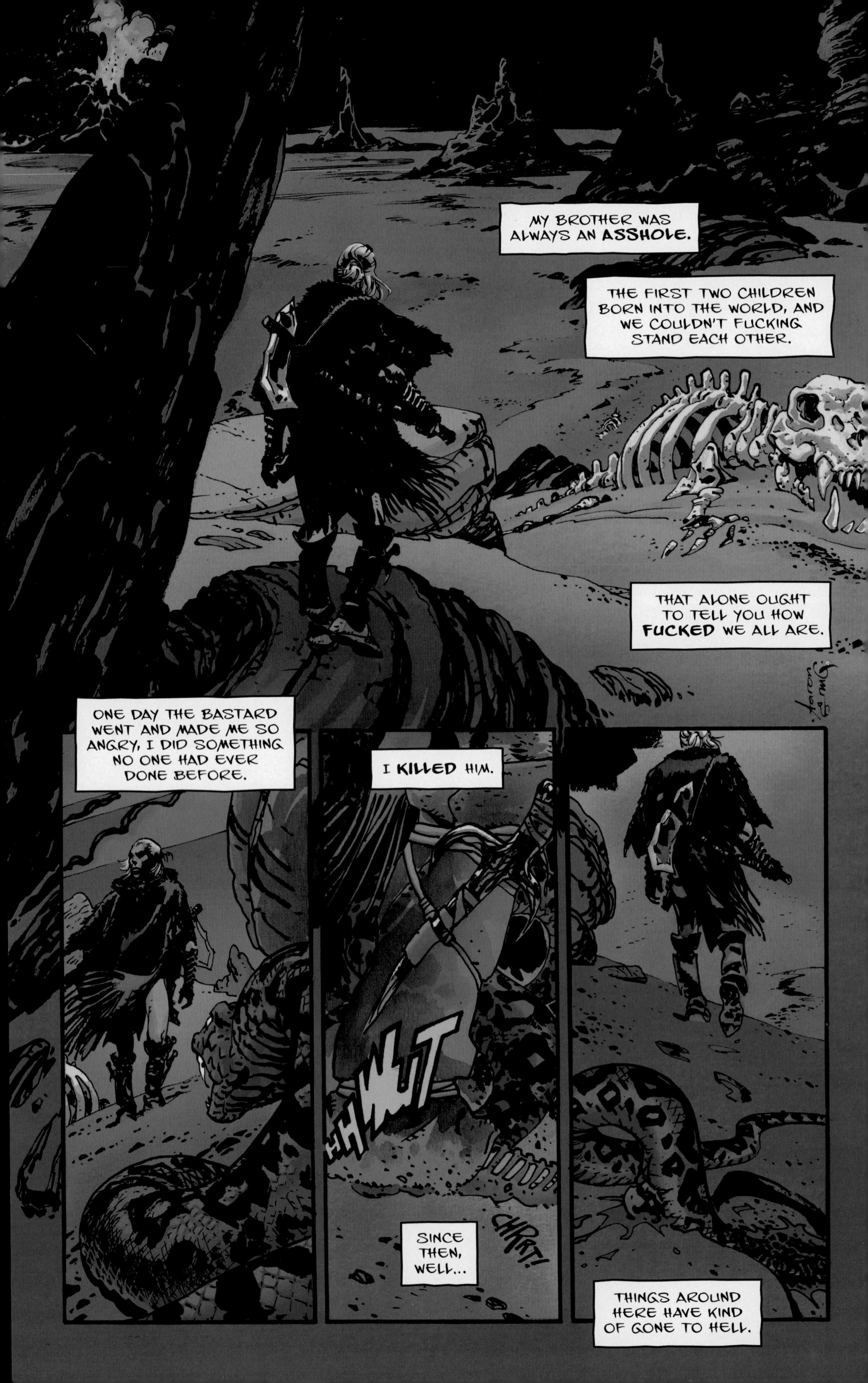
MY BROTHER WAS ALWAYS AN ASSHOLE.
THE FIRST TWO CHILDREN BORN INTO THE WORLD, AND WE COULDN'T FUCKING STAND EACH OTHER.
THAT ALONE OUGHT TO TELL YOU HOW FUCKED WE ALL ARE.
ONE DAY THE BASTARD WENT AND MADE ME SO ANGRY, I DID SOMETHING NO ONE HAD EVER DONE BEFORE.
I KILLED HIM.
HHWUT
SINCE THEN, WELL...
CHRRT!
THINGS AROUND HERE HAVE KIND OF GONE TO HELL.

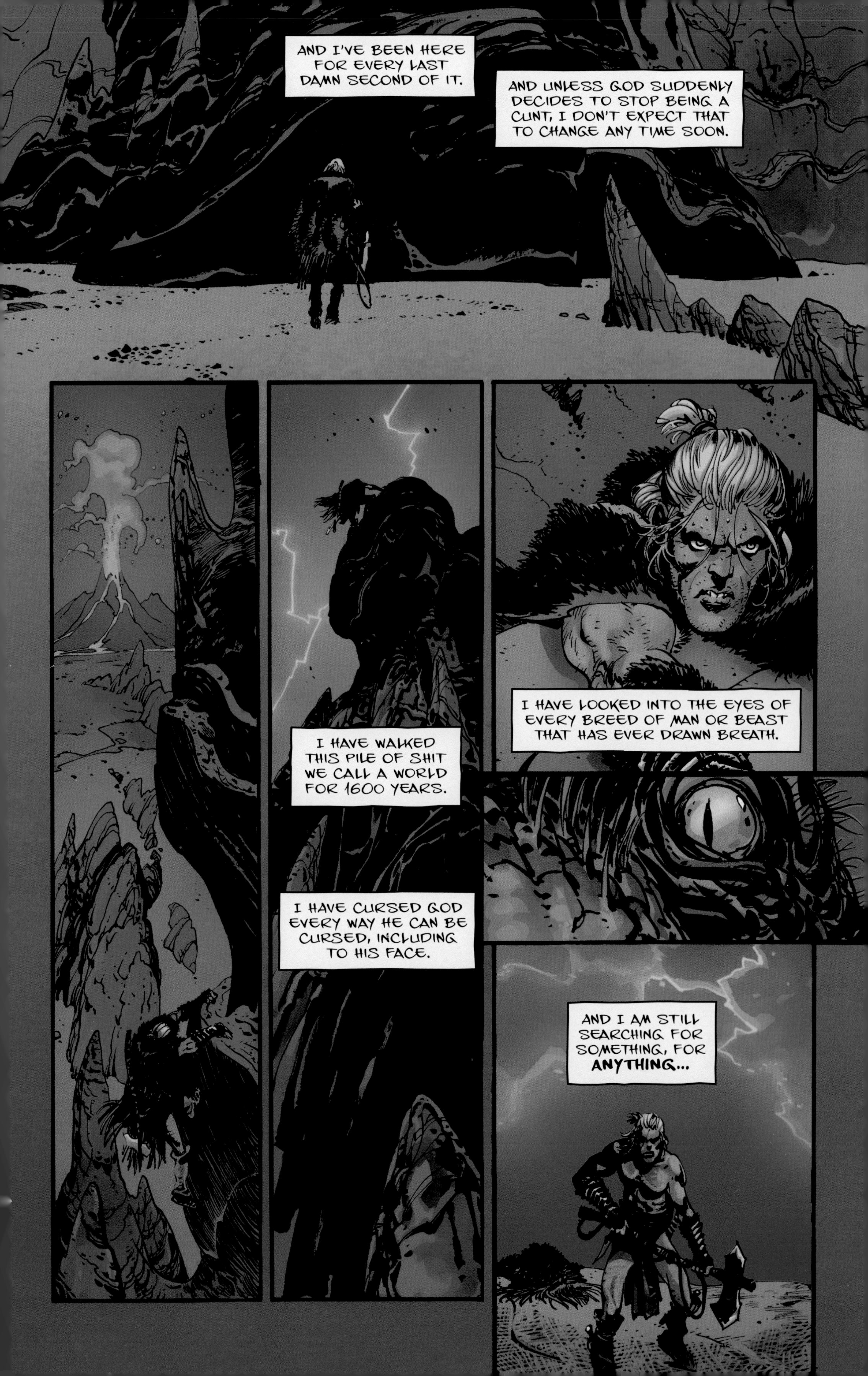
AND I'VE BEEN HERE FOR EVERY LAST DAMN SECOND OF IT.
AND UNLESS GOD SUDDENLY DECIDES TO STOP BEING A CUNT, I DON'T EXPECT THAT TO CHANGE ANY TIME SOON.
I HAVE WALKED THIS PILE OF SHIT WE CALL A WORLD FOR 1600 YEARS.
I HAVE CURSED GOD EVERY WAY HE CAN BE CURSED, INCLUDING TO HIS FACE.
I HAVE LOOKED INTO THE EYES OF EVERY BREED OF MAN OR BEAST THAT HAS EVER DRAWN BREATH.
AND I AM STILL SEARCHING FOR SOMETHING, FOR **ANYTHING...**

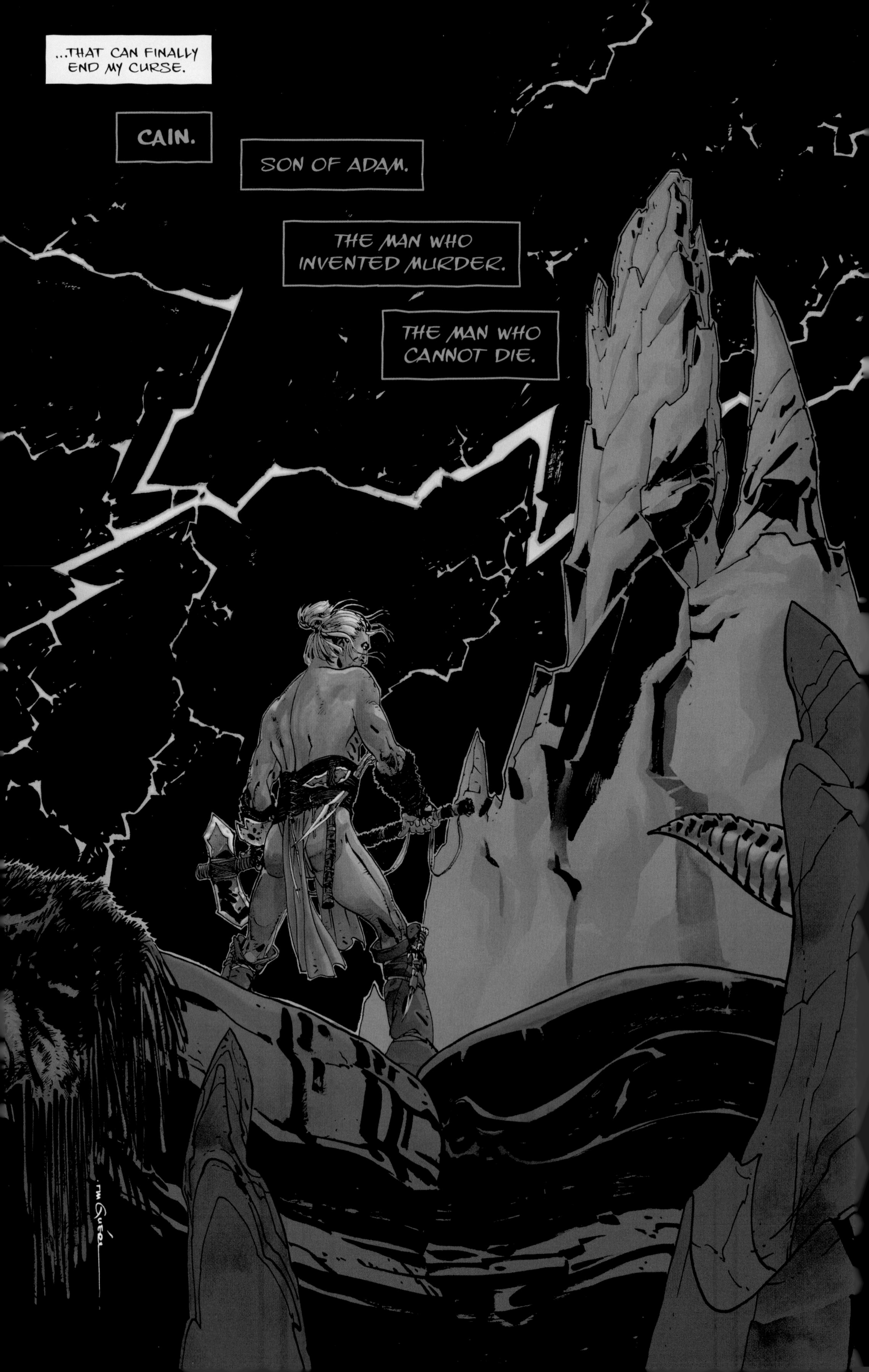

...THAT CAN FINALLY END MY CURSE.
CAIN.
SON OF ADAM.
THE MAN WHO INVENTED MURDER.
THE MAN WHO CANNOT DIE.

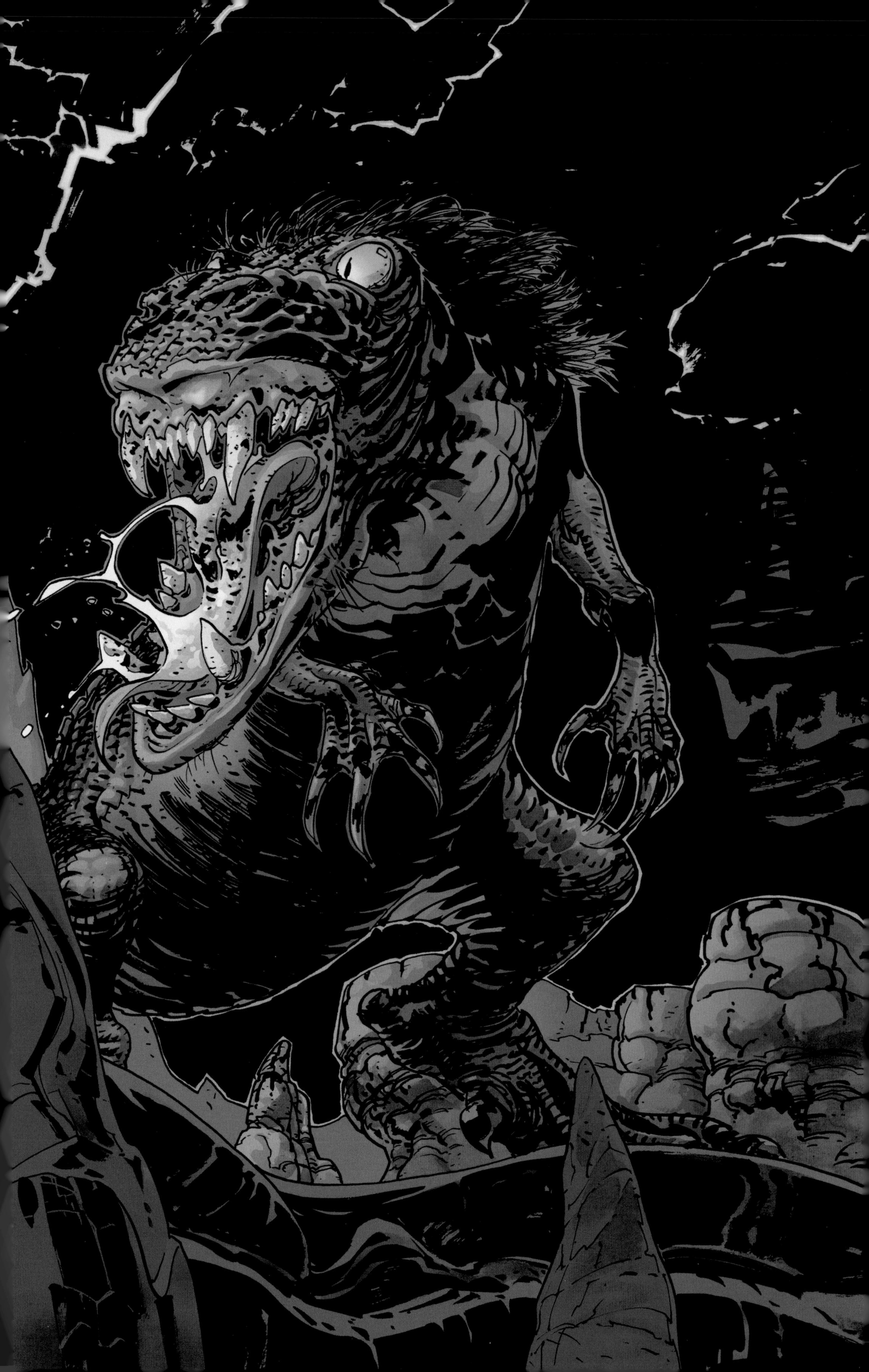

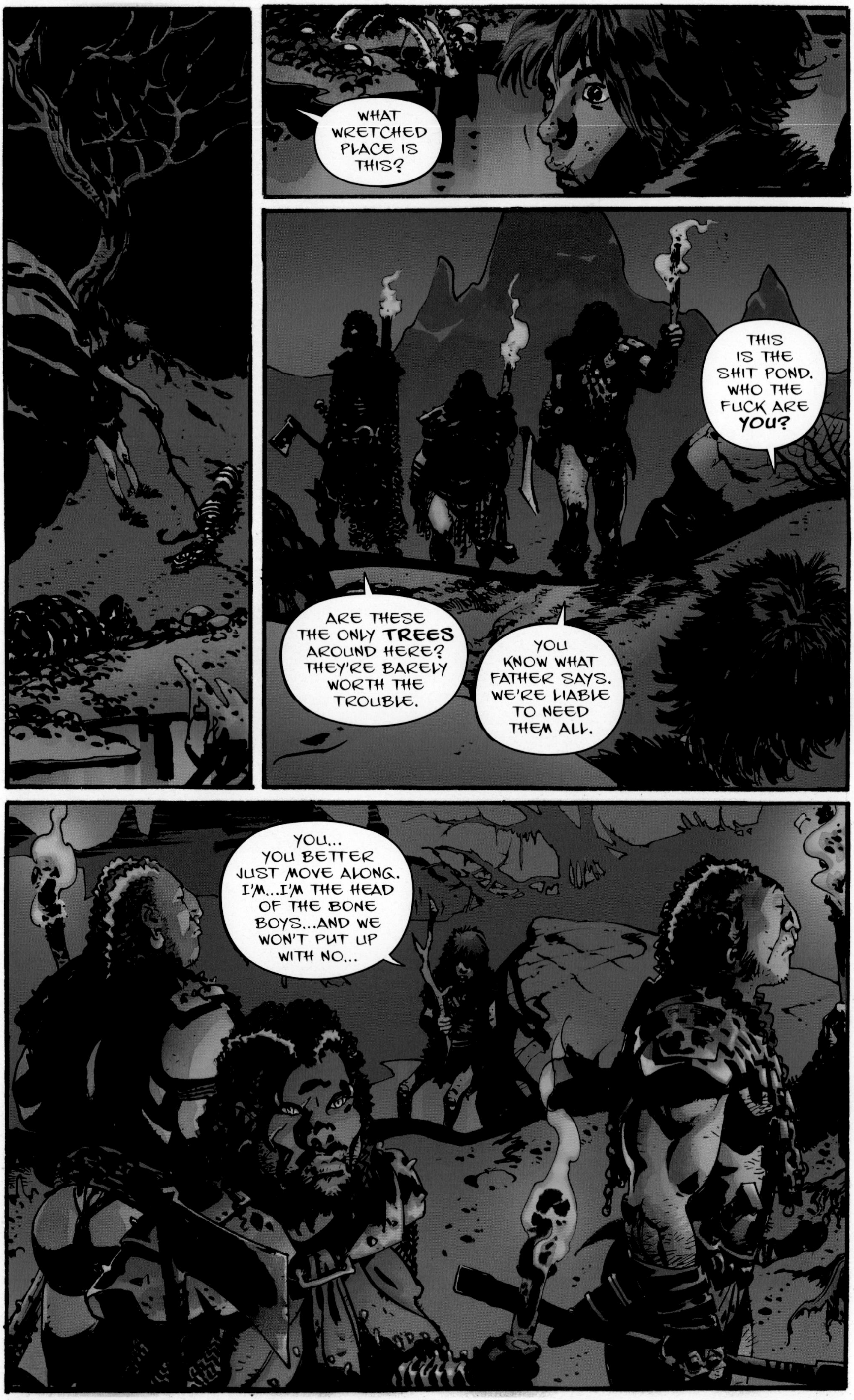
WHAT WRETCHED PLACE IS THIS?
THIS IS THE SHIT POND. WHO THE FUCK ARE YOU?
ARE THESE THE ONLY TREES AROUND HERE? THEY'RE BARELY WORTH THE TROUBLE.
YOU KNOW WHAT FATHER SAYS. WE'RE LIABLE TO NEED THEM ALL.
YOU... YOU BETTER JUST MOVE ALONG. I'M...I'M THE HEAD OF THE BONE BOYS...AND WE WON'T PUT UP WITH NO...

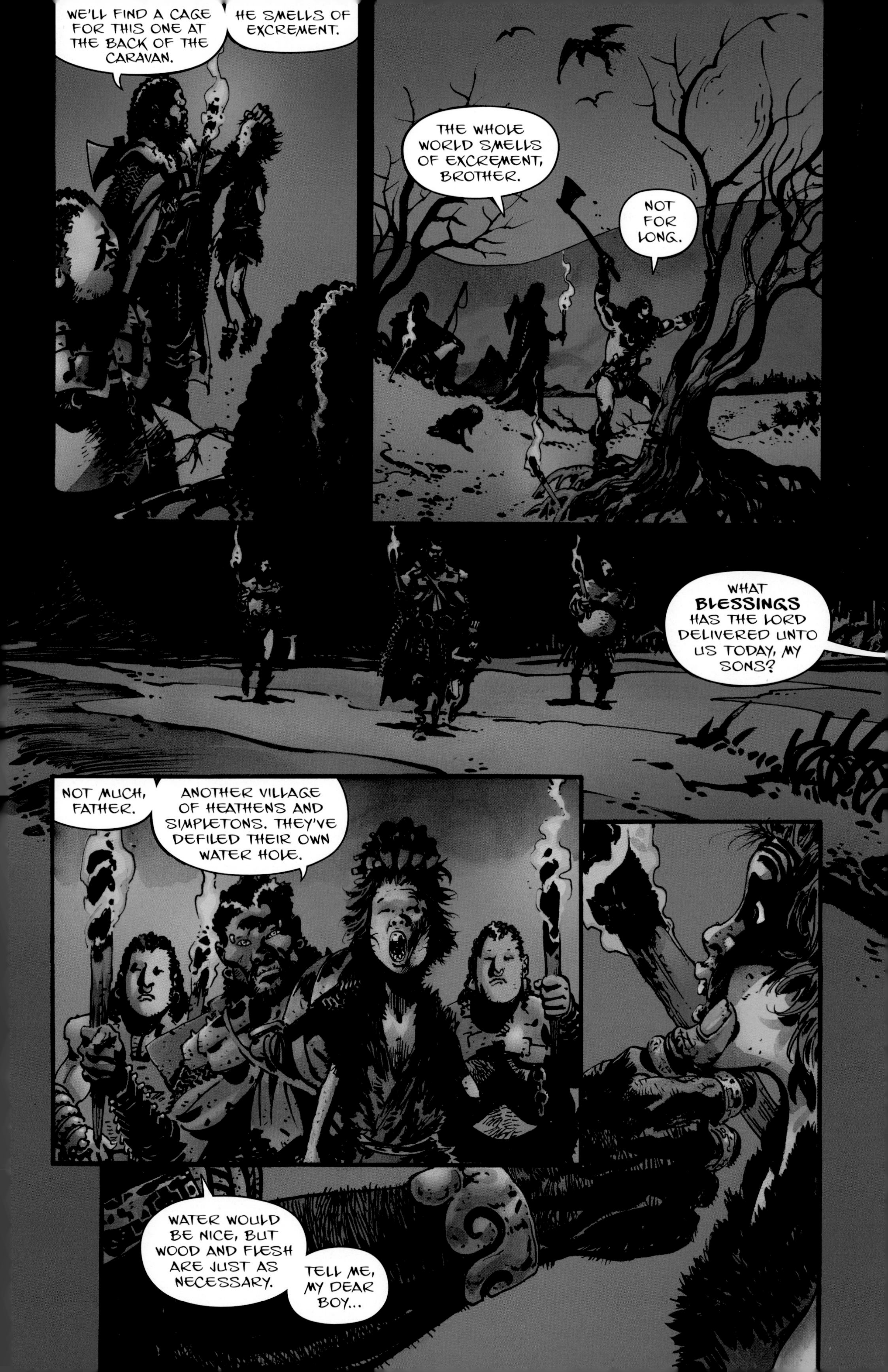
WE'LL FIND A CAGE FOR THIS ONE AT THE BACK OF THE CARAVAN.
HE SMELLS OF EXCREMENT.
THE WHOLE WORLD SMELLS OF EXCREMENT, BROTHER.
NOT FOR LONG.
WHAT BLESSINGS HAS THE LORD DELIVERED UNTO US TODAY, MY SONS?
NOT MUCH, FATHER.
ANOTHER VILLAGE OF HEATHENS AND SIMPLETONS. THEY'VE DEFILED THEIR OWN WATER HOLE.
WATER WOULD BE NICE, BUT WOOD AND FLESH ARE JUST AS NECESSARY.
TELL ME, MY DEAR BOY...

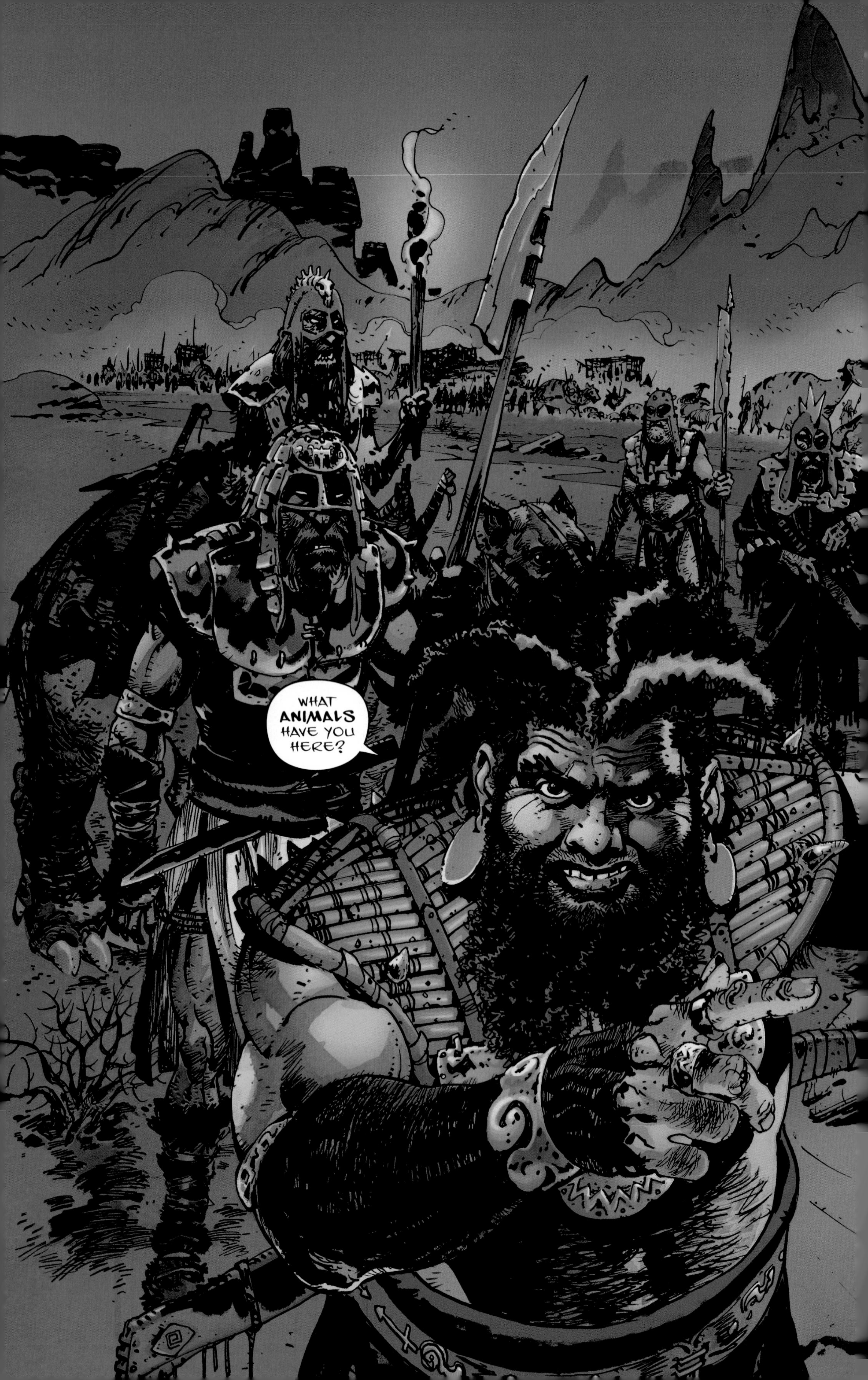
WHAT **ANIMALS** HAVE YOU HERE?

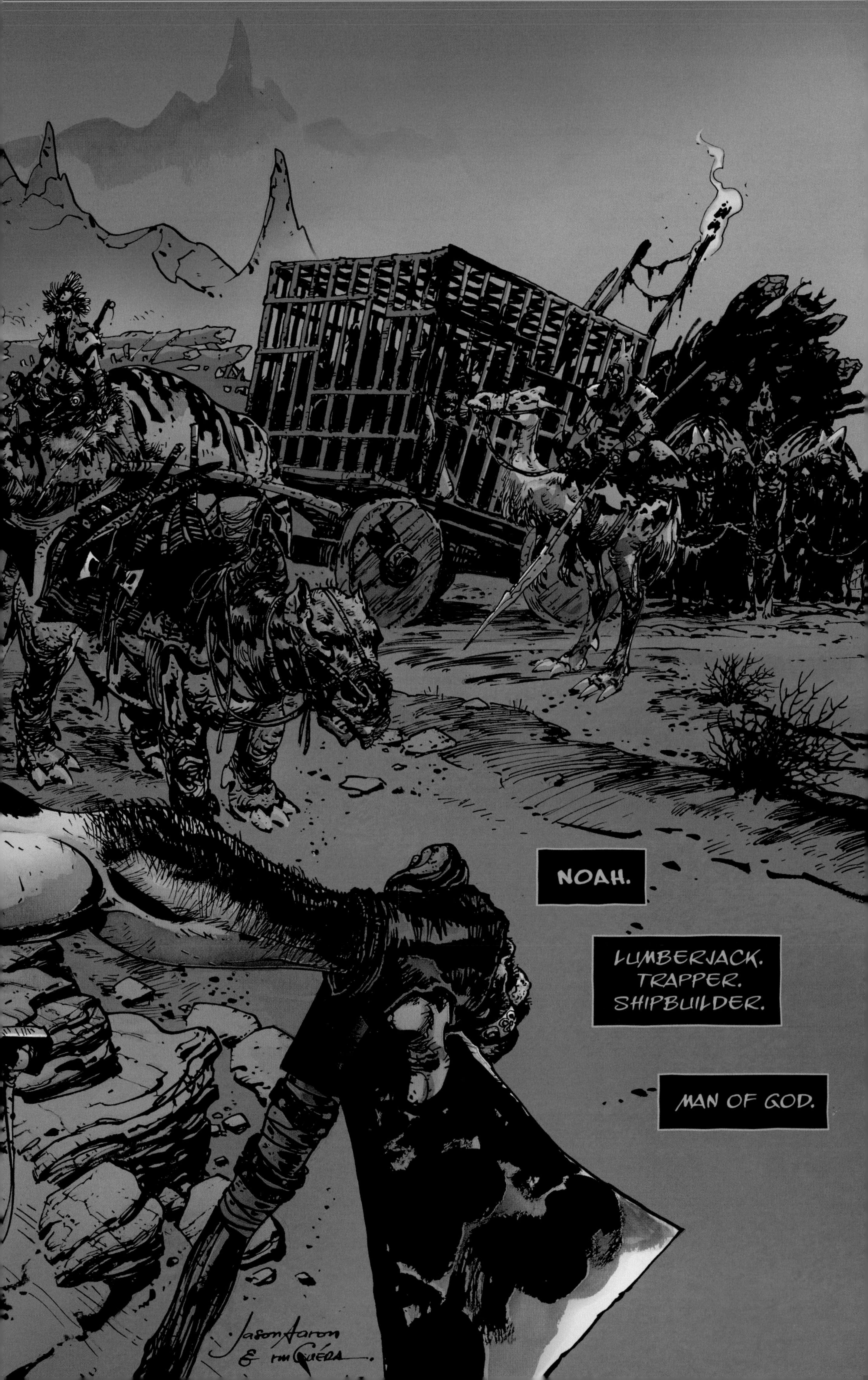
NOAH.
LUMBERJACK. TRAPPER. SHIPBUILDER.
MAN OF GOD.

chapter two

The Beasts of the Field

AND THE EARTH WAS
FILLED WITH VIOLENCE.

GENESIS 6:11

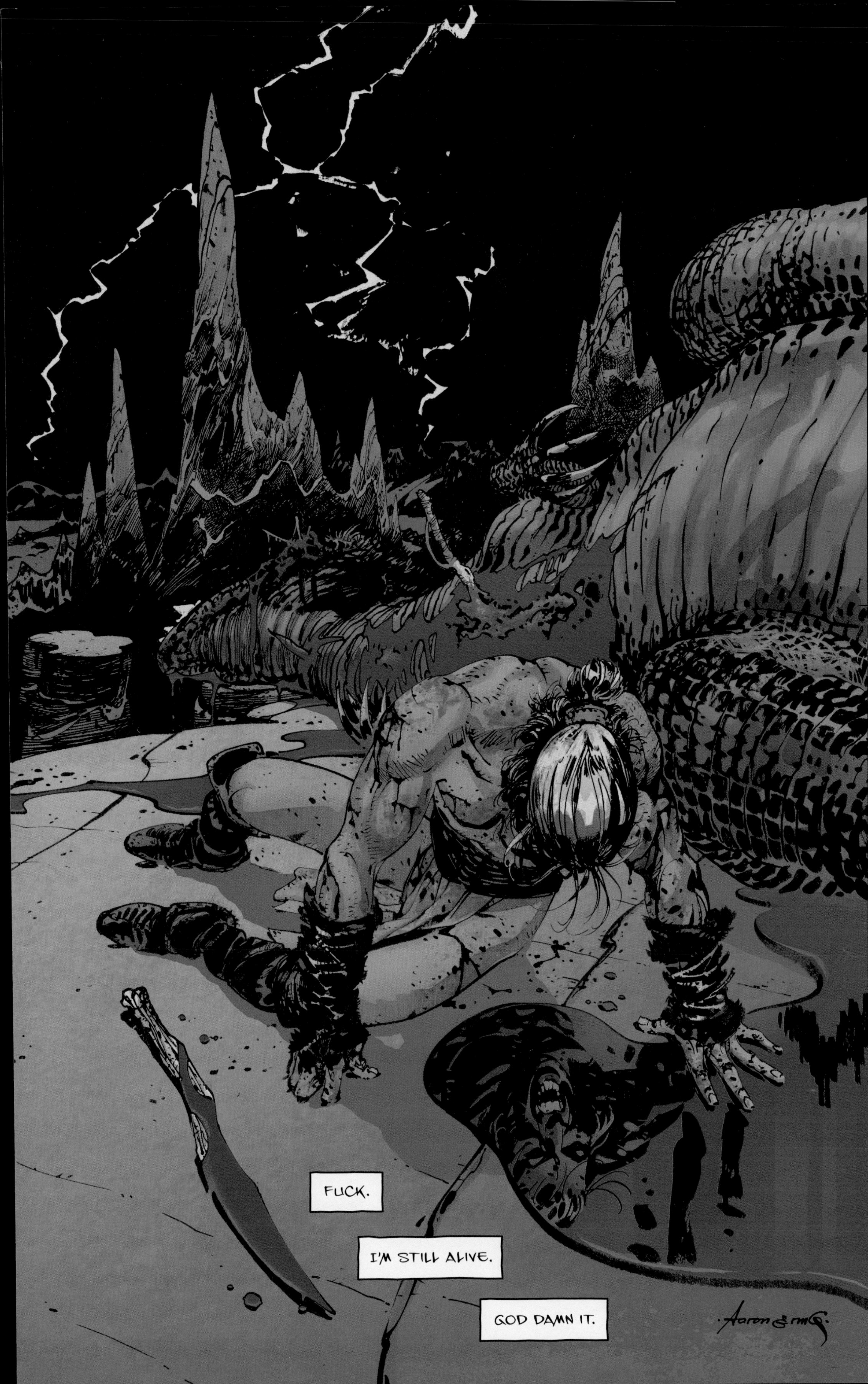
FUCK.
I'M STILL ALIVE.
GOD DAMN IT.
Aaron & rmG.

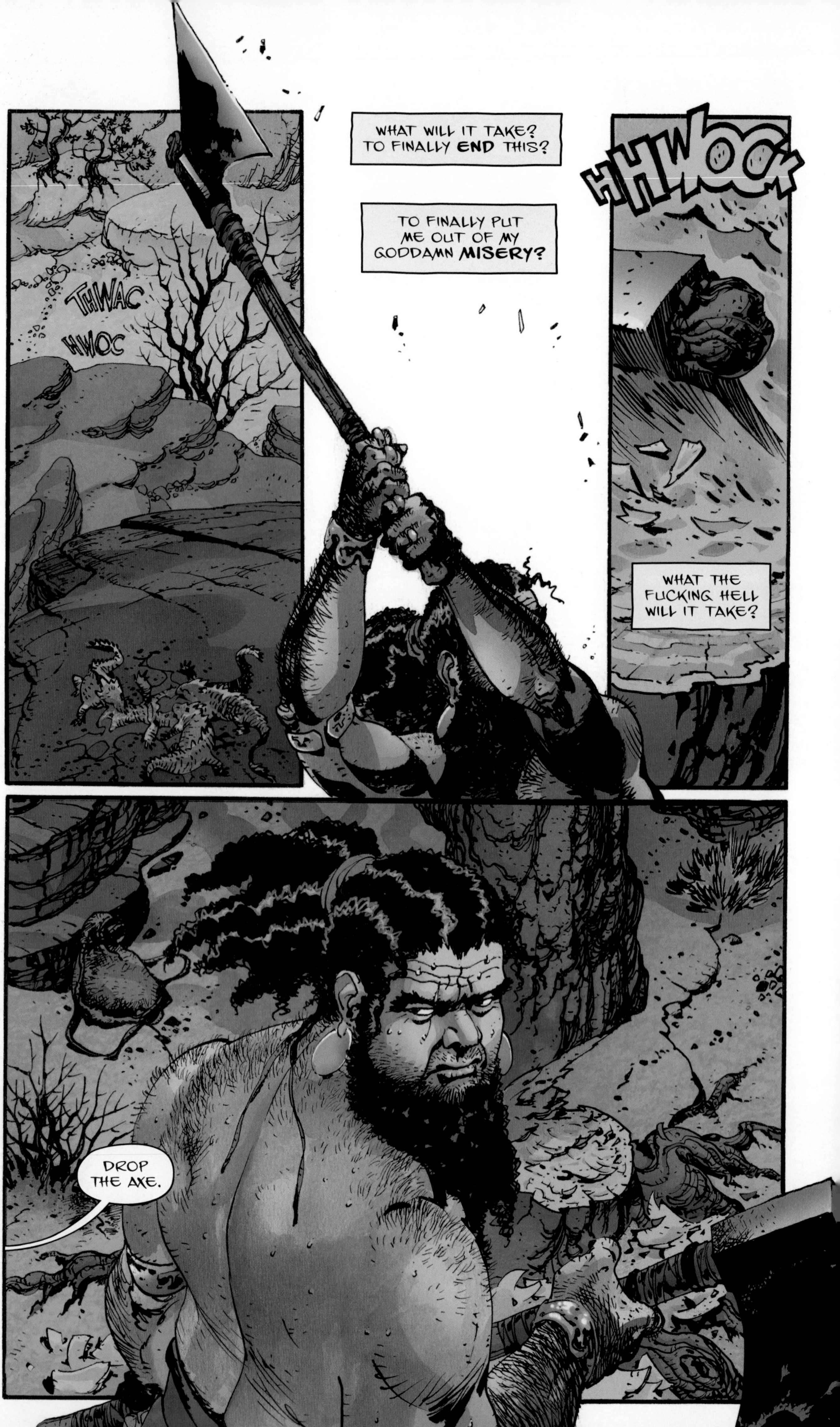
WHAT WILL IT TAKE? TO FINALLY END THIS?
TO FINALLY PUT ME OUT OF MY GODDAMN MISERY?
THWAC
HWOC
HHWOCK
WHAT THE FUCKING HELL WILL IT TAKE?
DROP THE AXE.

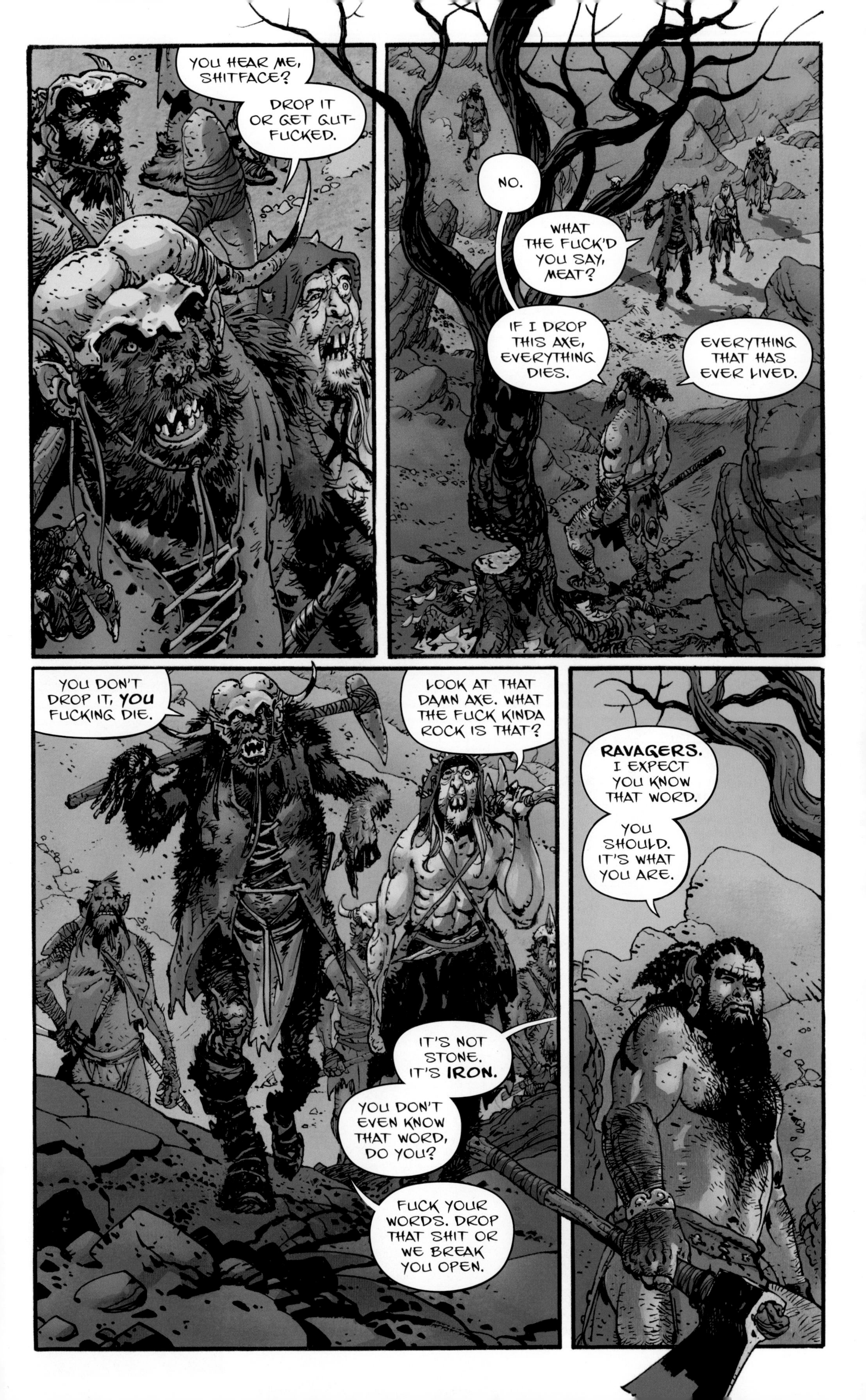
YOU HEAR ME, SHITFACE?
DROP IT OR GET GUT-FUCKED.
NO.
WHAT THE FUCK'D YOU SAY, MEAT?
IF I DROP THIS AXE, EVERYTHING DIES.
EVERYTHING THAT HAS EVER LIVED.
YOU DON'T DROP IT, **YOU** FUCKING DIE.
LOOK AT THAT DAMN AXE. WHAT THE FUCK KINDA ROCK IS THAT?
IT'S NOT STONE. IT'S **IRON**.
YOU DON'T EVEN KNOW THAT WORD, DO YOU?
FUCK YOUR WORDS. DROP THAT SHIT OR WE BREAK YOU OPEN.
RAVAGERS. I EXPECT YOU KNOW THAT WORD.
YOU SHOULD. IT'S WHAT YOU ARE.

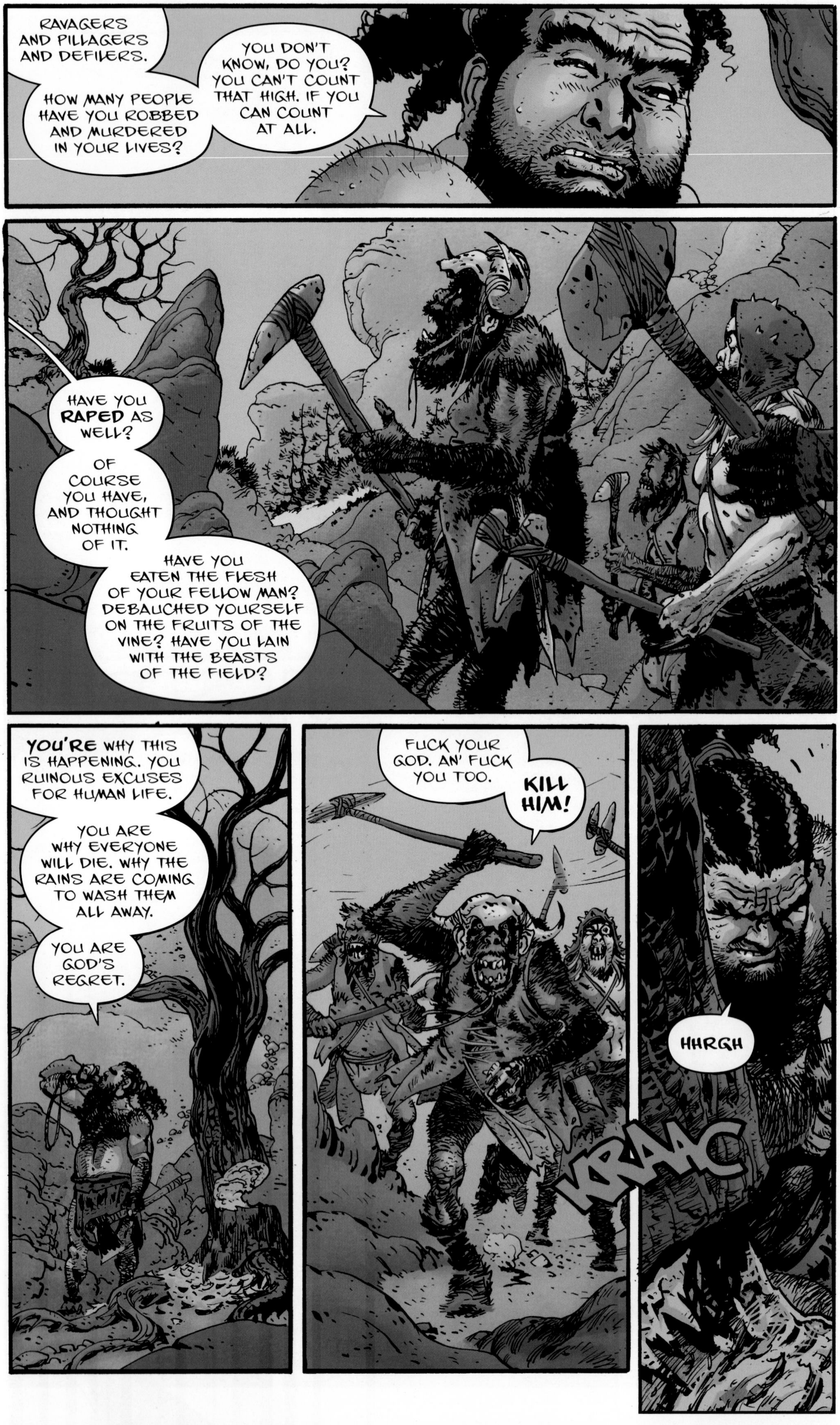

RAVAGERS AND PILLAGERS AND DEFILERS.
HOW MANY PEOPLE HAVE YOU ROBBED AND MURDERED IN YOUR LIVES?
YOU DON'T KNOW, DO YOU? YOU CAN'T COUNT THAT HIGH. IF YOU CAN COUNT AT ALL.
HAVE YOU **RAPED** AS WELL?
OF COURSE YOU HAVE, AND THOUGHT NOTHING OF IT.
HAVE YOU EATEN THE FLESH OF YOUR FELLOW MAN? DEBAUCHED YOURSELF ON THE FRUITS OF THE VINE? HAVE YOU LAIN WITH THE BEASTS OF THE FIELD?
YOU'RE WHY THIS IS HAPPENING. YOU RUINOUS EXCUSES FOR HUMAN LIFE.
YOU ARE WHY EVERYONE WILL DIE. WHY THE RAINS ARE COMING TO WASH THEM ALL AWAY.
YOU ARE GOD'S REGRET.
FUCK YOUR GOD. AN' FUCK YOU TOO.
KILL HIM!
HHRGH
KRAAC

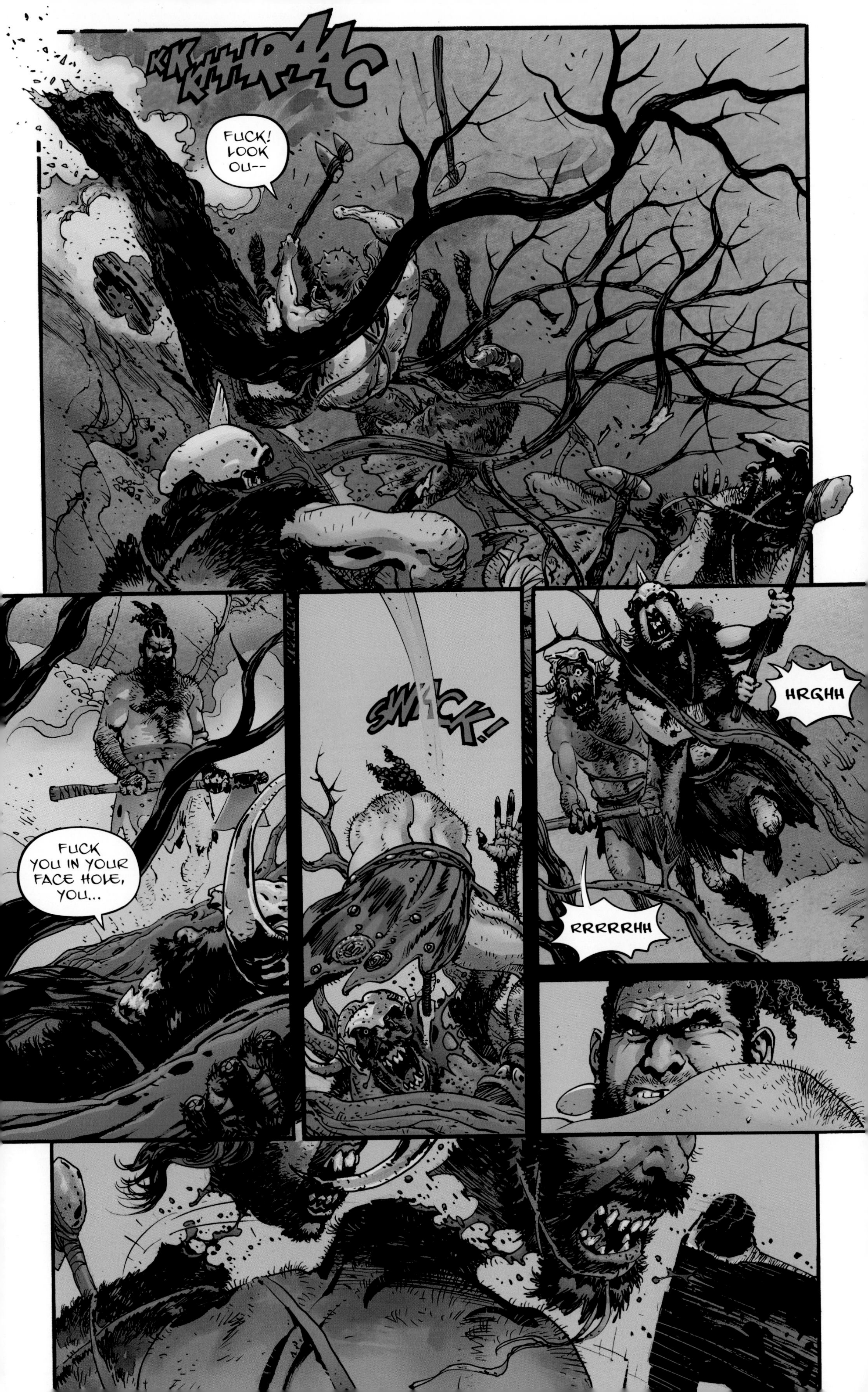
KKKHHRAAC
FUCK! LOOK OU--
FUCK YOU IN YOUR FACE HOLE, YOU...
SWACK!
HRGHH
RRRRRHH

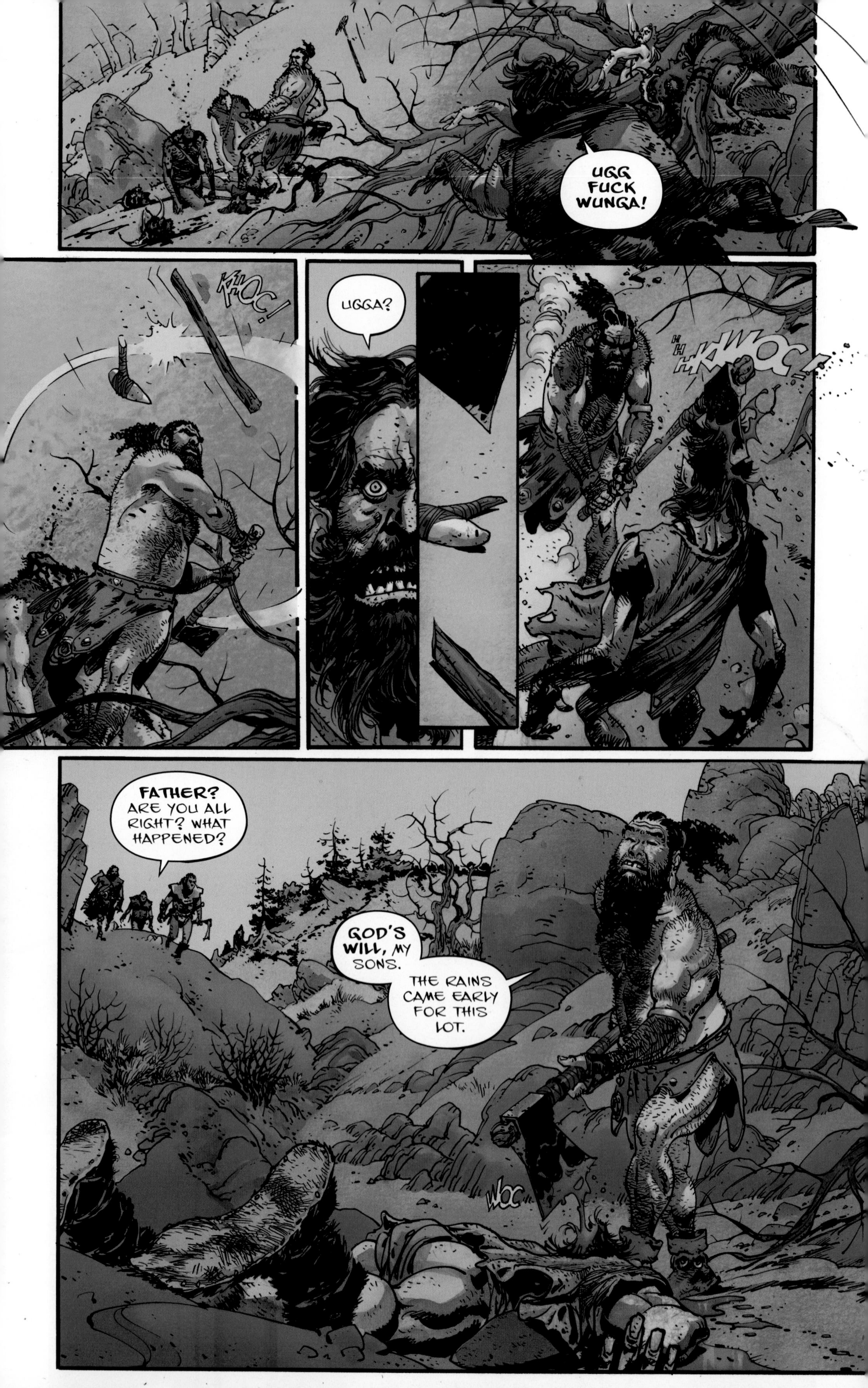
UGG FUCK WUNGA!
KTHOC!
UGGA?
HHHKWOC!
FATHER? ARE YOU ALL RIGHT? WHAT HAPPENED?
GOD'S WILL, MY SONS.
THE RAINS CAME EARLY FOR THIS LOT.
WOC

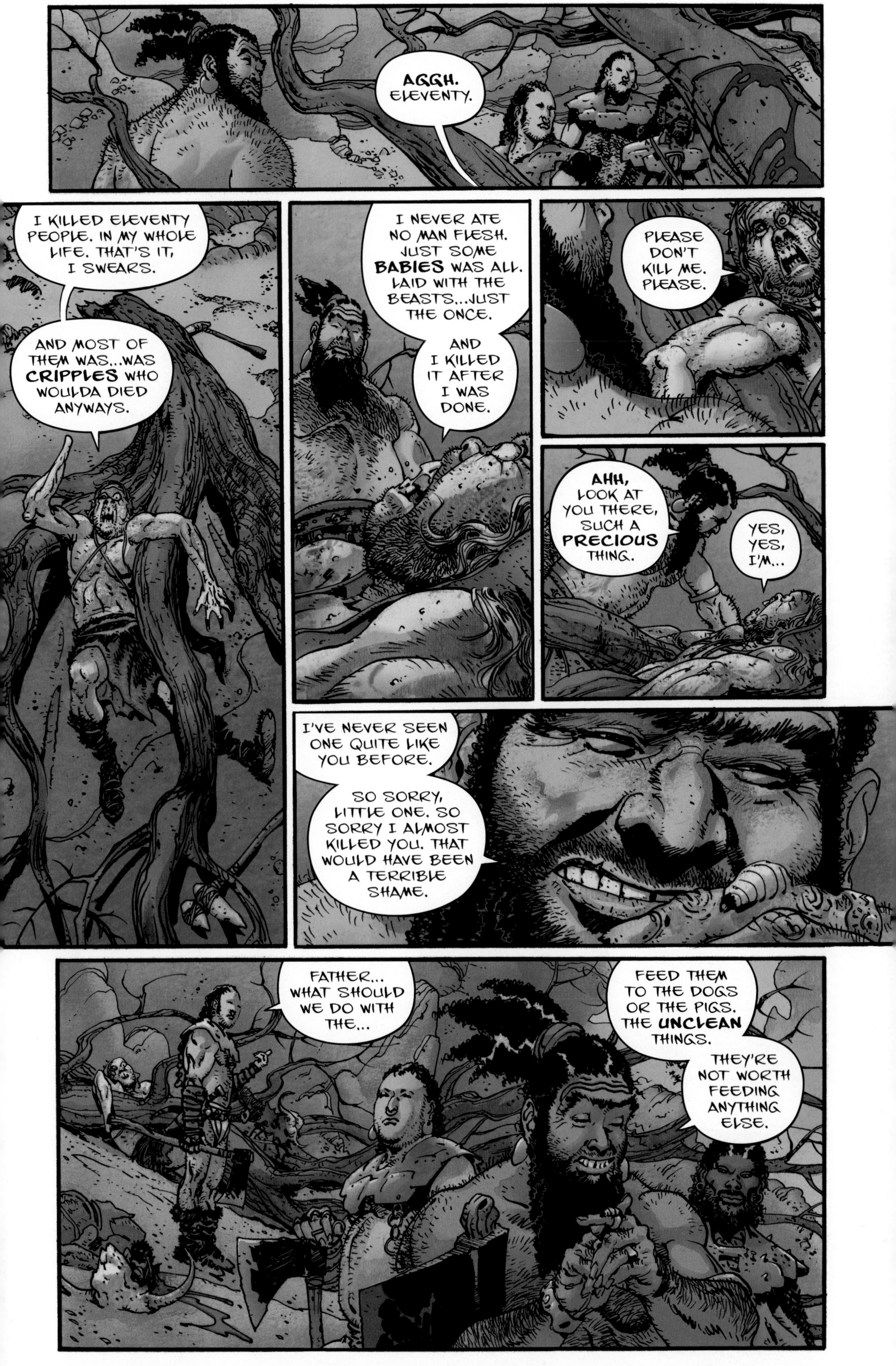

AGGH. ELEVENTY.
I KILLED ELEVENTY PEOPLE. IN MY WHOLE LIFE. THAT'S IT, I SWEARS.
AND MOST OF THEM WAS...WAS CRIPPLES WHO WOULDA DIED ANYWAYS.
I NEVER ATE NO MAN FLESH. JUST SOME BABIES WAS ALL. LAID WITH THE BEASTS...JUST THE ONCE.
AND I KILLED IT AFTER I WAS DONE.
PLEASE DON'T KILL ME. PLEASE.
AHH, LOOK AT YOU THERE, SUCH A PRECIOUS THING.
YES, YES, I'M...
I'VE NEVER SEEN ONE QUITE LIKE YOU BEFORE.
SO SORRY, LITTLE ONE. SO SORRY I ALMOST KILLED YOU. THAT WOULD HAVE BEEN A TERRIBLE SHAME.
FATHER... WHAT SHOULD WE DO WITH THE...
FEED THEM TO THE DOGS OR THE PIGS. THE UNCLEAN THINGS.
THEY'RE NOT WORTH FEEDING ANYTHING ELSE.

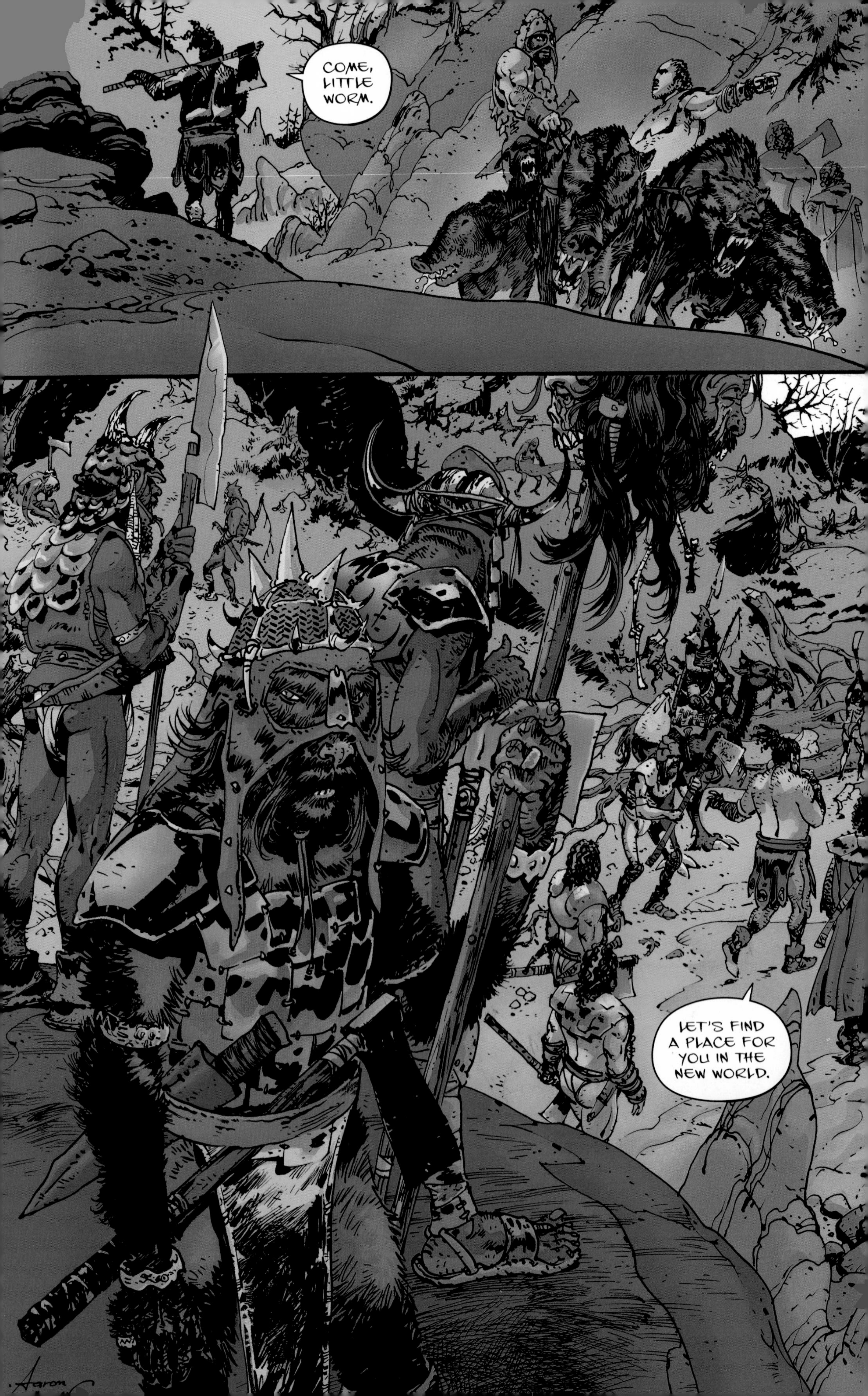
COME, LITTLE WORM.
LET'S FIND A PLACE FOR YOU IN THE NEW WORLD.
Aaron

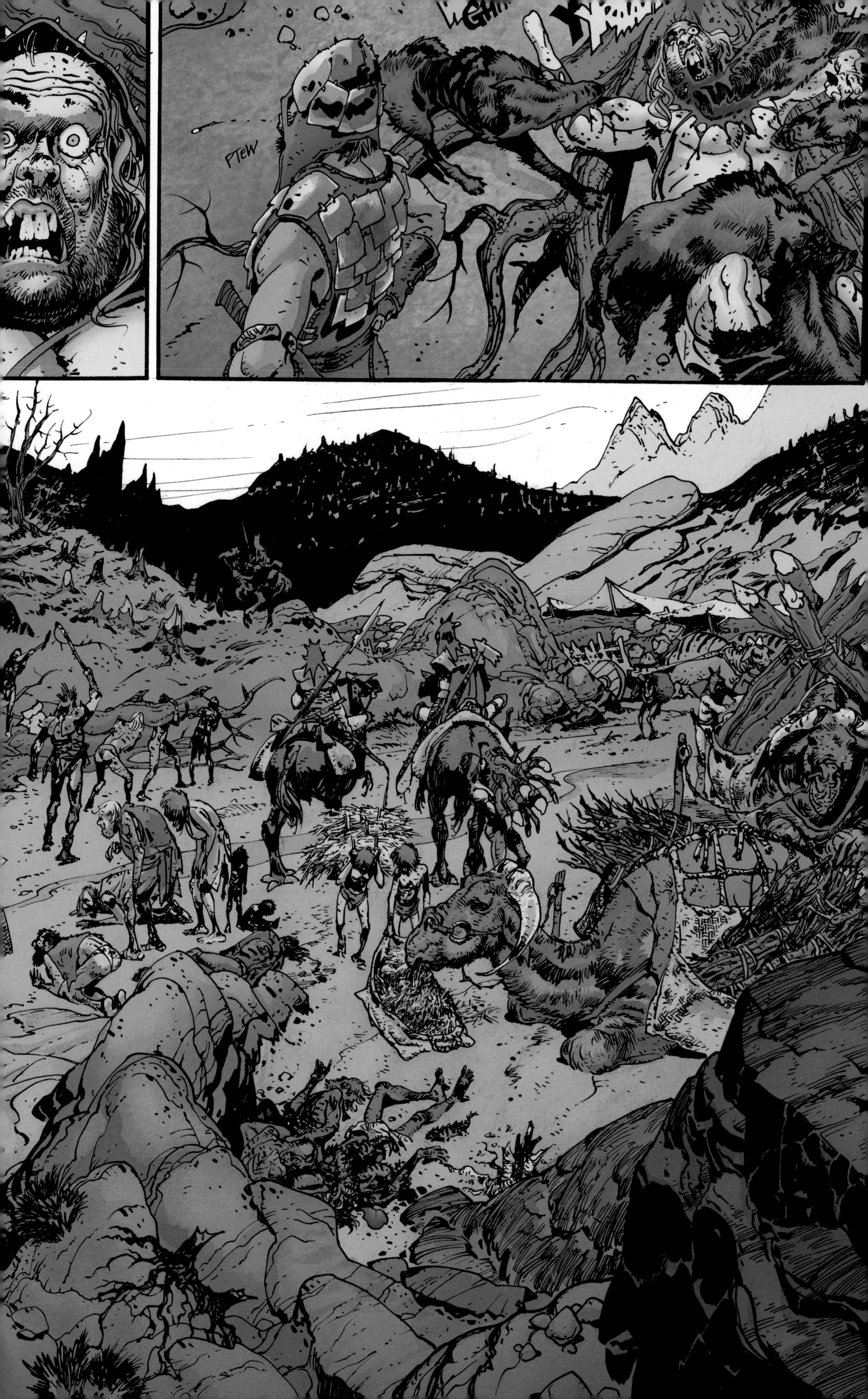
PTEW

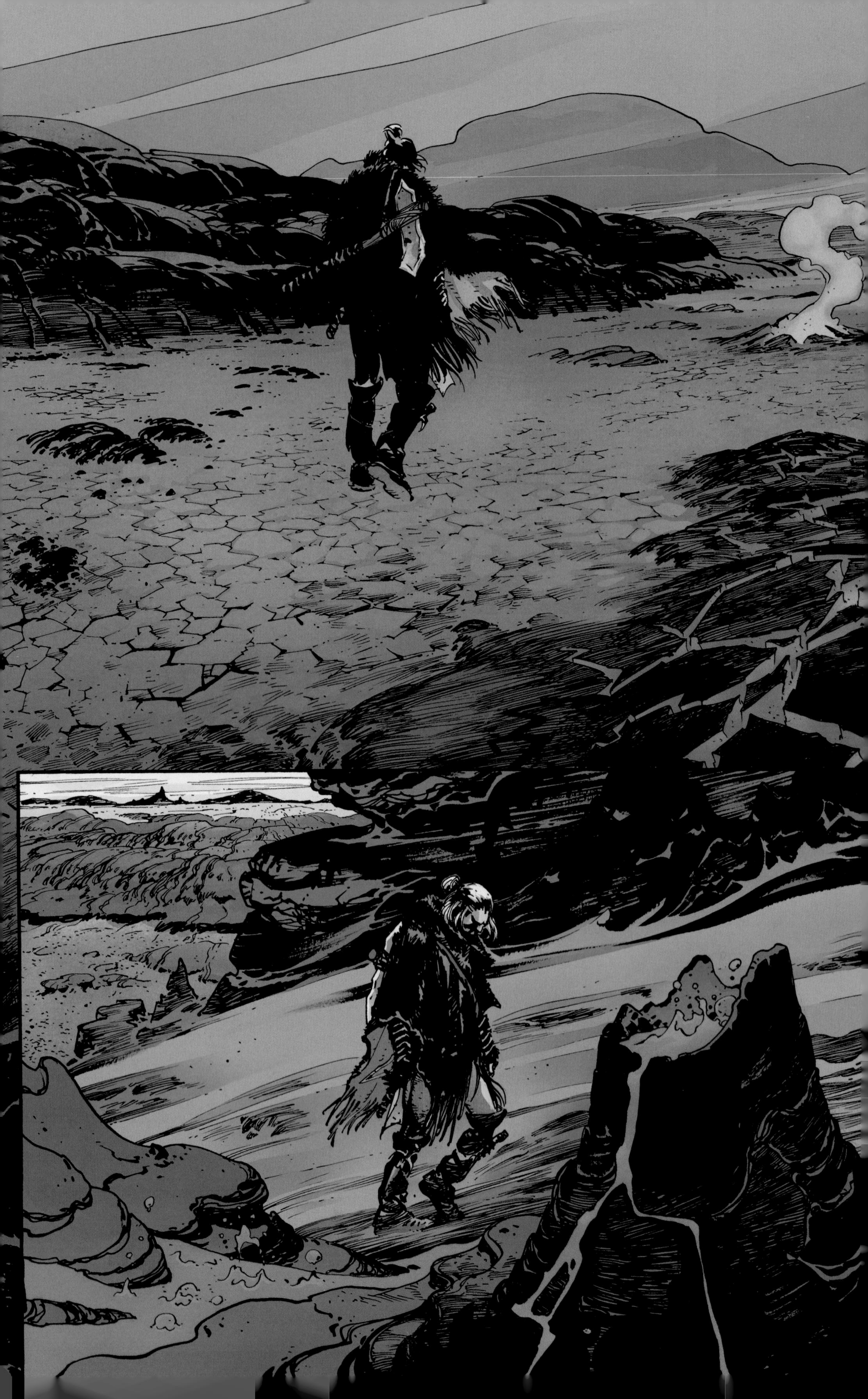

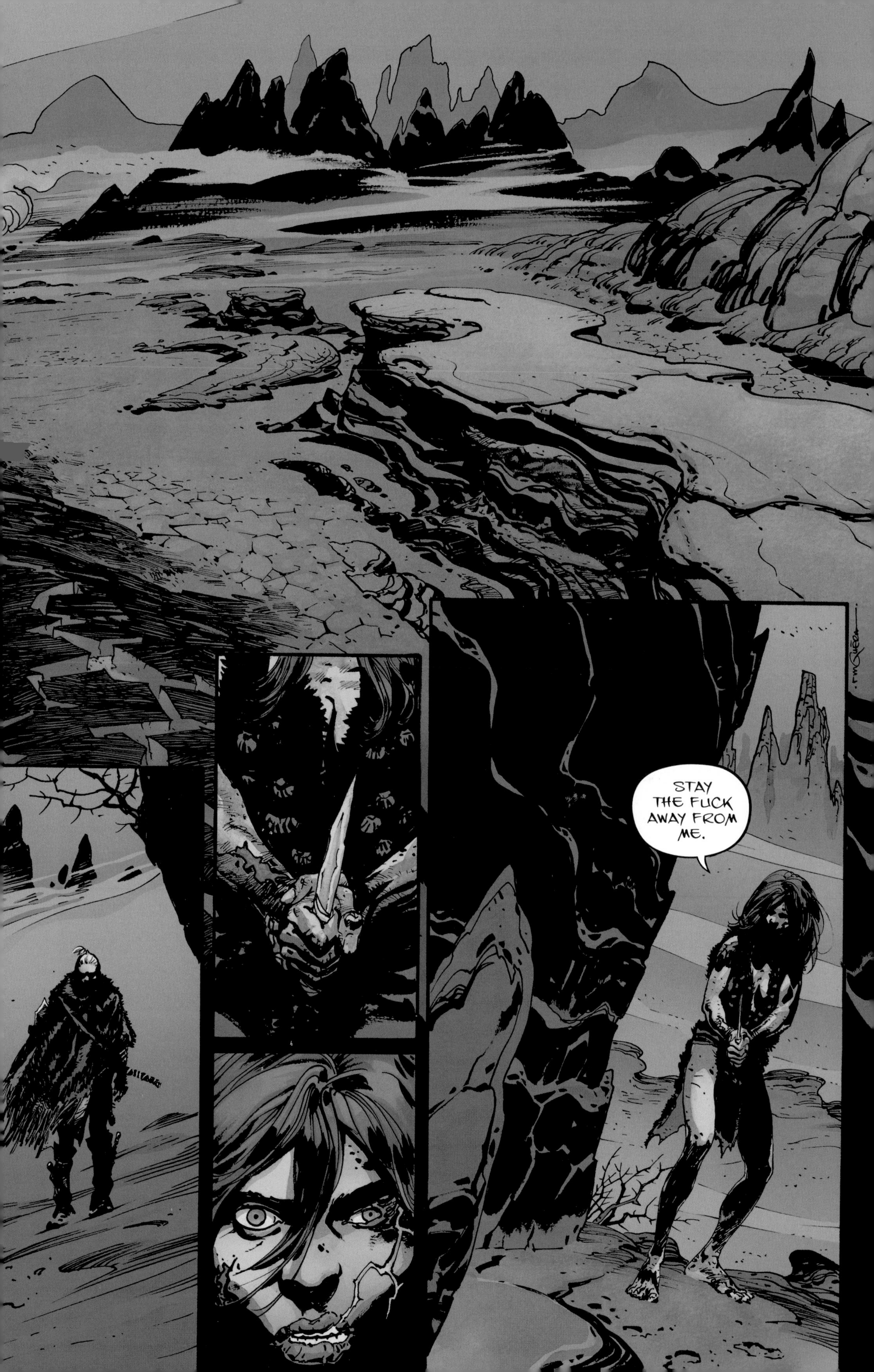
STAY THE FUCK AWAY FROM ME.

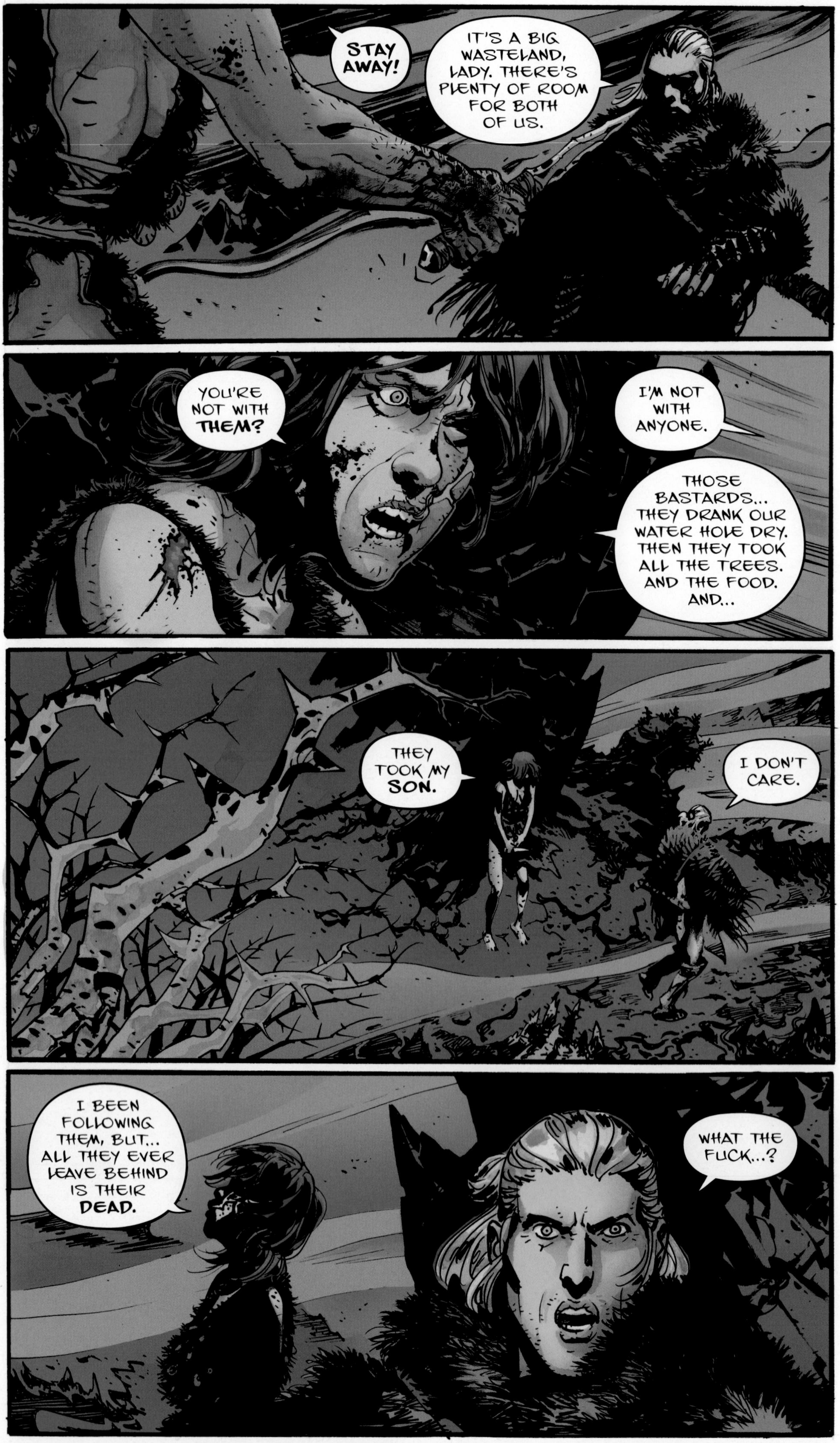
STAY AWAY!
IT'S A BIG WASTELAND, LADY. THERE'S PLENTY OF ROOM FOR BOTH OF US.
YOU'RE NOT WITH THEM?
I'M NOT WITH ANYONE.
THOSE BASTARDS... THEY DRANK OUR WATER HOLE DRY. THEN THEY TOOK ALL THE TREES. AND THE FOOD. AND...
THEY TOOK MY SON.
I DON'T CARE.
I BEEN FOLLOWING THEM, BUT... ALL THEY EVER LEAVE BEHIND IS THEIR DEAD.
WHAT THE FUCK...?

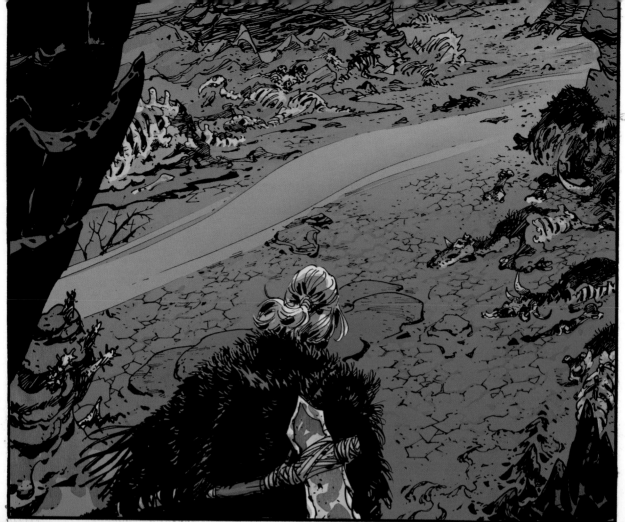

THESE **ANIMALS**... CAME FROM **VERY** FAR AWAY.

THERE WERE MORE.

MORE BEASTS THAN I KNEW THERE WERE IN THE WORLD.

SOME WERE IN CAGES. SOME THEY RODE.

MOVING CAGES? YOU MEAN THEY HAD **WHEELS**?

WHAT ARE WHEELS?

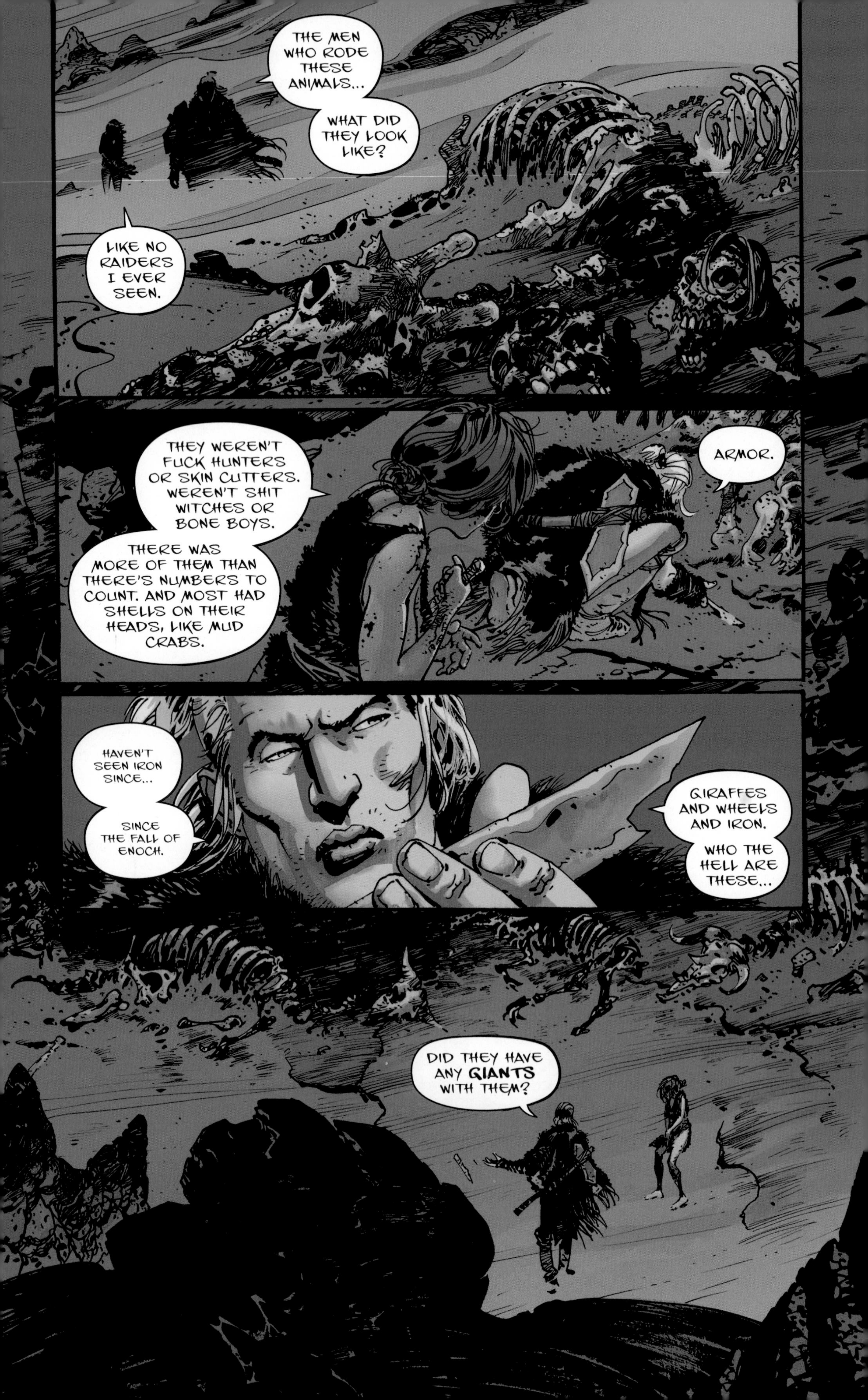
THE MEN WHO RODE THESE ANIMALS...
WHAT DID THEY LOOK LIKE?
LIKE NO RAIDERS I EVER SEEN.
THEY WEREN'T FUCK HUNTERS OR SKIN CUTTERS. WEREN'T SHIT WITCHES OR BONE BOYS.
THERE WAS MORE OF THEM THAN THERE'S NUMBERS TO COUNT. AND MOST HAD SHELLS ON THEIR HEADS, LIKE MUD CRABS.
ARMOR.
HAVEN'T SEEN IRON SINCE...
SINCE THE FALL OF ENOCH.
GIRAFFES AND WHEELS AND IRON.
WHO THE HELL ARE THESE...
DID THEY HAVE ANY GIANTS WITH THEM?

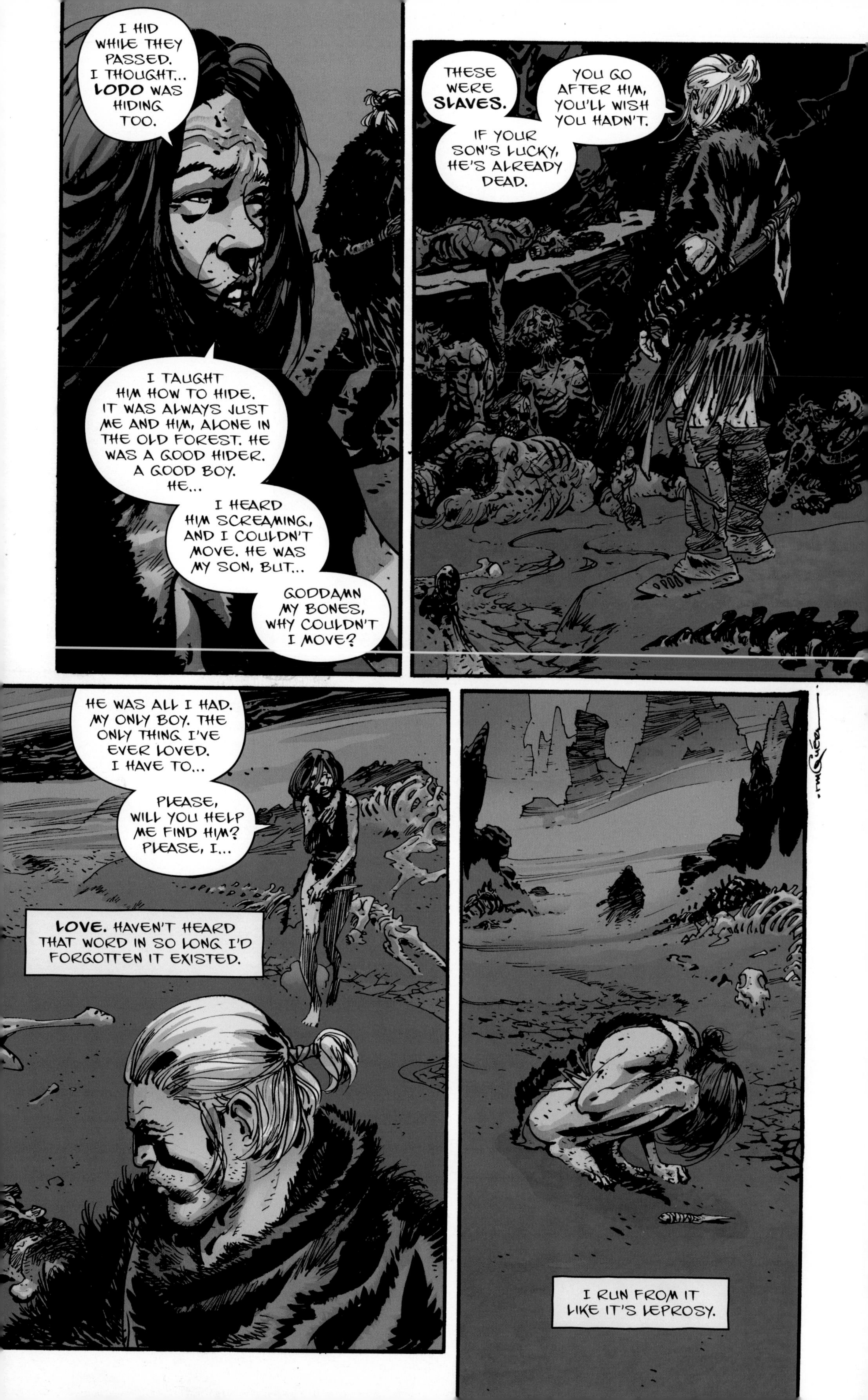
I HID WHILE THEY PASSED. I THOUGHT... LODO WAS HIDING TOO.
I TAUGHT HIM HOW TO HIDE. IT WAS ALWAYS JUST ME AND HIM, ALONE IN THE OLD FOREST. HE WAS A GOOD HIDER. A GOOD BOY. HE...
I HEARD HIM SCREAMING, AND I COULDN'T MOVE. HE WAS MY SON, BUT...
GODDAMN MY BONES, WHY COULDN'T I MOVE?
THESE WERE SLAVES.
YOU GO AFTER HIM, YOU'LL WISH YOU HADN'T.
IF YOUR SON'S LUCKY, HE'S ALREADY DEAD.
HE WAS ALL I HAD. MY ONLY BOY. THE ONLY THING I'VE EVER LOVED. I HAVE TO...
PLEASE, WILL YOU HELP ME FIND HIM? PLEASE, I...
LOVE. HAVEN'T HEARD THAT WORD IN SO LONG I'D FORGOTTEN IT EXISTED.
I RUN FROM IT LIKE IT'S LEPROSY.

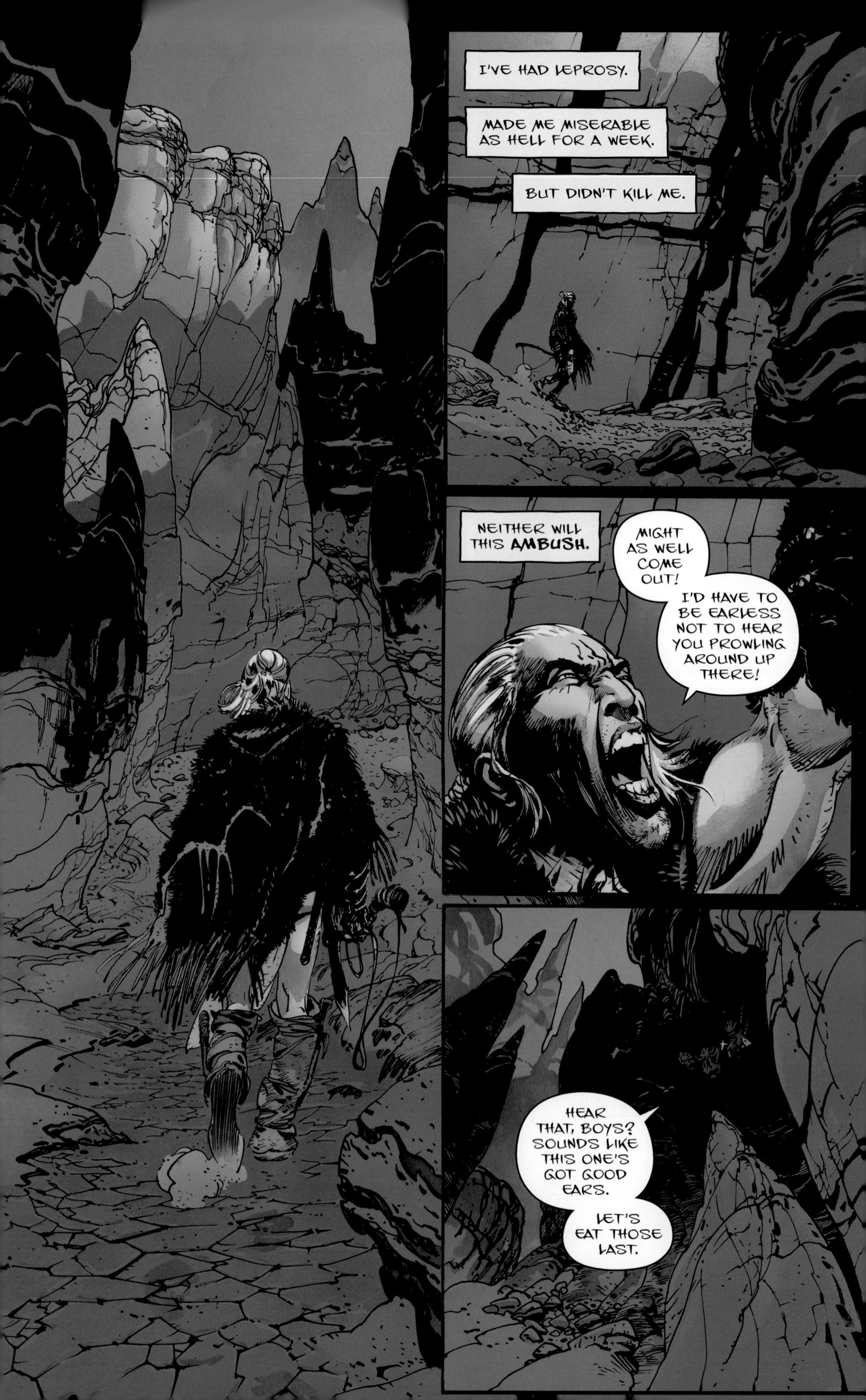
I'VE HAD LEPROSY.
MADE ME MISERABLE AS HELL FOR A WEEK.
BUT DIDN'T KILL ME.
NEITHER WILL THIS **AMBUSH.**
MIGHT AS WELL COME OUT!
I'D HAVE TO BE EARLESS NOT TO HEAR YOU PROWLING AROUND UP THERE!
HEAR THAT, BOYS? SOUNDS LIKE THIS ONE'S GOT GOOD EARS.
LET'S EAT THOSE LAST.

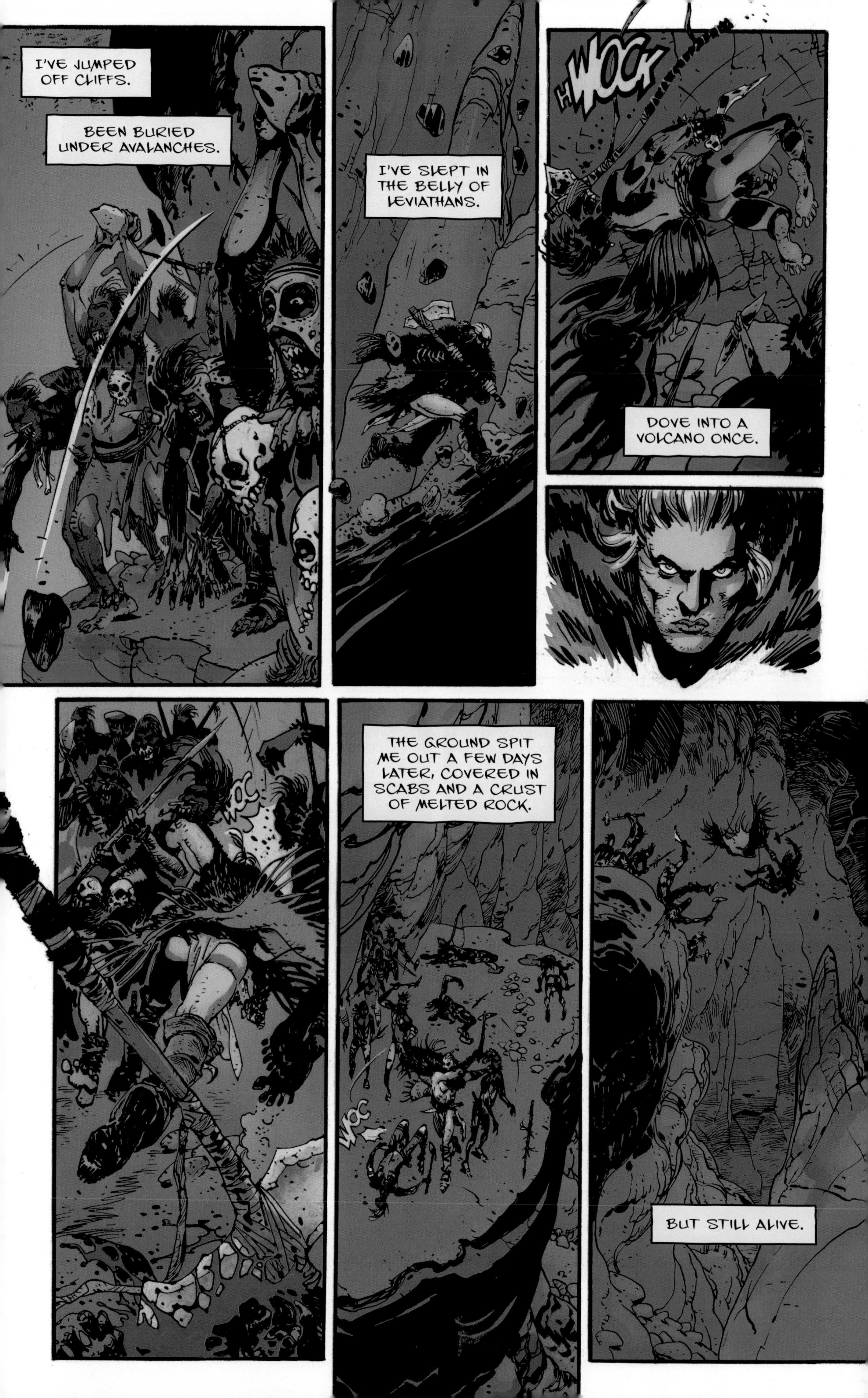
I'VE JUMPED OFF CLIFFS.
BEEN BURIED UNDER AVALANCHES.
I'VE SLEPT IN THE BELLY OF LEVIATHANS.
HWOCK
DOVE INTO A VOLCANO ONCE.
WOC
THE GROUND SPIT ME OUT A FEW DAYS LATER, COVERED IN SCABS AND A CRUST OF MELTED ROCK.
WOC
BUT STILL ALIVE.

I'VE SEEN EVERYTHING THIS WORLD HAS TO OFFER.

EVERY DEPRAVITY. EVERY DANGER. EVERY MONSTER, HUMAN OR OTHERWISE.

AND **NONE** OF IT COULD KILL ME.

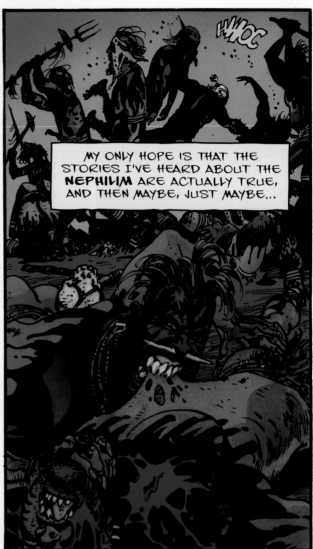

HWWOC

MY ONLY HOPE IS THAT THE STORIES I'VE HEARD ABOUT THE **NEPHILIM** ARE ACTUALLY TRUE, AND THEN MAYBE, JUST MAYBE...

I CAN FINALLY PUT AN END TO THIS FUCKING CURSE.

FINALLY KNOW WHAT IT'S LIKE TO BE MURDERED.

PLEASE, FUCKING GODDAMN GOD, LET ME BE MURDERED.

THE FUCKER'S CUTTING US TO PIECES!

BRING OUT THE FUCKING **DOGS!**

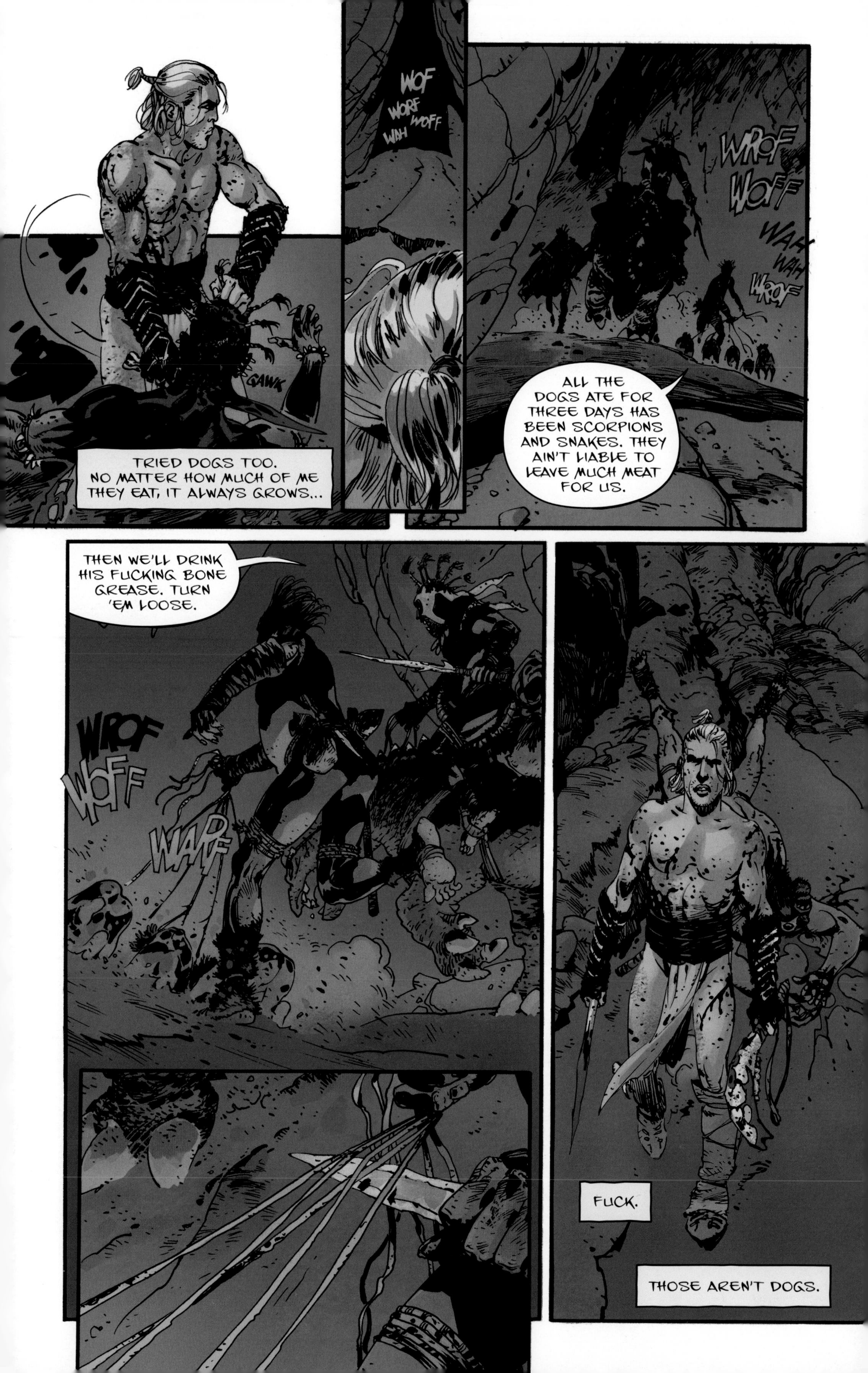
GAWK
TRIED DOGS TOO. NO MATTER HOW MUCH OF ME THEY EAT, IT ALWAYS GROWS...
WOF
WORF WOFF
WAH
WROF
WOFF
WAH
WAH
WROF
ALL THE DOGS ATE FOR THREE DAYS HAS BEEN SCORPIONS AND SNAKES. THEY AIN'T LIABLE TO LEAVE MUCH MEAT FOR US.
THEN WE'LL DRINK HIS FUCKING BONE GREASE. TURN 'EM LOOSE.
WROF
WOFF
WARF
FUCK.
THOSE AREN'T DOGS.

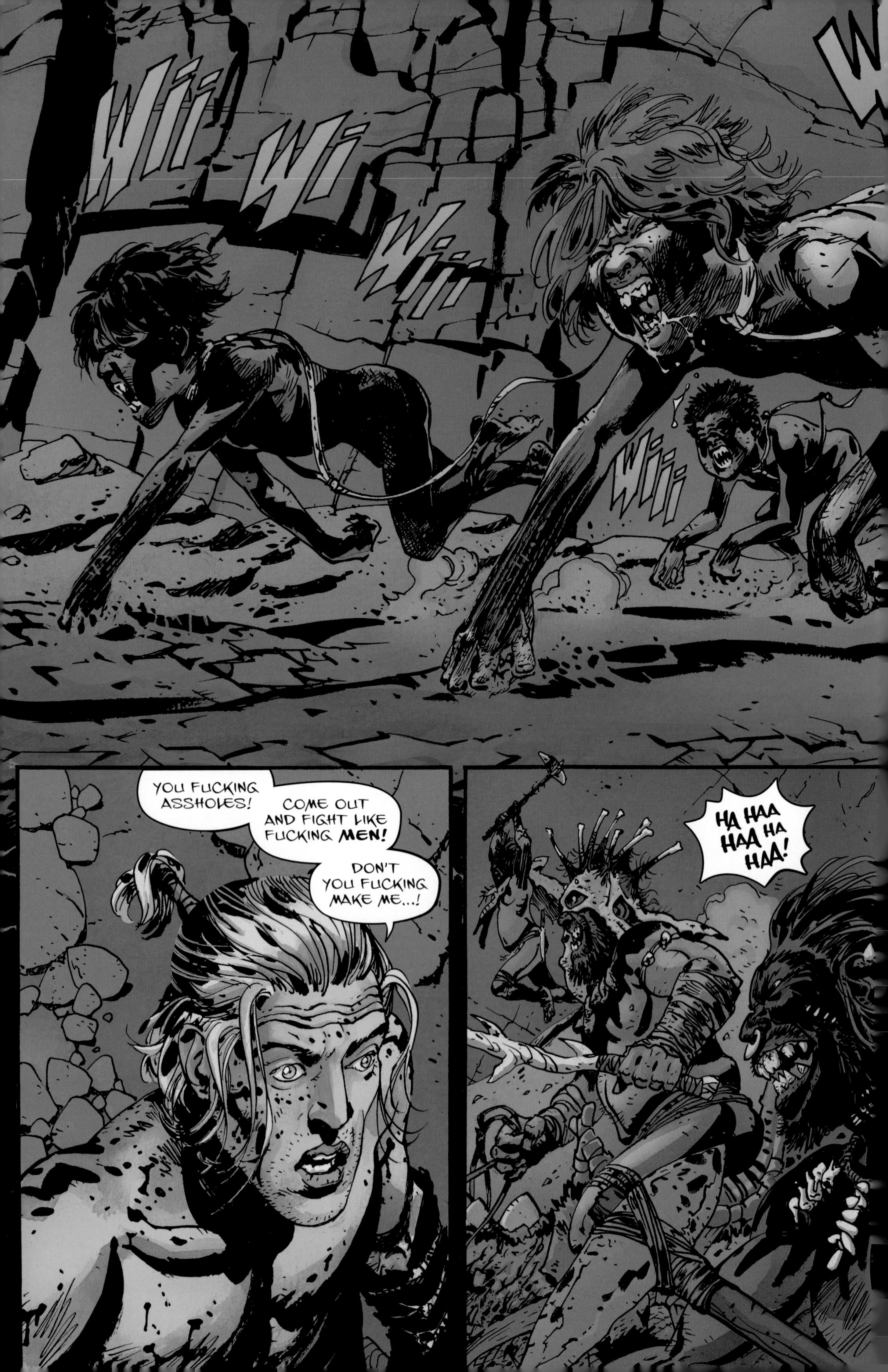
Wiii
Wi
Wiii
W
Wiii
YOU FUCKING ASSHOLES!
COME OUT AND FIGHT LIKE FUCKING **MEN!**
DON'T YOU FUCKING MAKE ME...!
HA HAA HAA HA HAA!

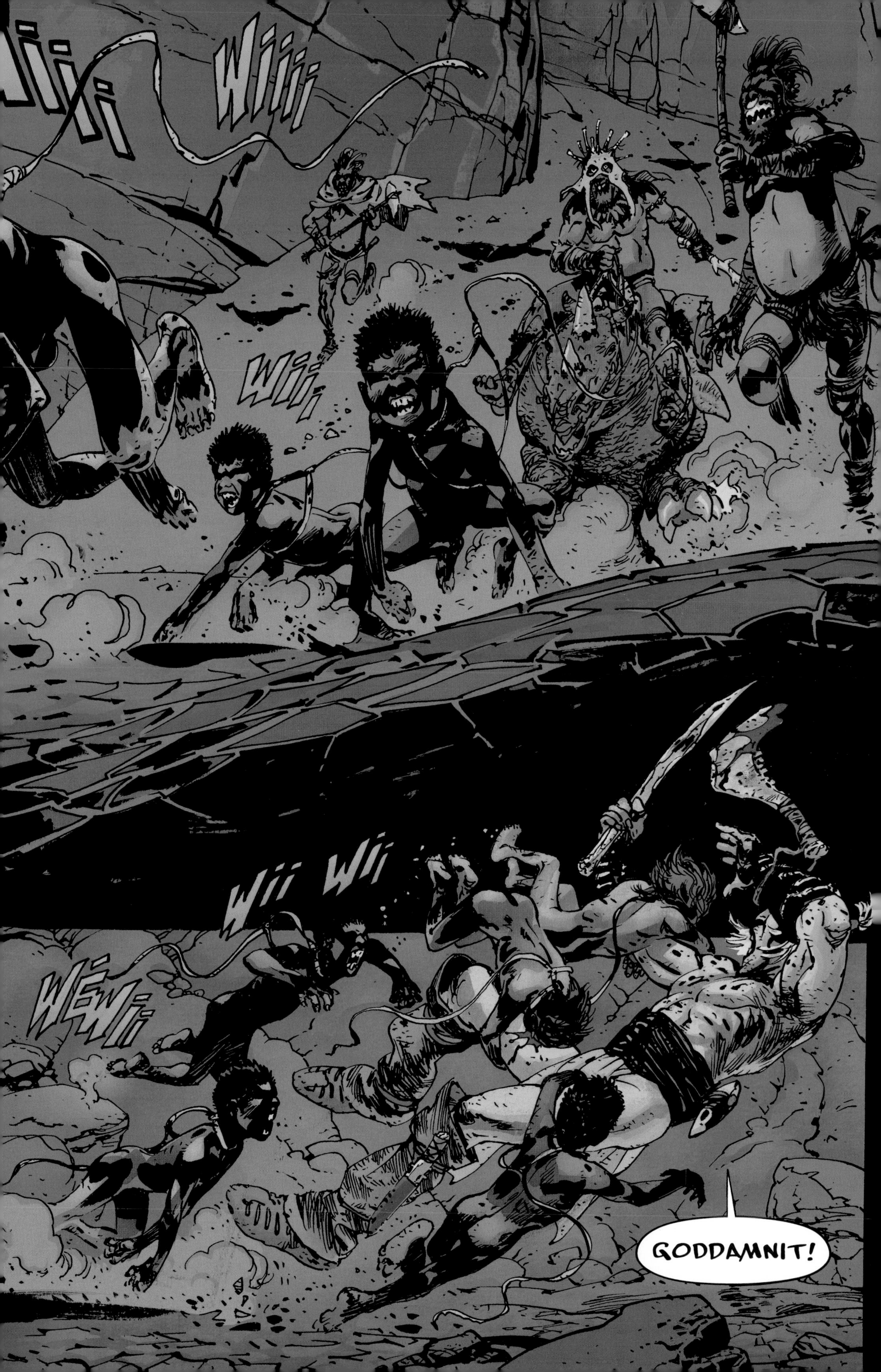

WIIII
WIII
WIII
WII WII
WÉWII
GODDAMNIT!

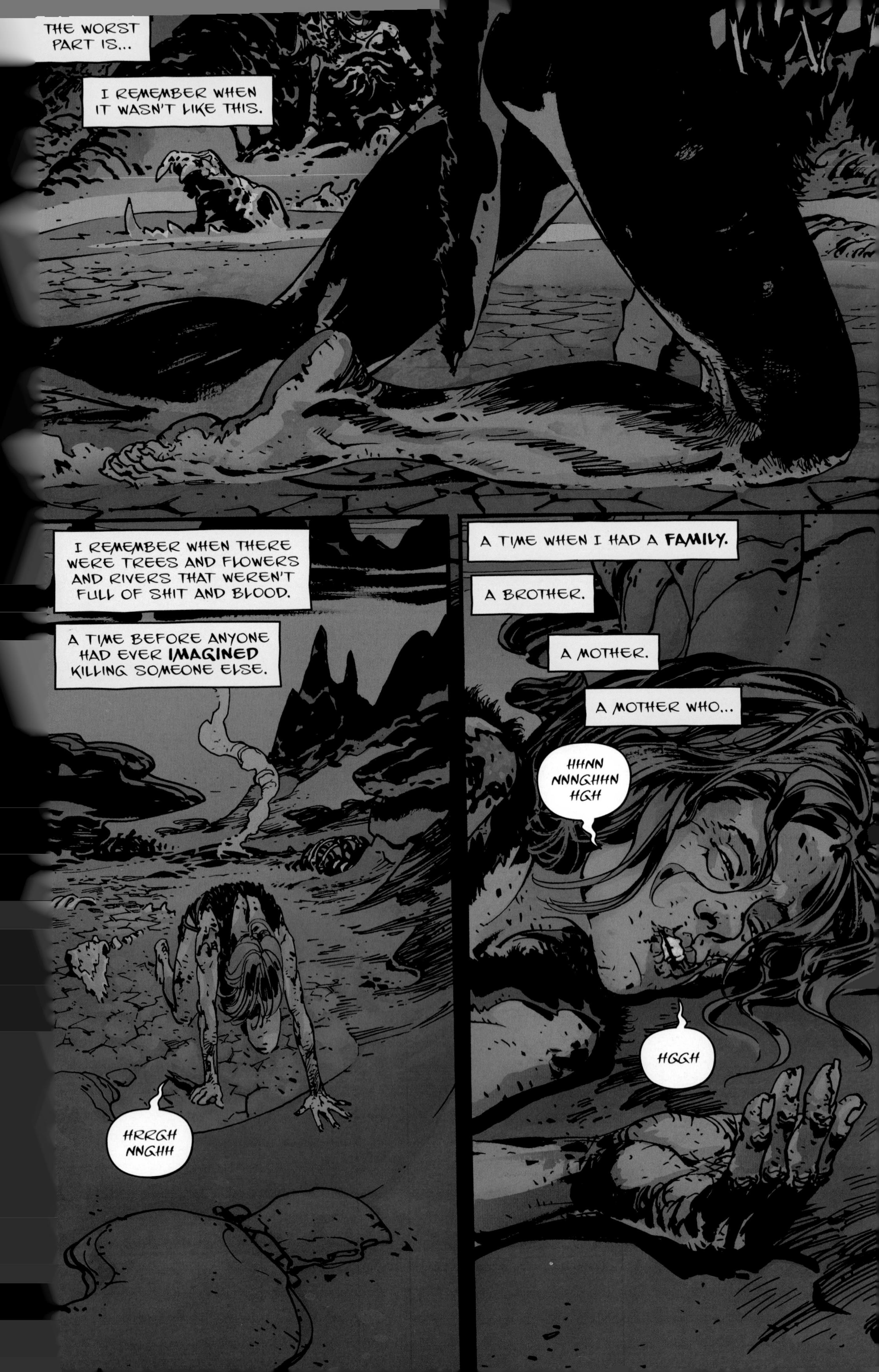
THE WORST PART IS...
I REMEMBER WHEN IT WASN'T LIKE THIS.
I REMEMBER WHEN THERE WERE TREES AND FLOWERS AND RIVERS THAT WEREN'T FULL OF SHIT AND BLOOD.
A TIME BEFORE ANYONE HAD EVER **IMAGINED** KILLING SOMEONE ELSE.
HRRGH NNGHH
A TIME WHEN I HAD A **FAMILY.**
A BROTHER.
A MOTHER.
A MOTHER WHO...
HHNN NNNGHHN HGH
HGGH

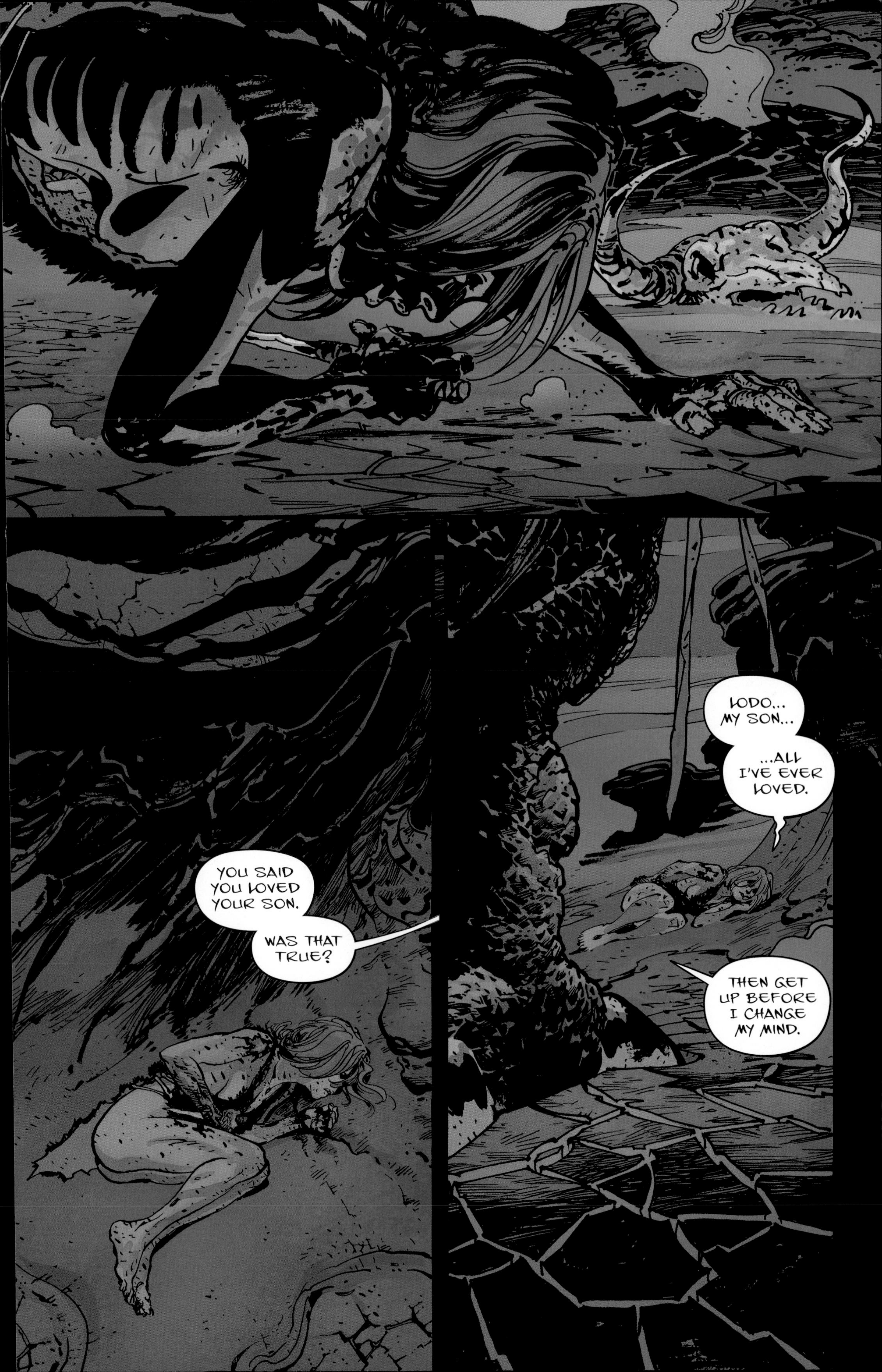
YOU SAID YOU LOVED YOUR SON.
WAS THAT TRUE?
LODO... MY SON...
...ALL I'VE EVER LOVED.
THEN GET UP BEFORE I CHANGE MY MIND.

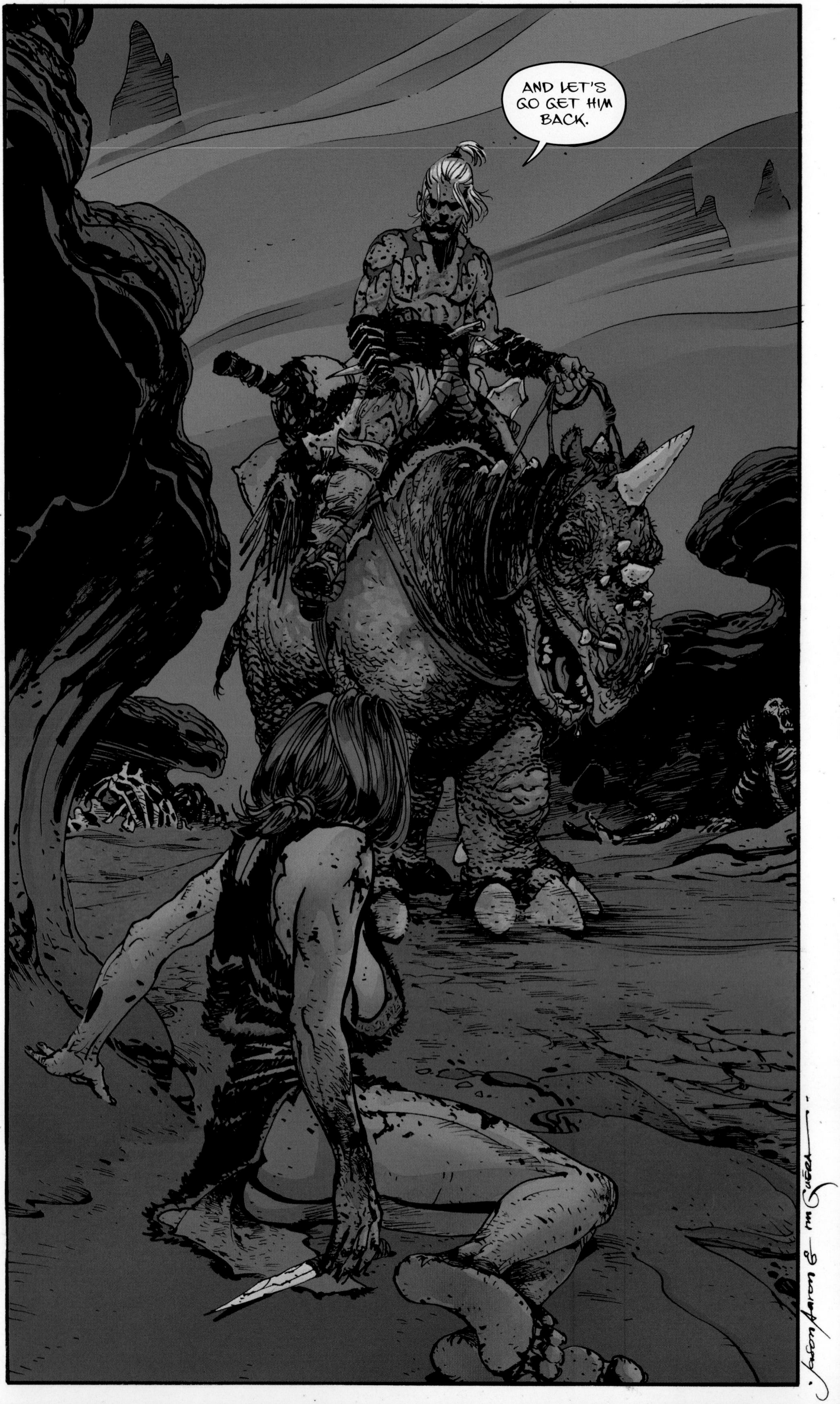
AND LET'S GO GET HIM BACK.

chapter three

The Children of Eden

*AND GOD BLESSED THEM,
AND GOD SAID UNTO THEM,
BE FRUITFUL, AND MULTIPLY,
AND REPLENISH THE EARTH,
AND SUBDUE IT.*

GENESIS 1:28

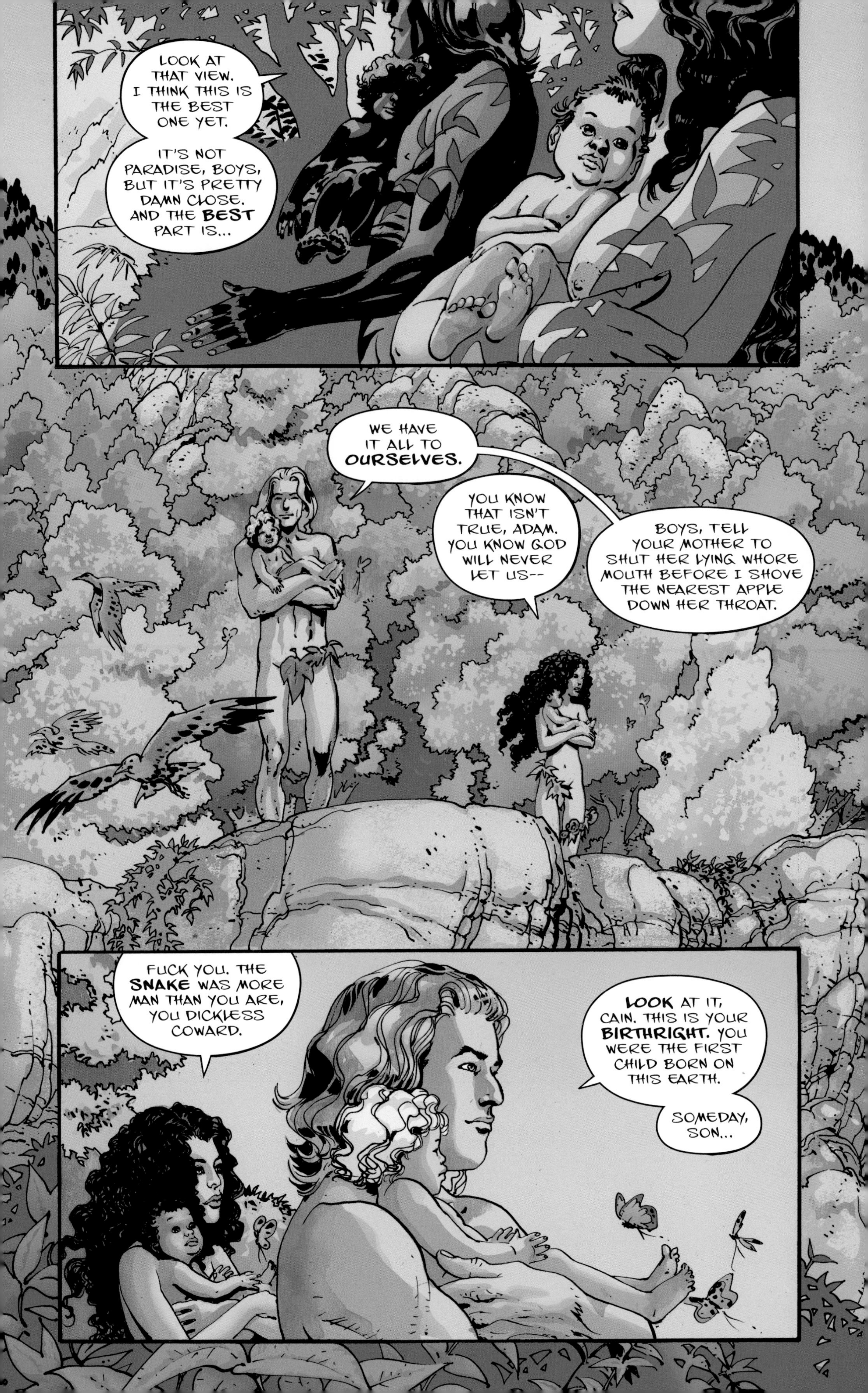
LOOK AT THAT VIEW. I THINK THIS IS THE BEST ONE YET.
IT'S NOT PARADISE, BOYS, BUT IT'S PRETTY DAMN CLOSE. AND THE **BEST** PART IS...
WE HAVE IT ALL TO **OURSELVES.**
YOU KNOW THAT ISN'T TRUE, ADAM. YOU KNOW GOD WILL NEVER LET US--
BOYS, TELL YOUR MOTHER TO SHUT HER LYING WHORE MOUTH BEFORE I SHOVE THE NEAREST APPLE DOWN HER THROAT.
FUCK YOU. THE **SNAKE** WAS MORE MAN THAN YOU ARE, YOU DICKLESS COWARD.
LOOK AT IT, CAIN. THIS IS YOUR **BIRTHRIGHT.** YOU WERE THE FIRST CHILD BORN ON THIS EARTH.
SOMEDAY, SON...

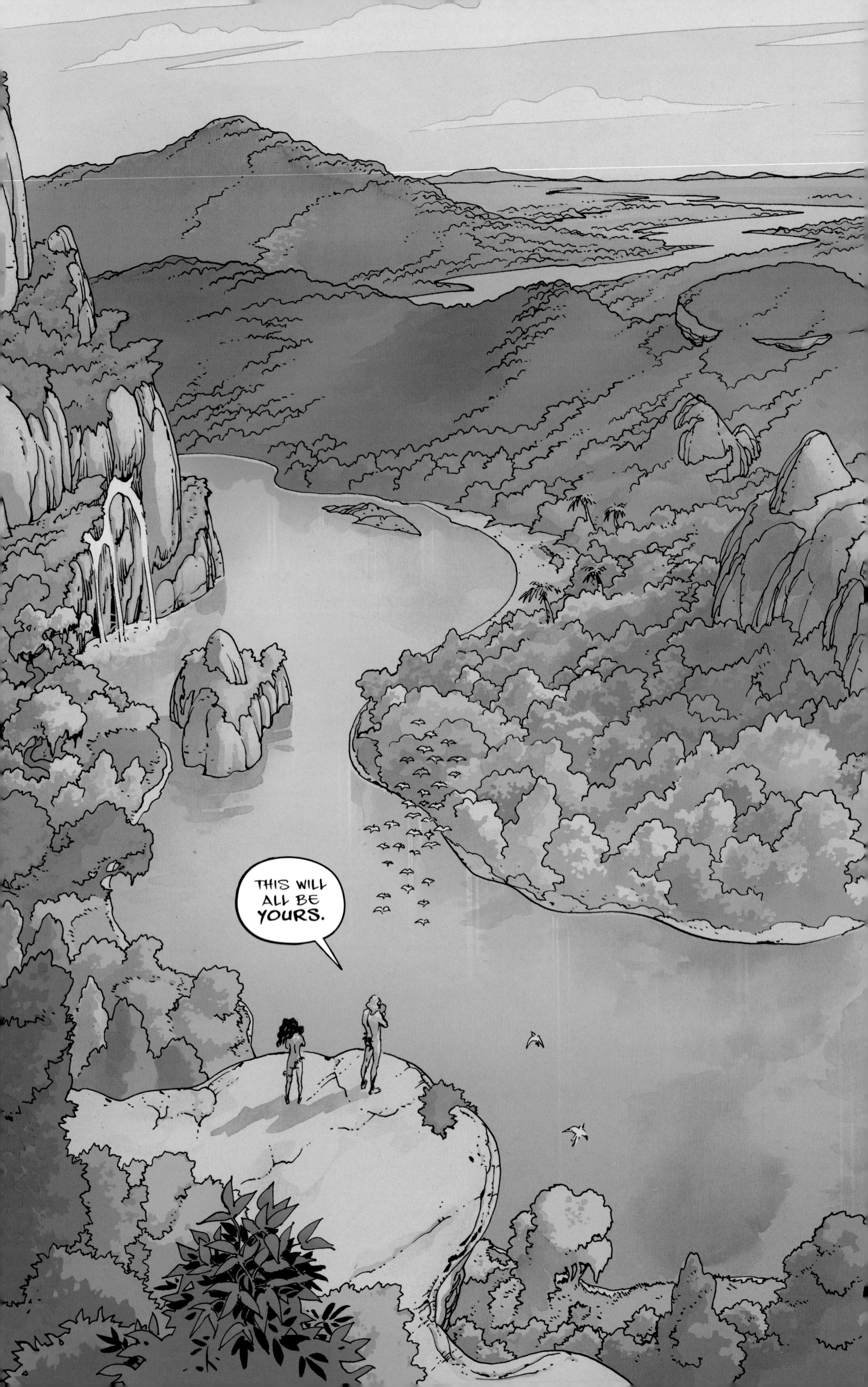
THIS WILL ALL BE YOURS.

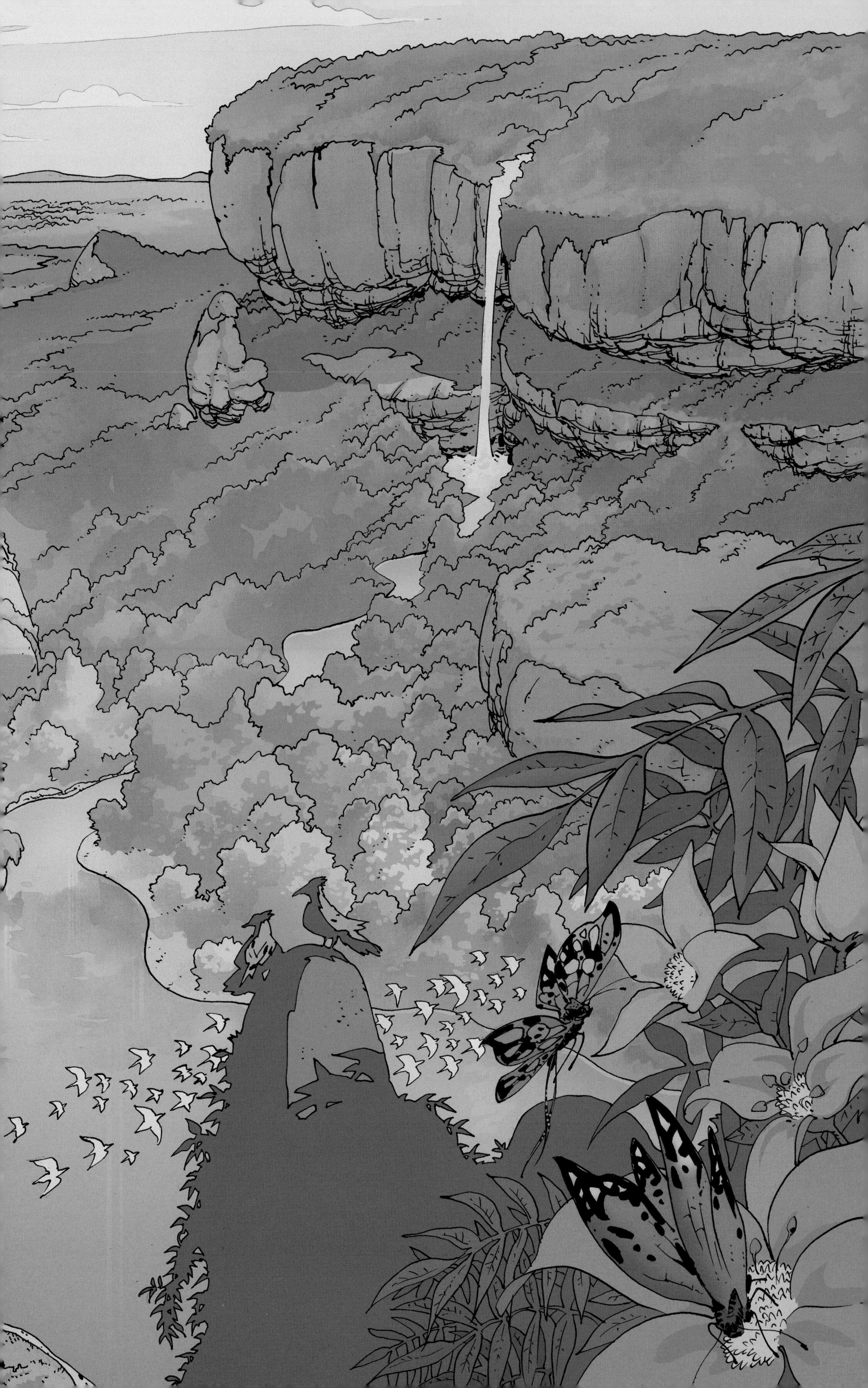

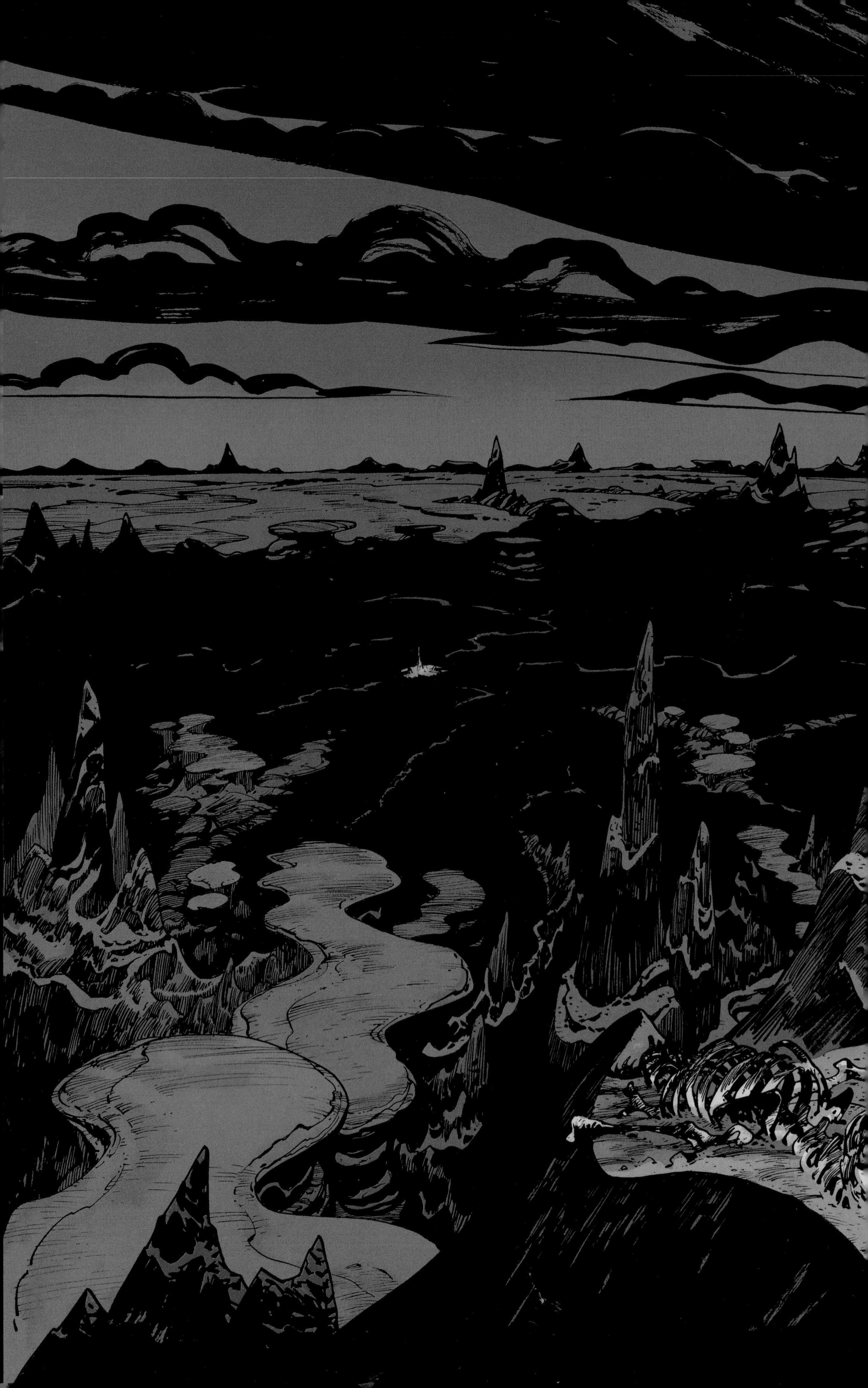

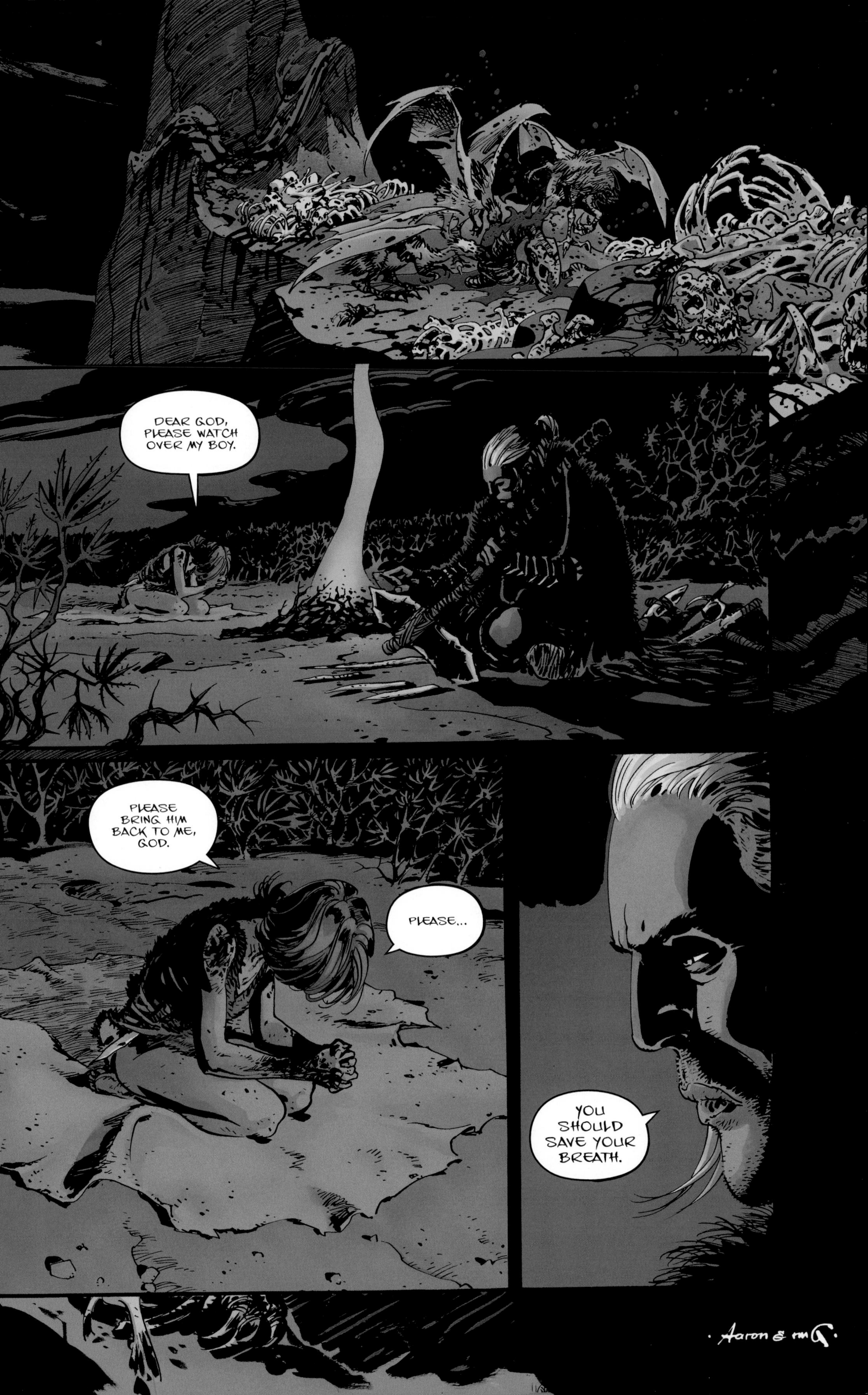
DEAR GOD, PLEASE WATCH OVER MY BOY.
PLEASE BRING HIM BACK TO ME, GOD.
PLEASE...
YOU SHOULD SAVE YOUR BREATH.
· Aaron & rmG ·

AM I NOT DOING IT RIGHT?
I'VE NEVER PRAYED BEFORE.
I SAW AN OLD WOMAN DO IT ONCE, WHEN SHE WAS CAUGHT BY SOME REAVERS.
AND WERE THE OLD WOMAN'S PRAYERS ANSWERED?
I DON'T THINK SO.
THEY KILLED HER FOR A VERY LONG TIME.
LIKE I SAID. SAVE YOUR BREATH.
SOME SAY GOD STILL WALKS THE LAND. THOUGH I'VE NEVER SEEN HIM.
YOU DON'T THINK HE CAN HEAR US ANYMORE?
OH, HE CAN HEAR YOU JUST FINE. HE HEARS **EVERYTHING.**
EVERY SCREAM. EVERY CRY. EVERY WHIMPER.
EVERY PLEA FOR MERCY.
FOR DEATH.
HE HEARS.
HE JUST DOESN'T GIVE A FUCK.
WHY DID YOU CHANGE YOUR MIND ABOUT HELPING ME?
NHRRCCC.

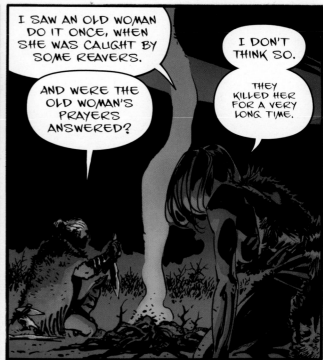

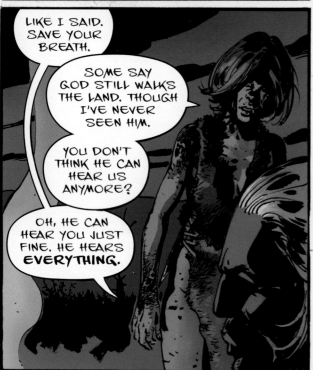

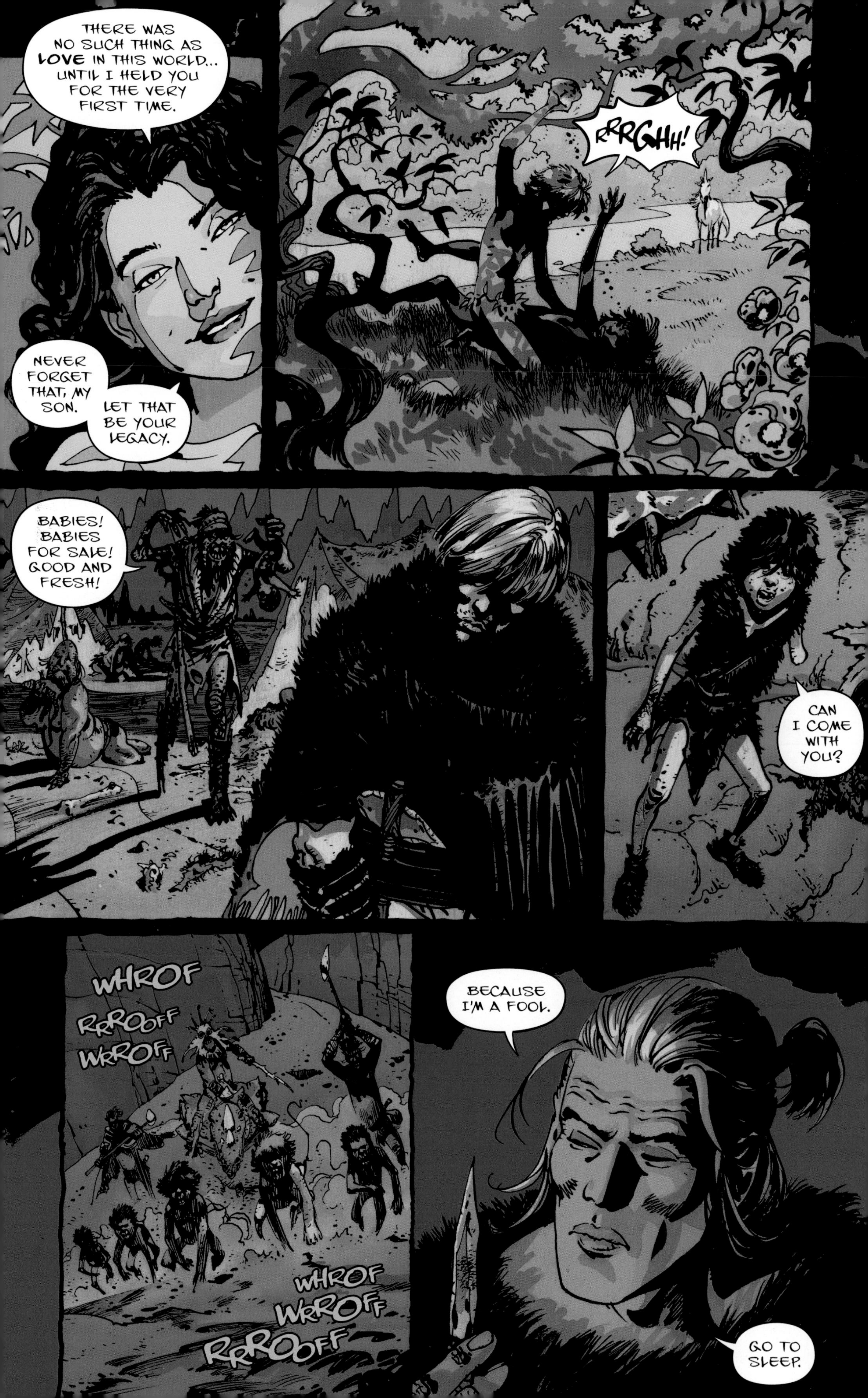
THERE WAS NO SUCH THING AS **LOVE** IN THIS WORLD... UNTIL I HELD YOU FOR THE VERY FIRST TIME.
NEVER FORGET THAT, MY SON.
LET THAT BE YOUR LEGACY.
RRRGHH!
BABIES! BABIES FOR SALE! GOOD AND FRESH!
CAN I COME WITH YOU?
WHROF
RRROOFF
WRROFF
BECAUSE I'M A FOOL.
WHROF
WRROFF
RRROOFF
GO TO SLEEP.

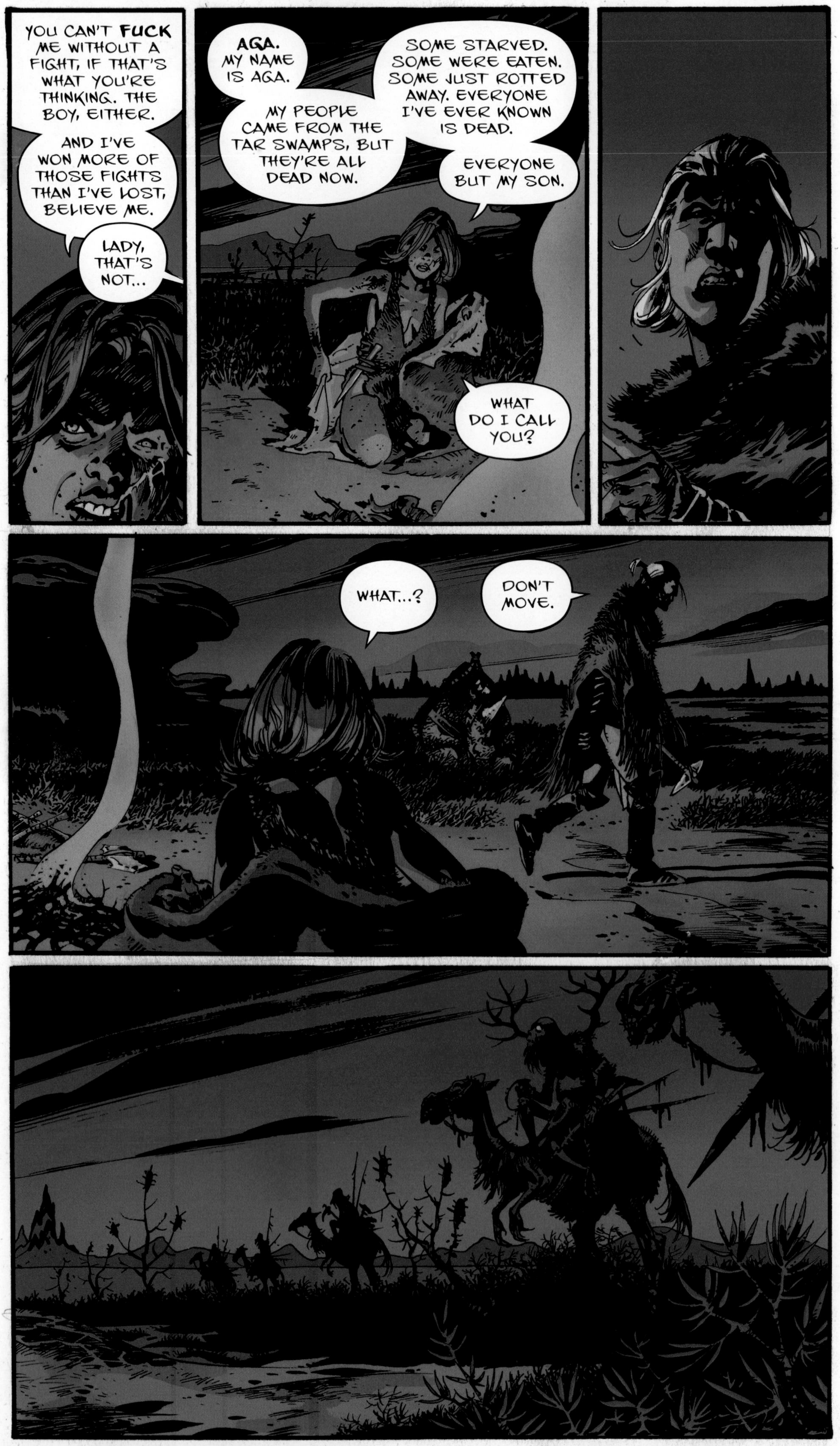
YOU CAN'T FUCK ME WITHOUT A FIGHT, IF THAT'S WHAT YOU'RE THINKING. THE BOY, EITHER.
AND I'VE WON MORE OF THOSE FIGHTS THAN I'VE LOST, BELIEVE ME.
LADY, THAT'S NOT...
AGA. MY NAME IS AGA.
MY PEOPLE CAME FROM THE TAR SWAMPS, BUT THEY'RE ALL DEAD NOW.
SOME STARVED. SOME WERE EATEN. SOME JUST ROTTED AWAY. EVERYONE I'VE EVER KNOWN IS DEAD.
EVERYONE BUT MY SON.
WHAT DO I CALL YOU?
WHAT...?
DON'T MOVE.

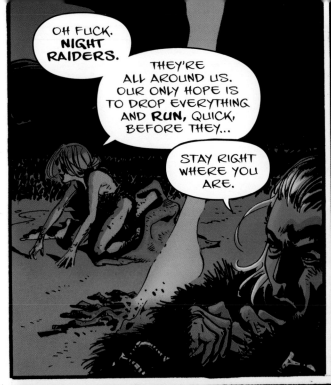

OH FUCK. **NIGHT RAIDERS.**

THEY'RE ALL AROUND US. OUR ONLY HOPE IS TO DROP EVERYTHING AND **RUN**, QUICK, BEFORE THEY...

STAY RIGHT WHERE YOU ARE.

BUT... WHAT ARE YOU...

...

HE'S **CRAZY.**

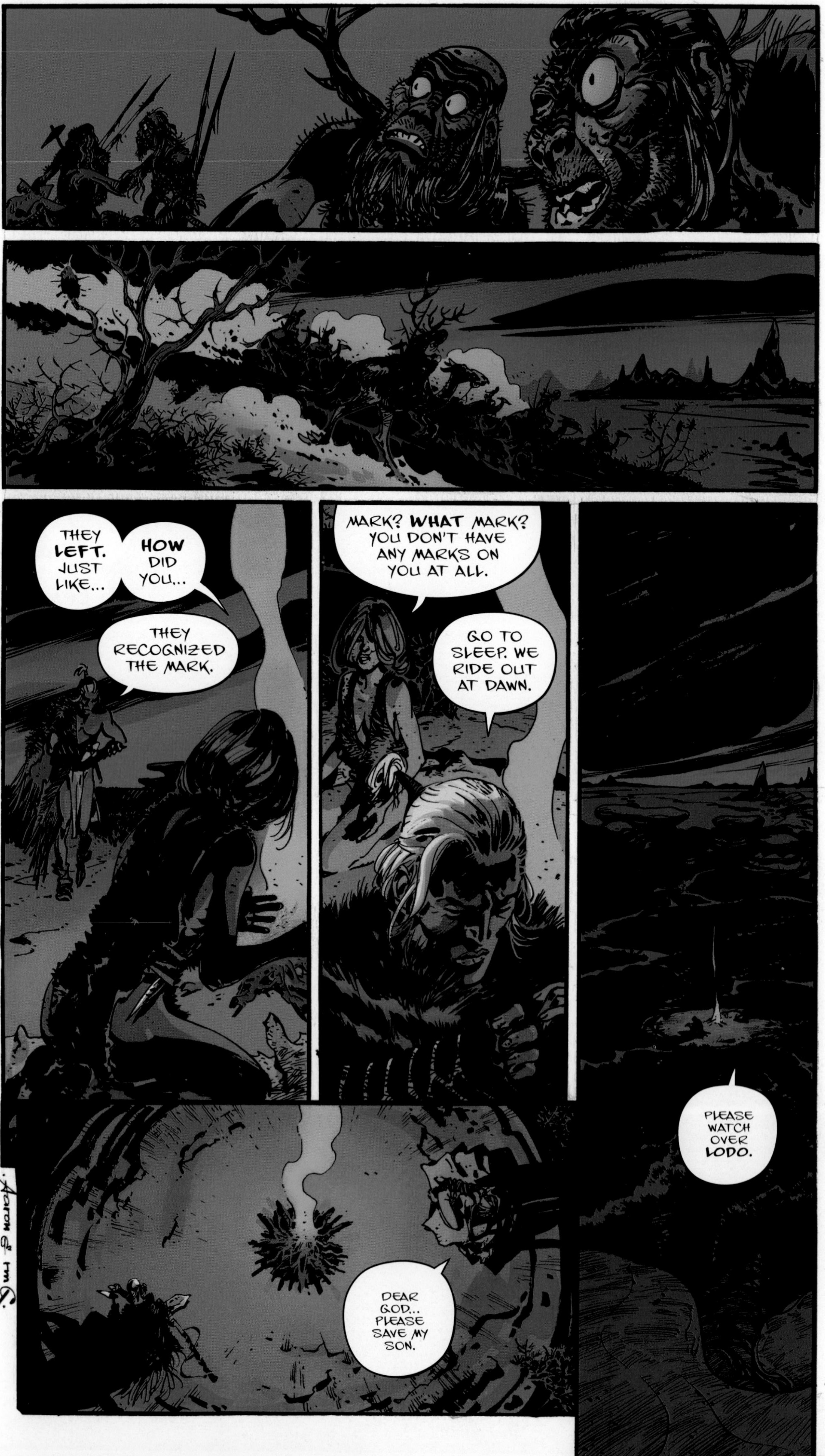
THEY LEFT. JUST LIKE...
HOW DID YOU...
THEY RECOGNIZED THE MARK.
MARK? WHAT MARK? YOU DON'T HAVE ANY MARKS ON YOU AT ALL.
GO TO SLEEP. WE RIDE OUT AT DAWN.
PLEASE WATCH OVER LODO.
DEAR GOD... PLEASE SAVE MY SON.

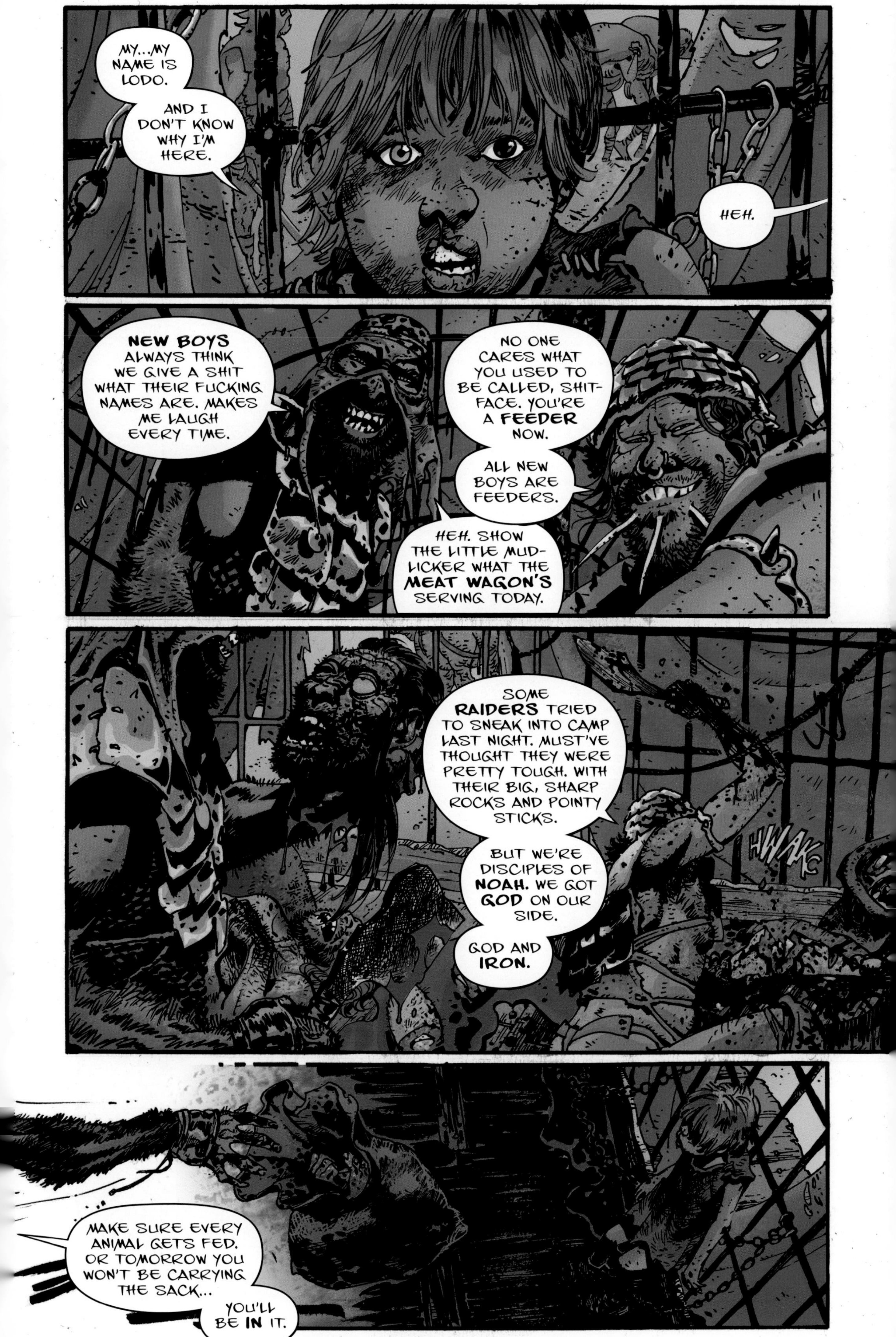
MY... MY NAME IS LODO.
AND I DON'T KNOW WHY I'M HERE.
HEH.
NEW BOYS ALWAYS THINK WE GIVE A SHIT WHAT THEIR FUCKING NAMES ARE. MAKES ME LAUGH EVERY TIME.
NO ONE CARES WHAT YOU USED TO BE CALLED, SHIT-FACE. YOU'RE A FEEDER NOW.
ALL NEW BOYS ARE FEEDERS.
HEH. SHOW THE LITTLE MUD-LICKER WHAT THE MEAT WAGON'S SERVING TODAY.
SOME RAIDERS TRIED TO SNEAK INTO CAMP LAST NIGHT. MUST'VE THOUGHT THEY WERE PRETTY TOUGH. WITH THEIR BIG, SHARP ROCKS AND POINTY STICKS.
BUT WE'RE DISCIPLES OF NOAH. WE GOT GOD ON OUR SIDE.
GOD AND IRON.
HWAKC
MAKE SURE EVERY ANIMAL GETS FED. OR TOMORROW YOU WON'T BE CARRYING THE SACK...
YOU'LL BE IN IT.

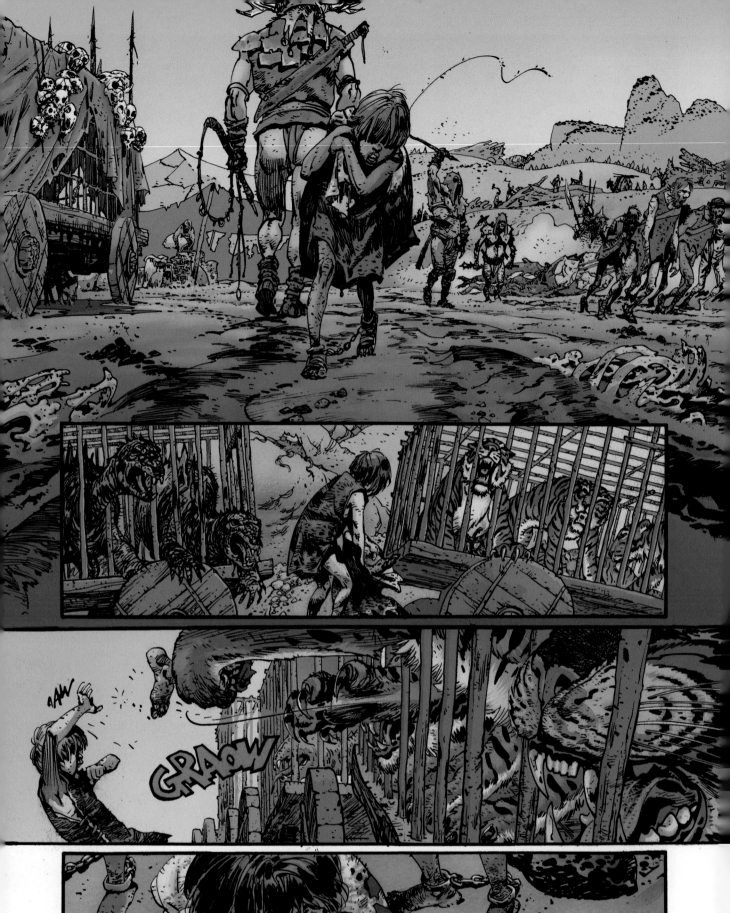

GAW

GRAOW

LOOK AT THIS LITTLE **SHIT BITCH** HERE.

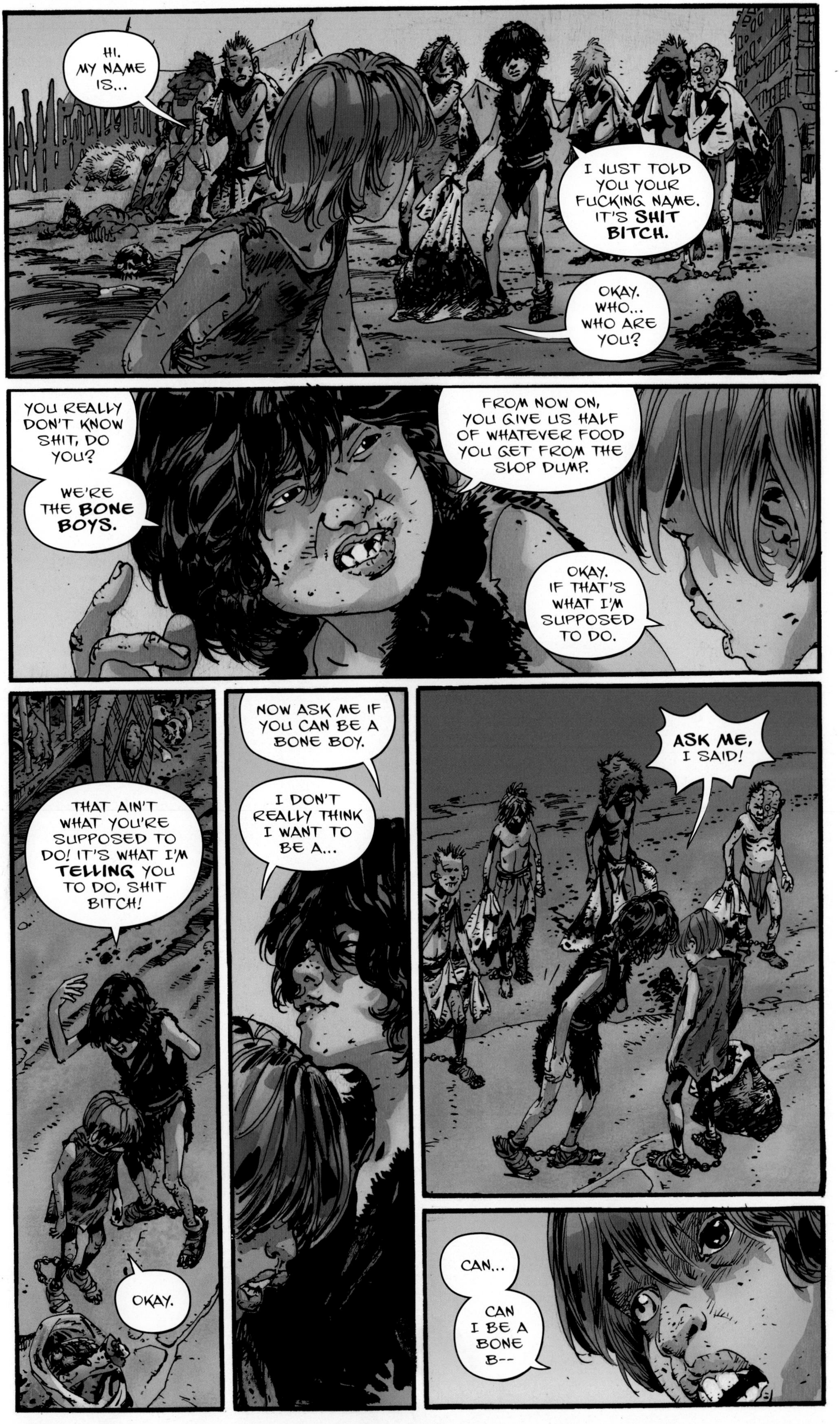
HI. MY NAME IS...
I JUST TOLD YOU YOUR FUCKING NAME. IT'S SHIT BITCH.
OKAY. WHO... WHO ARE YOU?
YOU REALLY DON'T KNOW SHIT, DO YOU?
WE'RE THE BONE BOYS.
FROM NOW ON, YOU GIVE US HALF OF WHATEVER FOOD YOU GET FROM THE SLOP DUMP.
OKAY. IF THAT'S WHAT I'M SUPPOSED TO DO.
THAT AIN'T WHAT YOU'RE SUPPOSED TO DO! IT'S WHAT I'M TELLING YOU TO DO, SHIT BITCH!
OKAY.
NOW ASK ME IF YOU CAN BE A BONE BOY.
I DON'T REALLY THINK I WANT TO BE A...
ASK ME, I SAID!
CAN...
CAN I BE A BONE B--

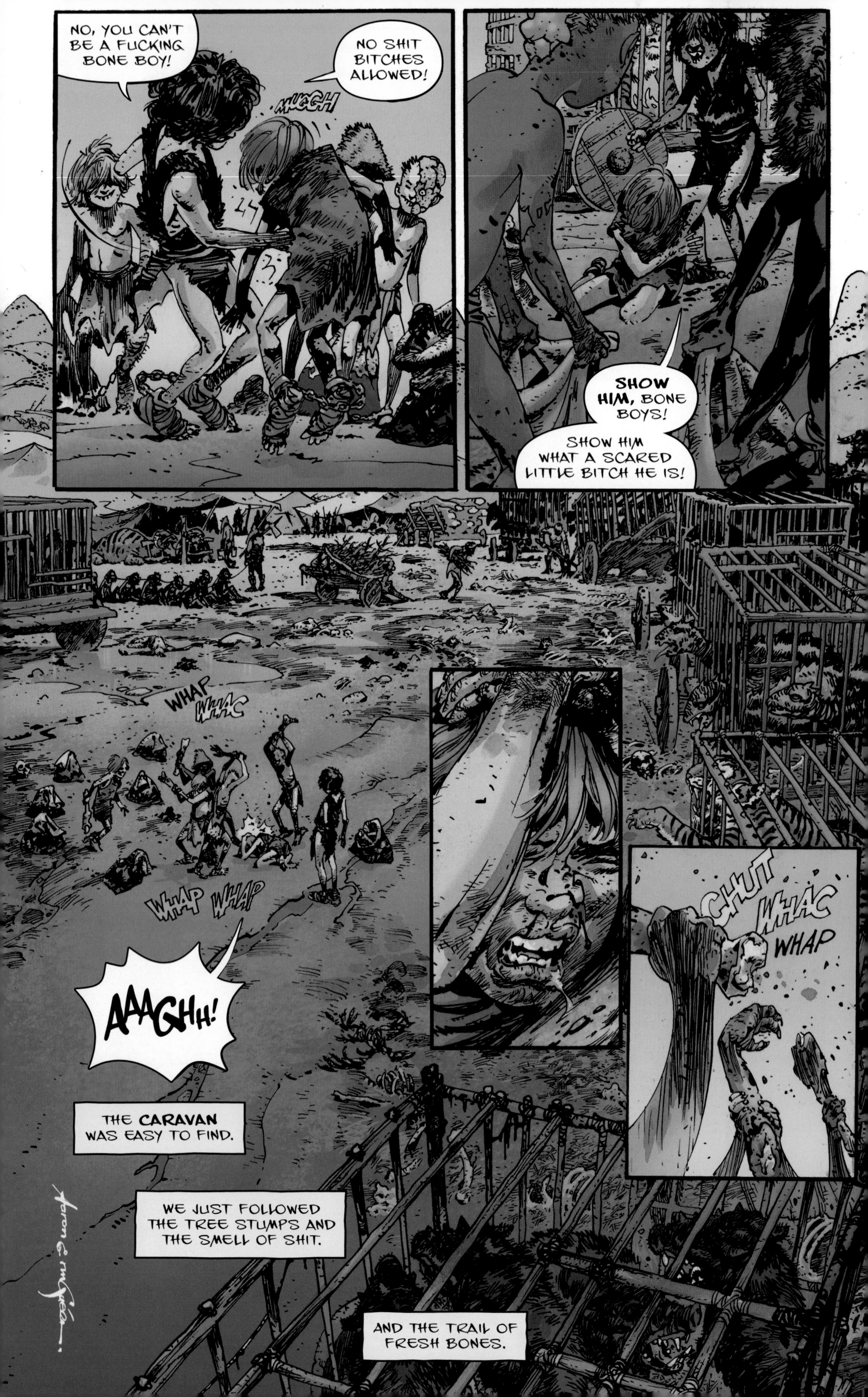
NO, YOU CAN'T BE A FUCKING BONE BOY!
NO SHIT BITCHES ALLOWED!
MUGGH
SHOW HIM, BONE BOYS!
SHOW HIM WHAT A SCARED LITTLE BITCH HE IS!
WHAP
WHAC
WHAP WHAP
AAAGHH!
CHUT
WHAC
WHAP
THE CARAVAN WAS EASY TO FIND.
WE JUST FOLLOWED THE TREE STUMPS AND THE SMELL OF SHIT.
AND THE TRAIL OF FRESH BONES.

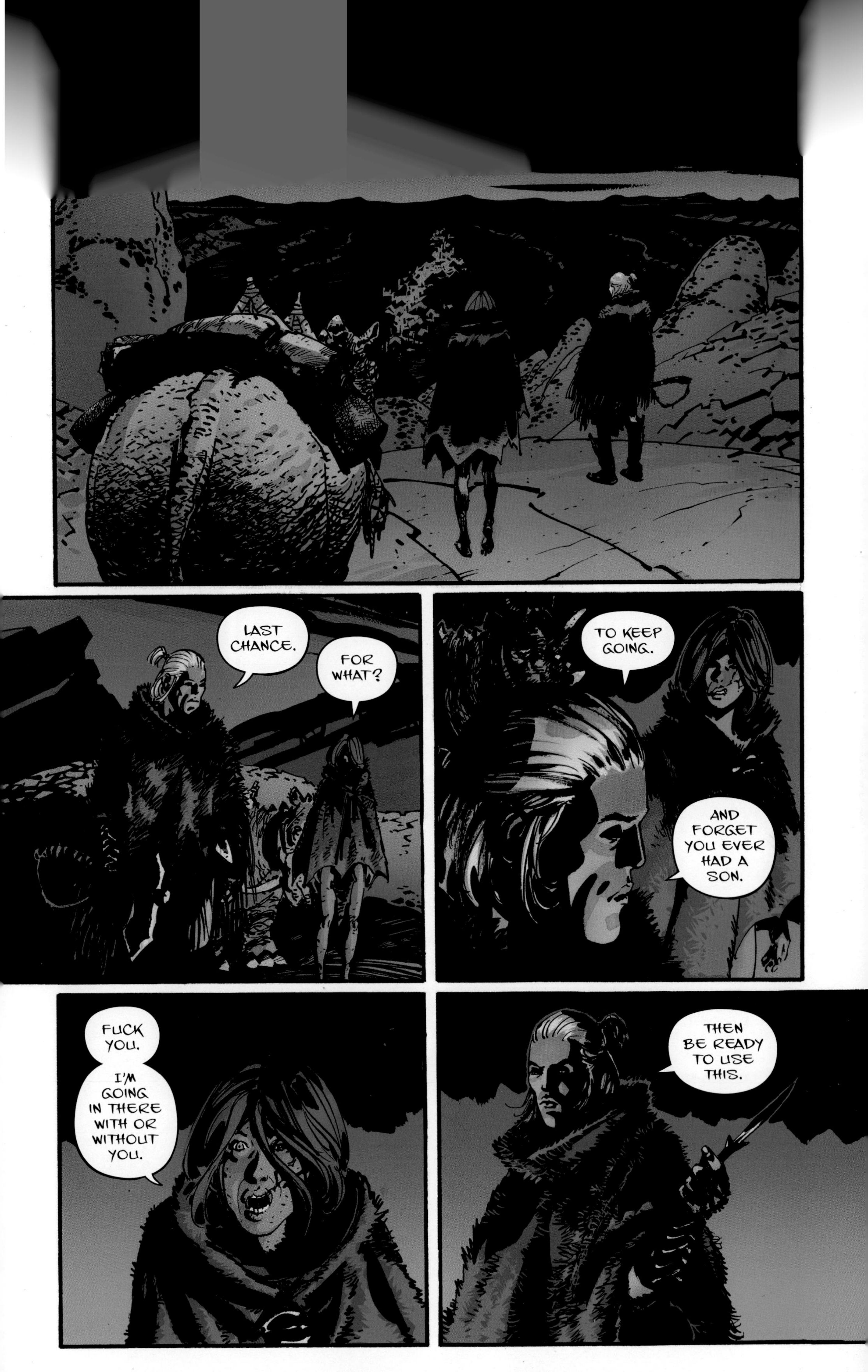
LAST CHANCE.
FOR WHAT?
TO KEEP GOING.
AND FORGET YOU EVER HAD A SON.
FUCK YOU.
I'M GOING IN THERE WITH OR WITHOUT YOU.
THEN BE READY TO USE THIS.

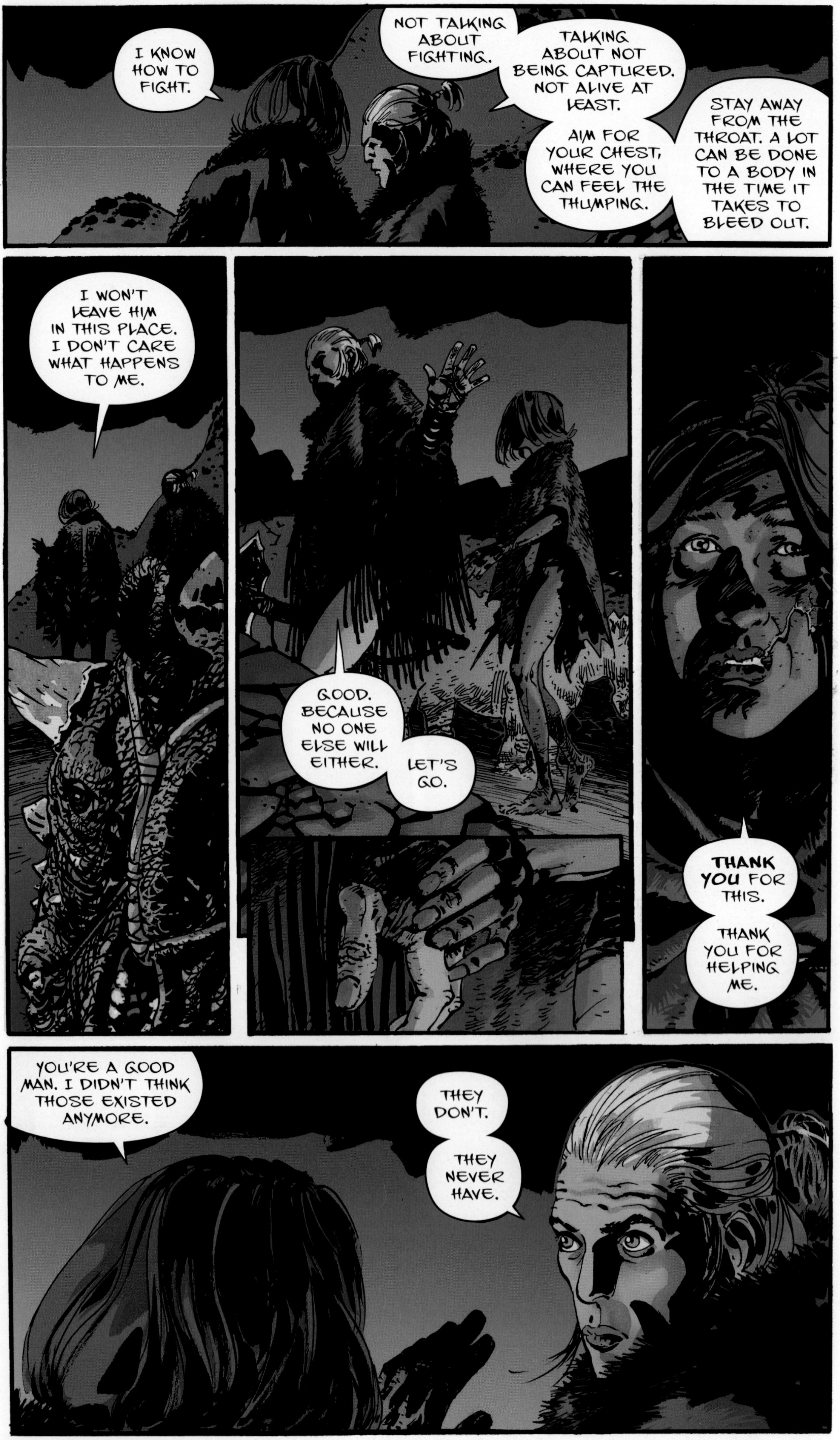

I KNOW HOW TO FIGHT.
NOT TALKING ABOUT FIGHTING.
TALKING ABOUT NOT BEING CAPTURED. NOT ALIVE AT LEAST.
AIM FOR YOUR CHEST, WHERE YOU CAN FEEL THE THUMPING.
STAY AWAY FROM THE THROAT. A LOT CAN BE DONE TO A BODY IN THE TIME IT TAKES TO BLEED OUT.
I WON'T LEAVE HIM IN THIS PLACE. I DON'T CARE WHAT HAPPENS TO ME.
GOOD. BECAUSE NO ONE ELSE WILL EITHER.
LET'S GO.
THANK YOU FOR THIS.
THANK YOU FOR HELPING ME.
YOU'RE A GOOD MAN. I DIDN'T THINK THOSE EXISTED ANYMORE.
THEY DON'T.
THEY NEVER HAVE.

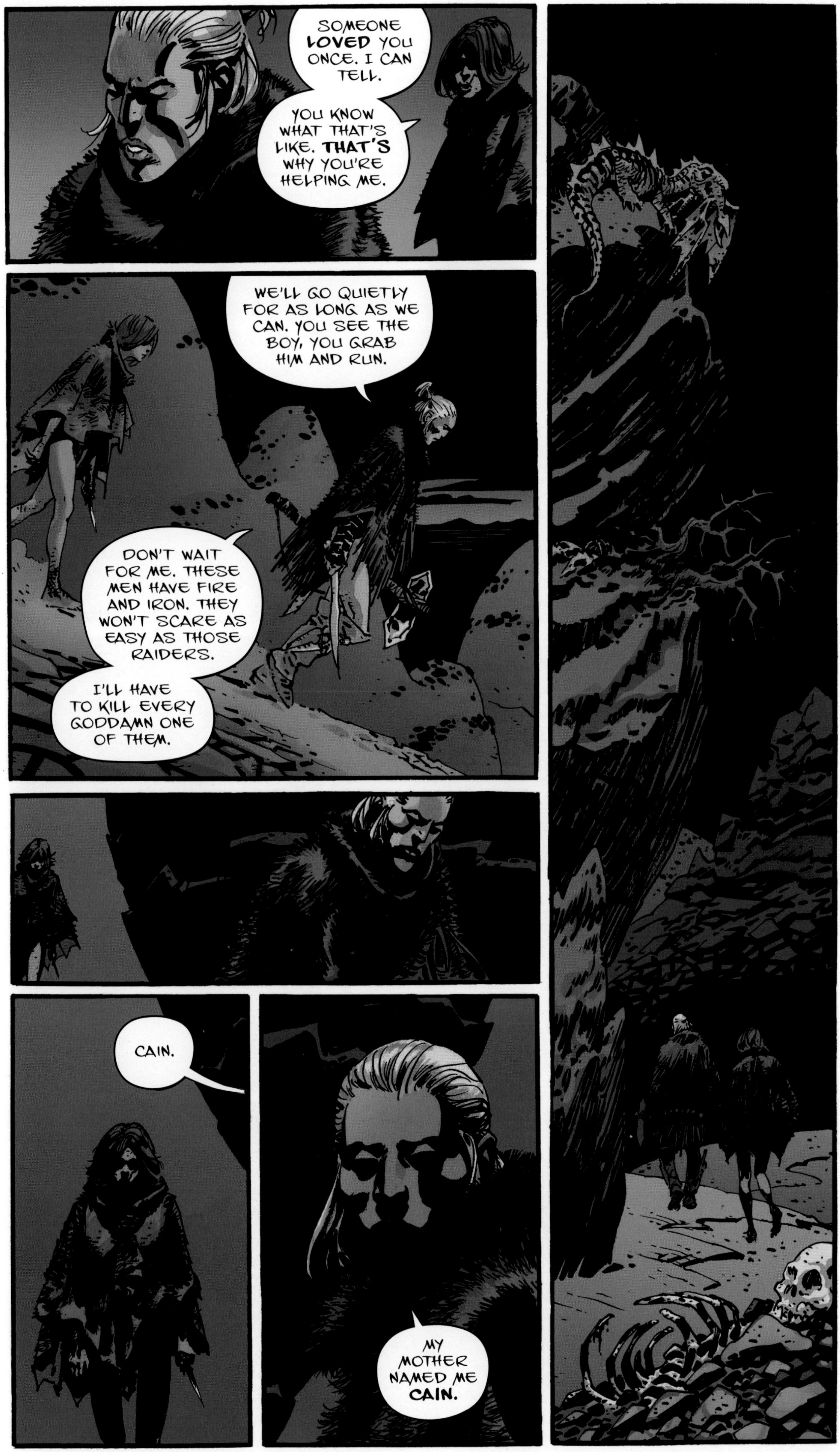
SOMEONE LOVED YOU ONCE. I CAN TELL.
YOU KNOW WHAT THAT'S LIKE. THAT'S WHY YOU'RE HELPING ME.
WE'LL GO QUIETLY FOR AS LONG AS WE CAN. YOU SEE THE BOY, YOU GRAB HIM AND RUN.
DON'T WAIT FOR ME. THESE MEN HAVE FIRE AND IRON. THEY WON'T SCARE AS EASY AS THOSE RAIDERS.
I'LL HAVE TO KILL EVERY GODDAMN ONE OF THEM.
CAIN.
MY MOTHER NAMED ME CAIN.

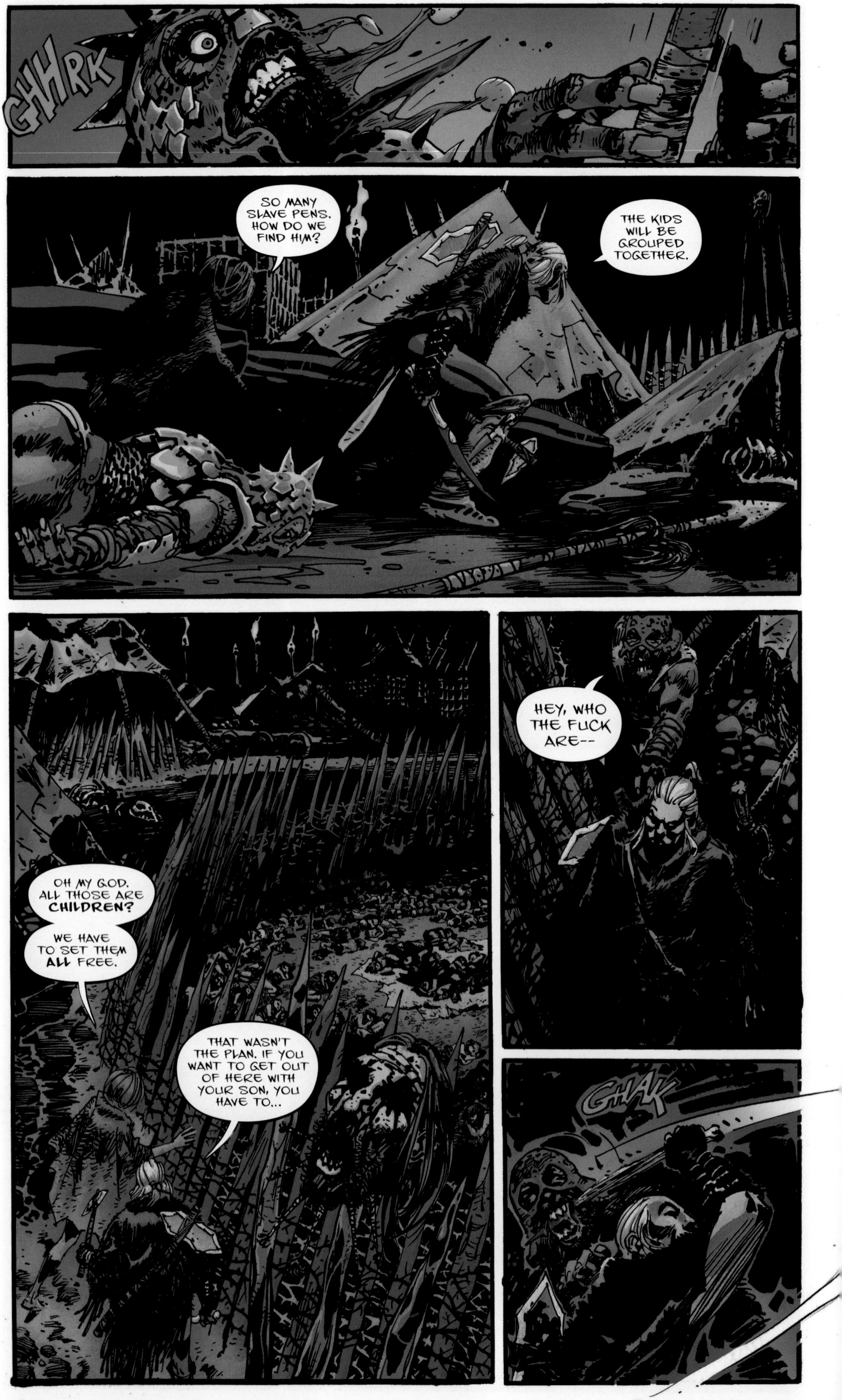
GHHRK
SO MANY SLAVE PENS. HOW DO WE FIND HIM?
THE KIDS WILL BE GROUPED TOGETHER.
OH MY GOD. ALL THOSE ARE **CHILDREN?**
WE HAVE TO SET THEM **ALL** FREE.
THAT WASN'T THE PLAN. IF YOU WANT TO GET OUT OF HERE WITH YOUR SON, YOU HAVE TO...
HEY, WHO THE FUCK ARE--
GHAK

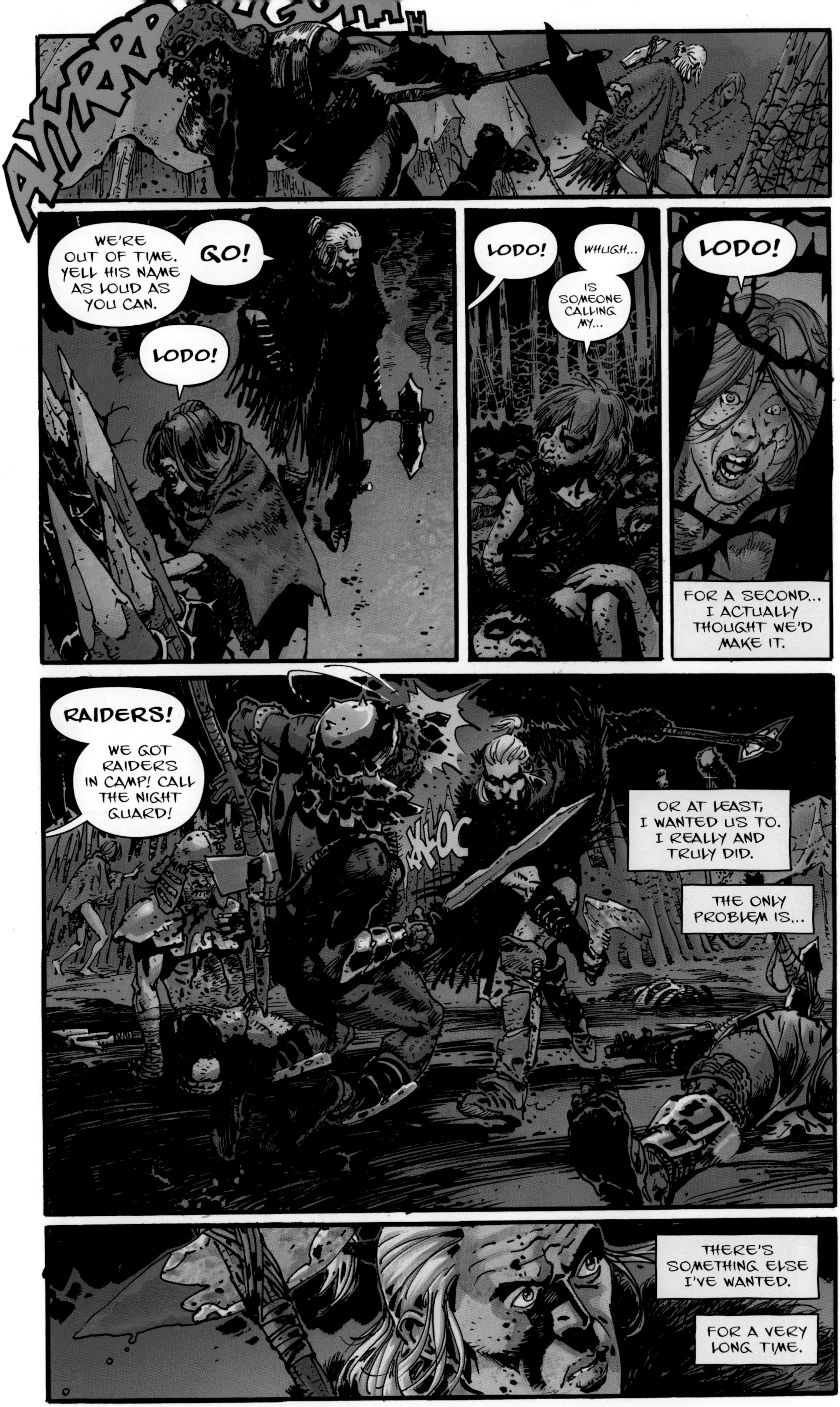
WE'RE OUT OF TIME. YELL HIS NAME AS LOUD AS YOU CAN.
GO!
LODO!
LODO!
WHUGH...
IS SOMEONE CALLING MY...
LODO!
FOR A SECOND... I ACTUALLY THOUGHT WE'D MAKE IT.
RAIDERS!
WE GOT RAIDERS IN CAMP! CALL THE NIGHT GUARD!
OR AT LEAST, I WANTED US TO. I REALLY AND TRULY DID.
THE ONLY PROBLEM IS...
THERE'S SOMETHING ELSE I'VE WANTED.
FOR A VERY LONG TIME.

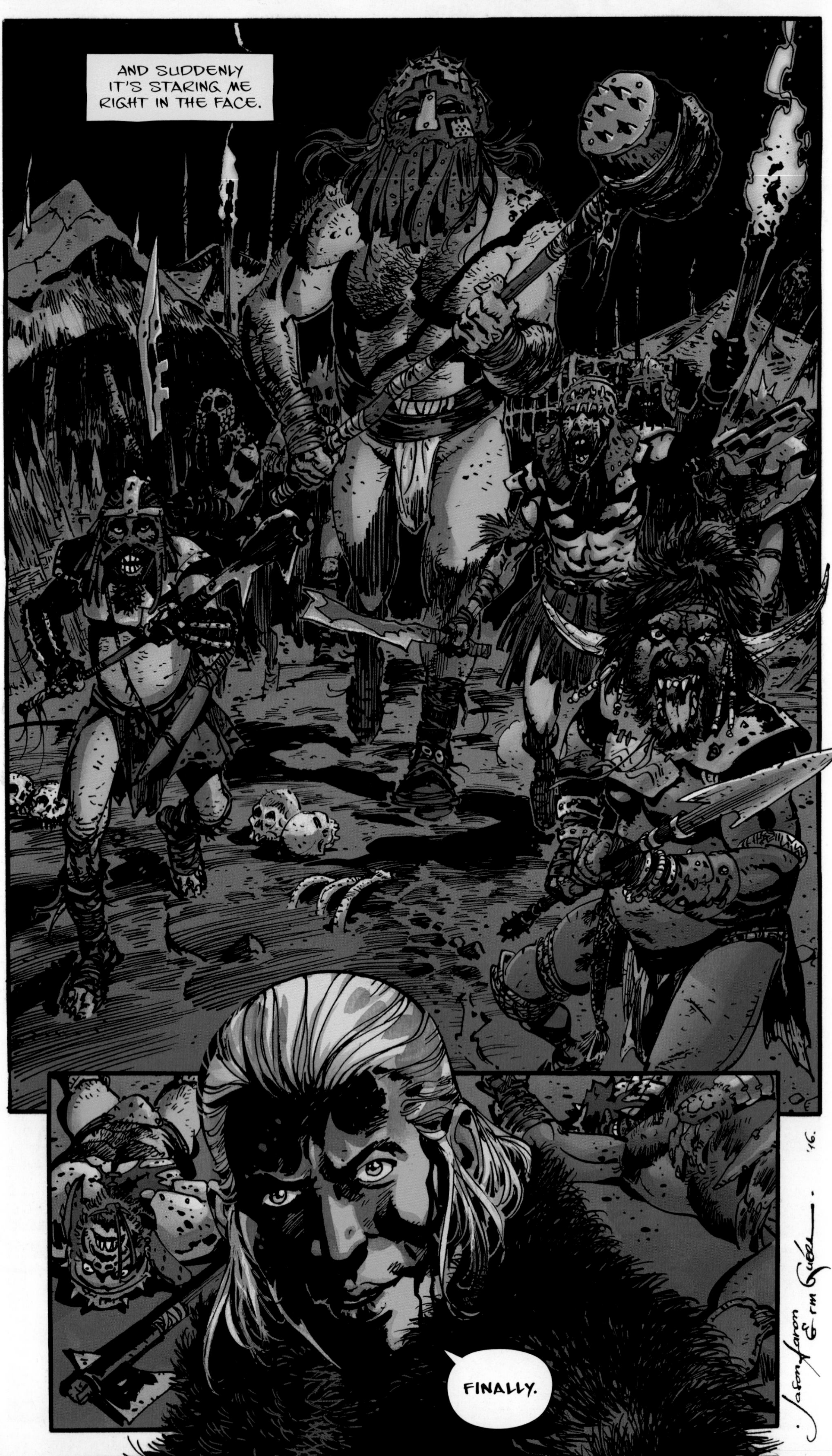
AND SUDDENLY IT'S STARING ME RIGHT IN THE FACE.
FINALLY.

chapter four

The Covenant of Noah

WOE UNTO THEM!
FOR THEY HAVE GONE
IN THE WAY OF CAIN.

JUDE 1:11

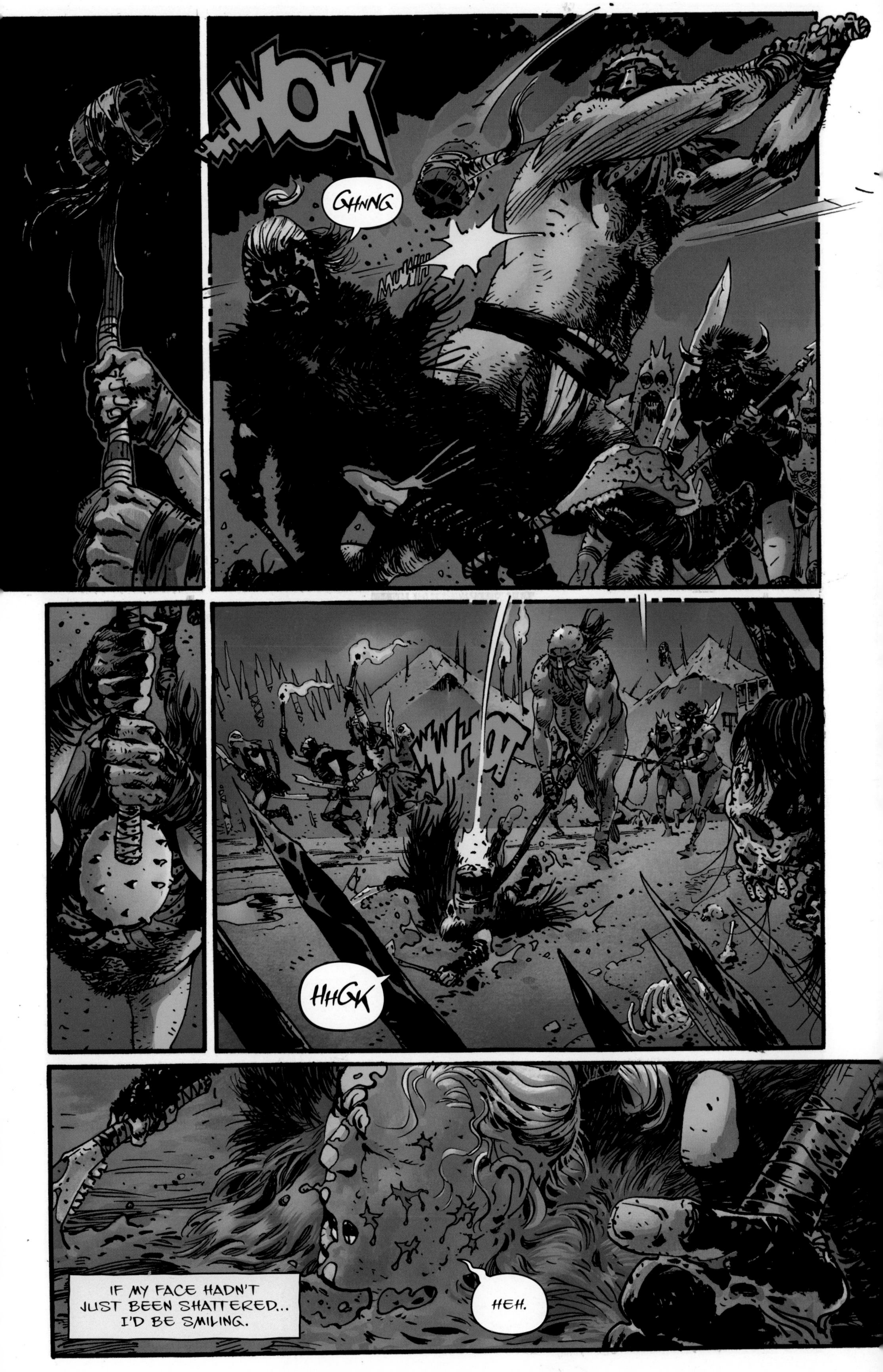
WOK
GHNNG
WHOT
HHGK
IF MY FACE HADN'T JUST BEEN SHATTERED... I'D BE SMILING.
HEH.

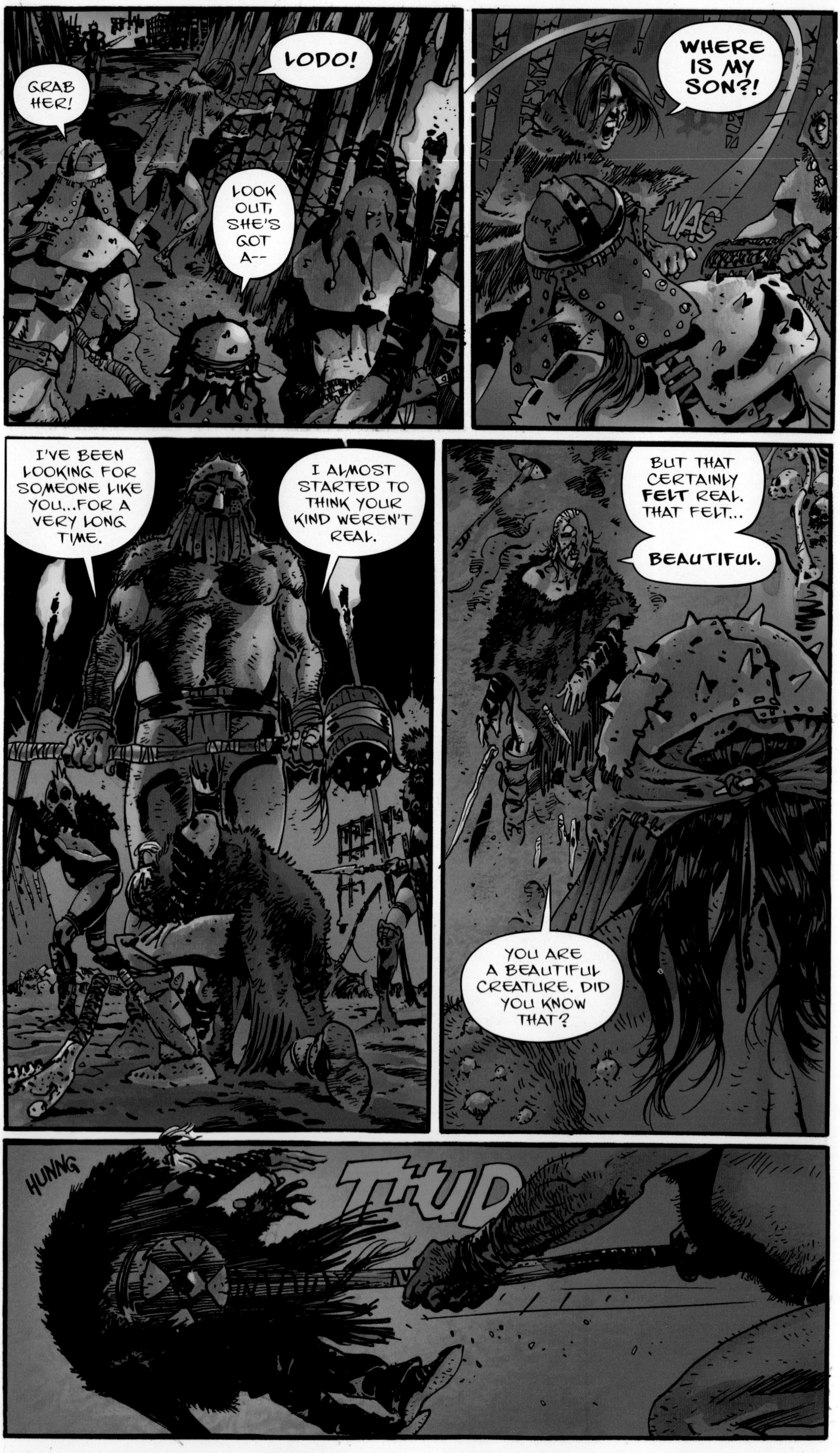
LODO!
GRAB HER!
LOOK OUT, SHE'S GOT A--
WHERE IS MY SON?!
WAC
I'VE BEEN LOOKING FOR SOMEONE LIKE YOU...FOR A VERY LONG TIME.
I ALMOST STARTED TO THINK YOUR KIND WEREN'T REAL.
BUT THAT CERTAINLY FELT REAL. THAT FELT...
BEAUTIFUL.
YOU ARE A BEAUTIFUL CREATURE. DID YOU KNOW THAT?
HUNNG
THUD

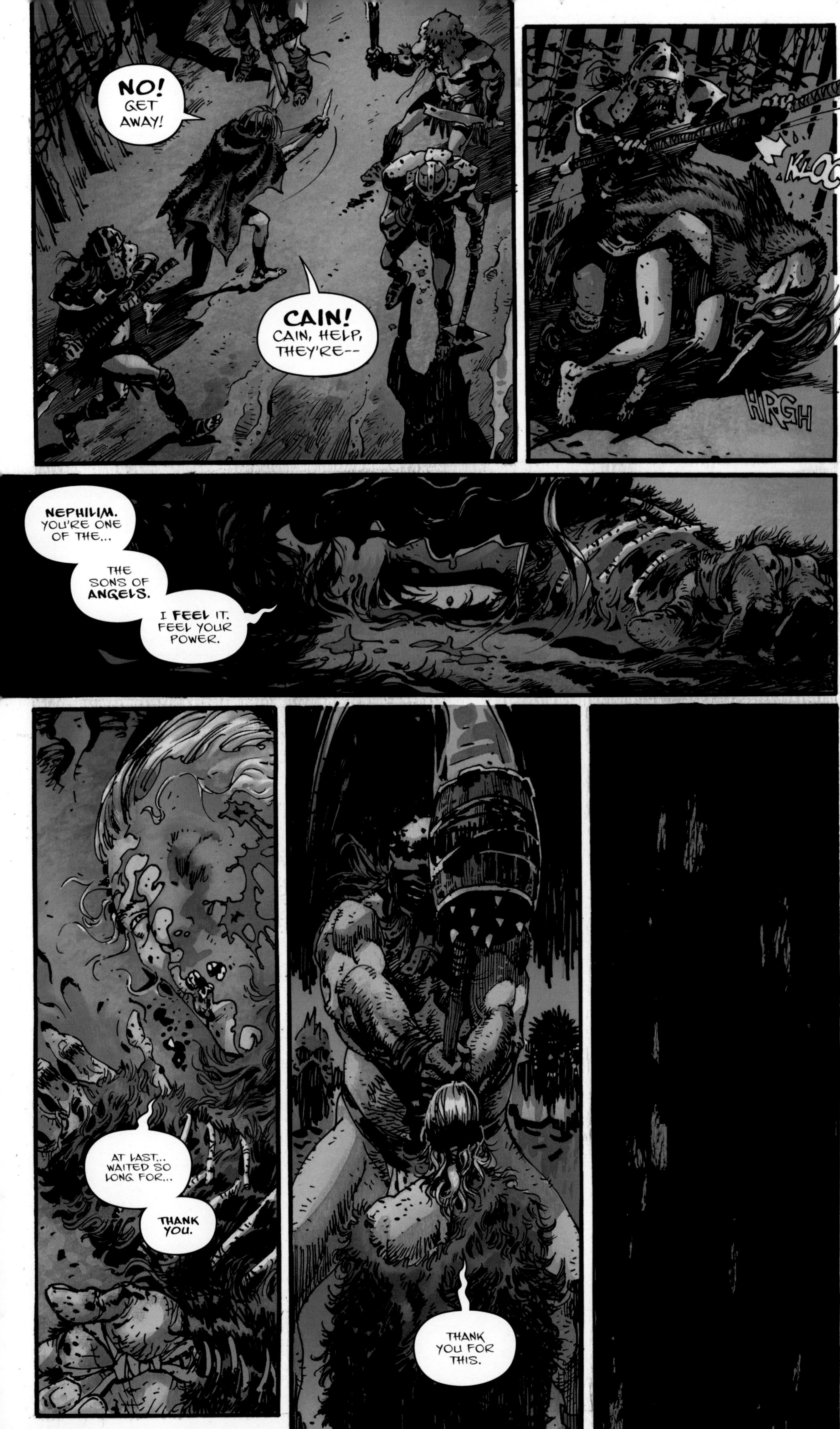
NO! GET AWAY!
CAIN! CAIN, HELP, THEY'RE--
KLOC
HRGH
NEPHILIM. YOU'RE ONE OF THE...
THE SONS OF ANGELS.
I FEEL IT. FEEL YOUR POWER.
AT LAST... WAITED SO LONG FOR...
THANK YOU.
THANK YOU FOR THIS.

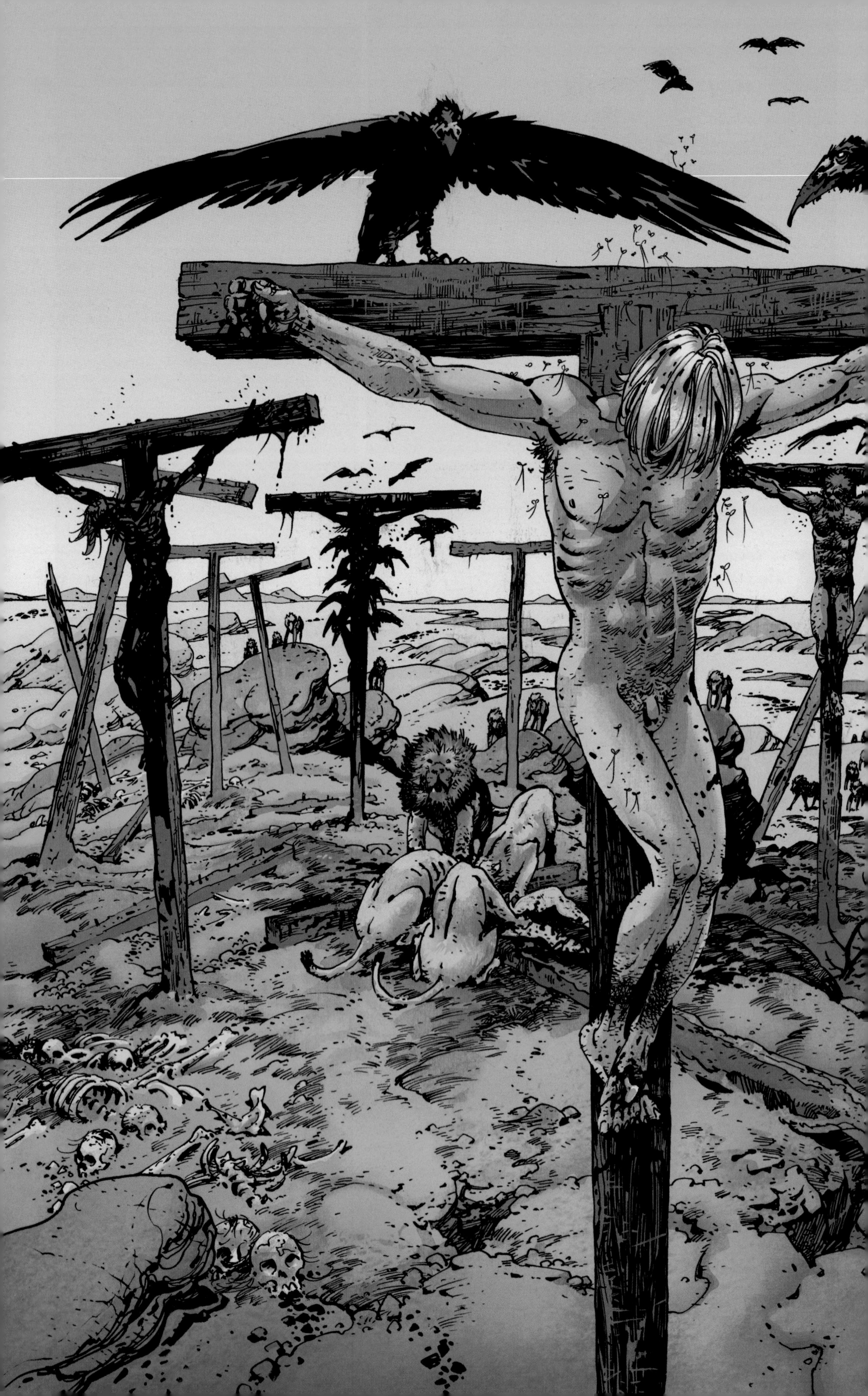

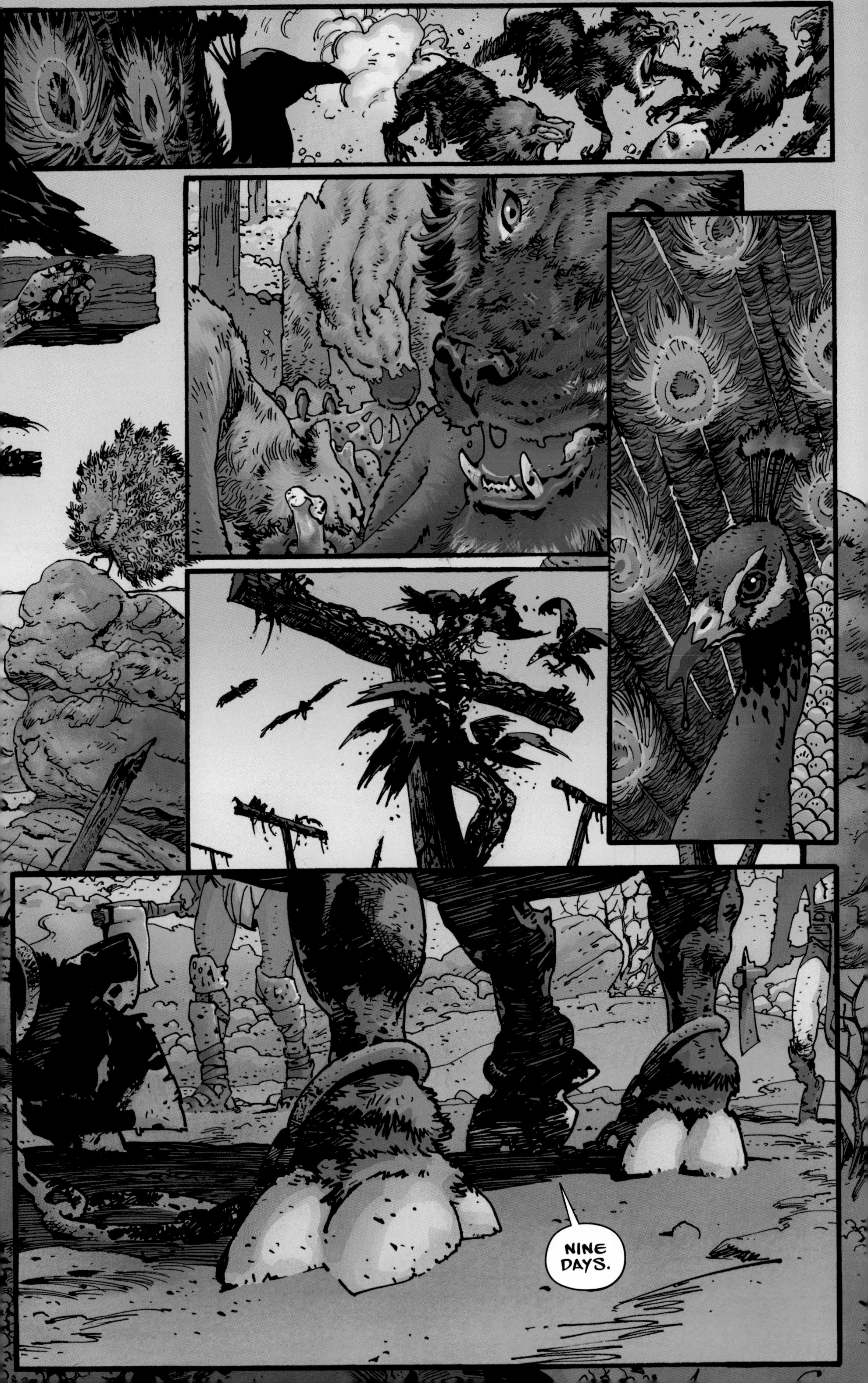
NINE DAYS.

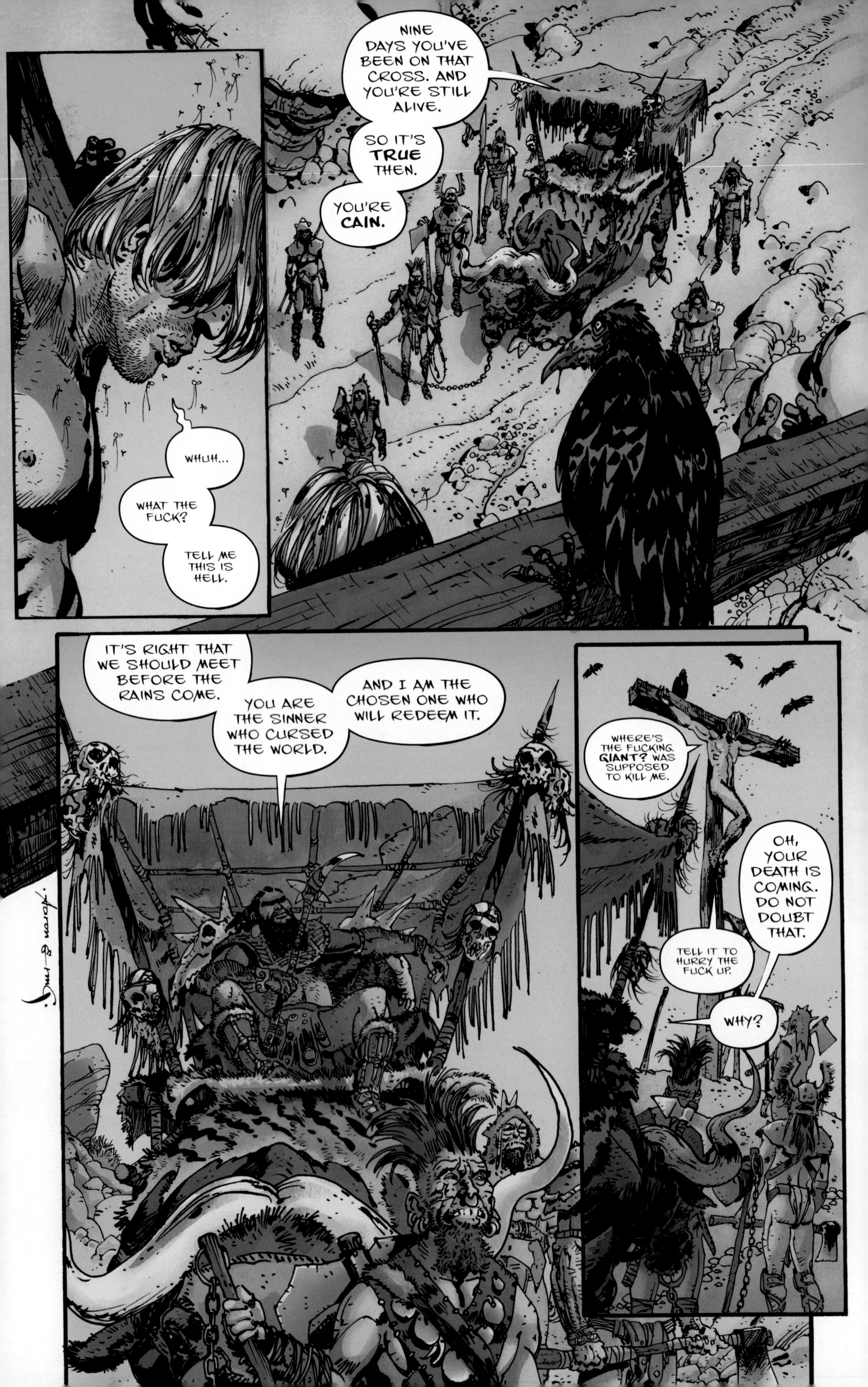

WHUH...
WHAT THE FUCK?
TELL ME THIS IS HELL.
NINE DAYS YOU'VE BEEN ON THAT CROSS. AND YOU'RE STILL ALIVE.
SO IT'S **TRUE** THEN.
YOU'RE **CAIN.**
IT'S RIGHT THAT WE SHOULD MEET BEFORE THE RAINS COME.
YOU ARE THE SINNER WHO CURSED THE WORLD.
AND I AM THE CHOSEN ONE WHO WILL REDEEM IT.
WHERE'S THE FUCKING **GIANT?** WAS SUPPOSED TO KILL ME.
OH, YOUR DEATH IS COMING. DO NOT DOUBT THAT.
TELL IT TO HURRY THE FUCK UP.
WHY?

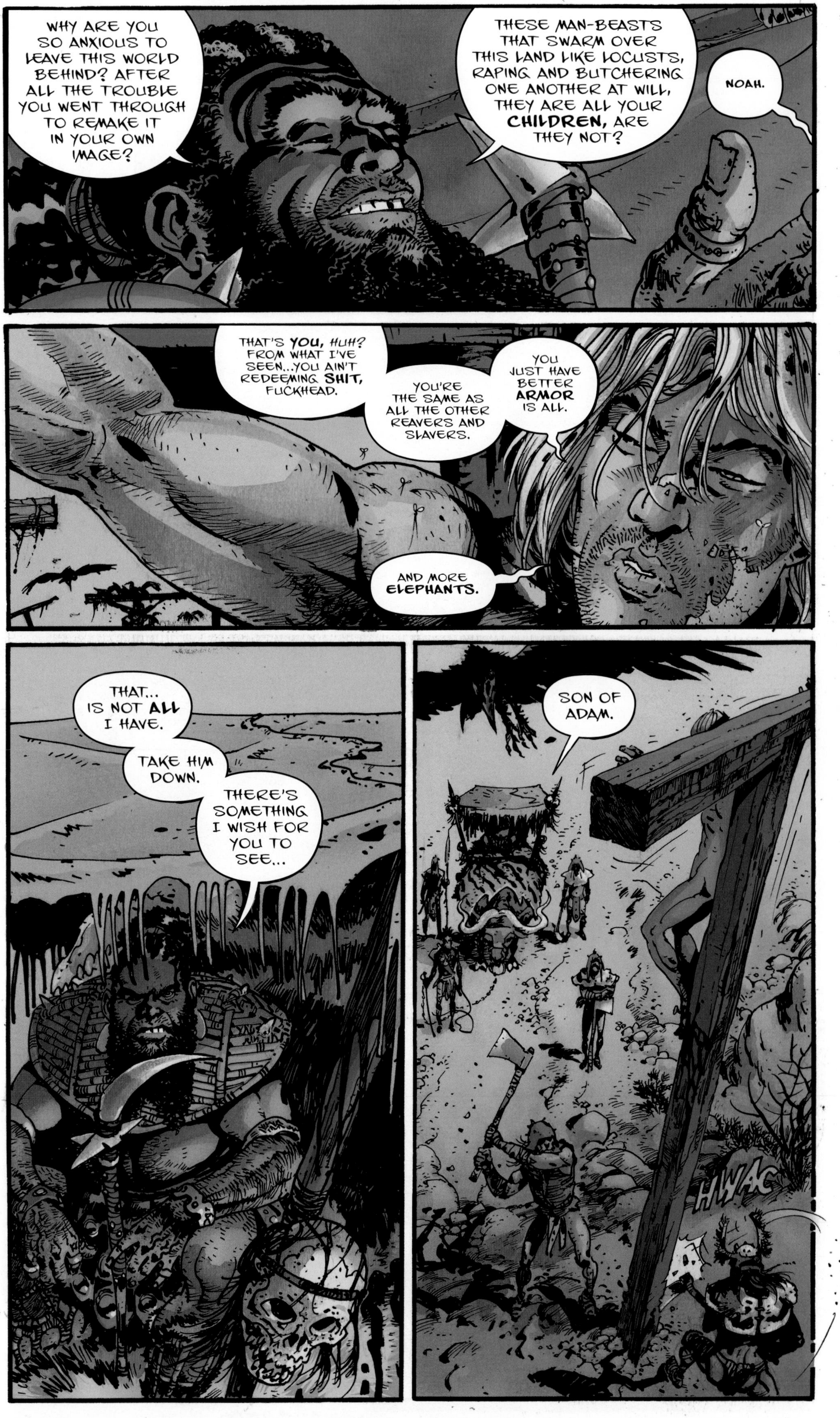
WHY ARE YOU SO ANXIOUS TO LEAVE THIS WORLD BEHIND? AFTER ALL THE TROUBLE YOU WENT THROUGH TO REMAKE IT IN YOUR OWN IMAGE?
THESE MAN-BEASTS THAT SWARM OVER THIS LAND LIKE LOCUSTS, RAPING AND BUTCHERING ONE ANOTHER AT WILL, THEY ARE ALL YOUR CHILDREN, ARE THEY NOT?
NOAH.
THAT'S YOU, HUH? FROM WHAT I'VE SEEN...YOU AIN'T REDEEMING SHIT, FUCKHEAD.
YOU'RE THE SAME AS ALL THE OTHER REAVERS AND SLAVERS.
YOU JUST HAVE BETTER ARMOR IS ALL.
AND MORE ELEPHANTS.
THAT... IS NOT ALL I HAVE.
TAKE HIM DOWN.
THERE'S SOMETHING I WISH FOR YOU TO SEE...
SON OF ADAM.
HWAC

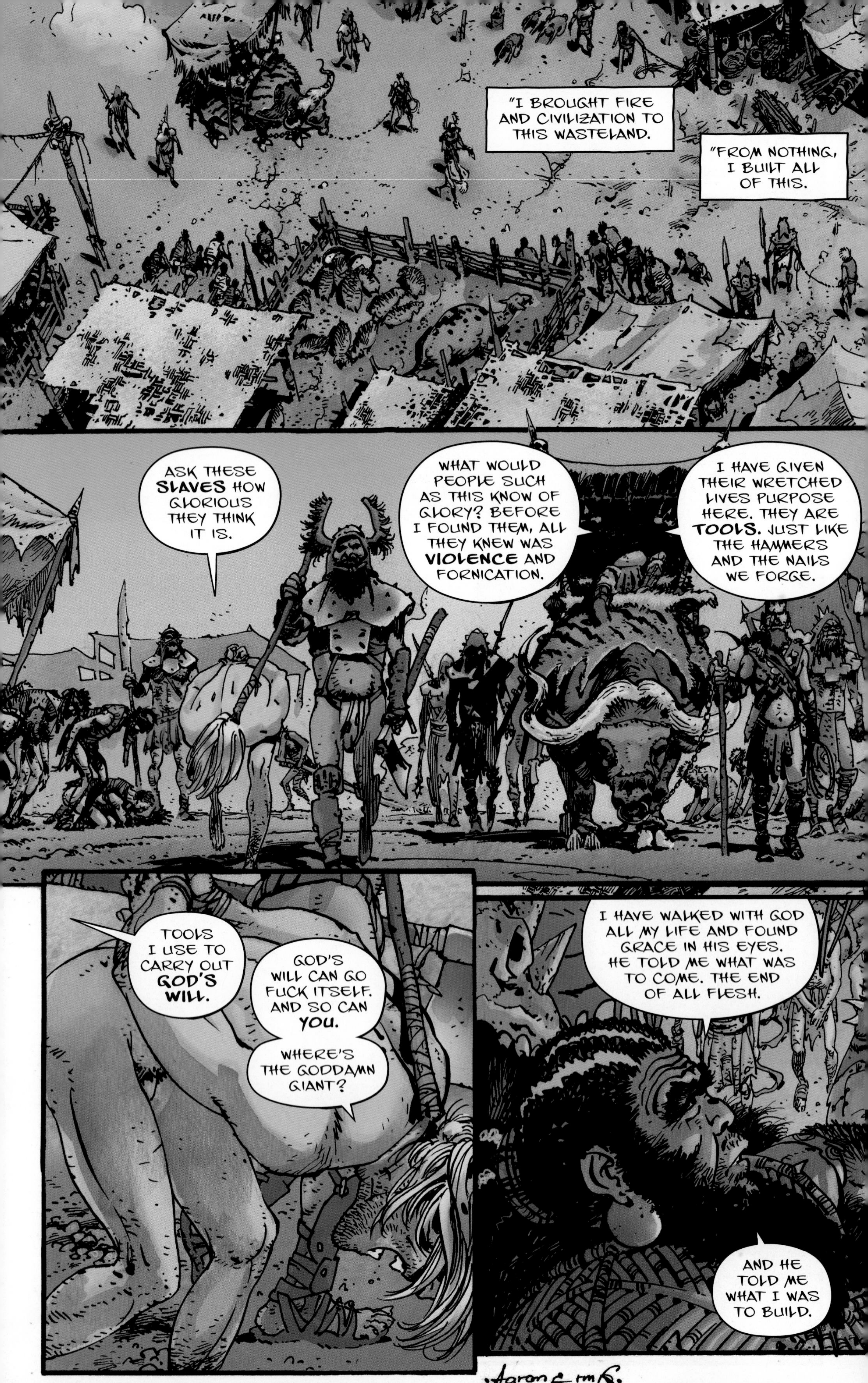
"I BROUGHT FIRE AND CIVILIZATION TO THIS WASTELAND.
"FROM NOTHING, I BUILT ALL OF THIS.
ASK THESE **SLAVES** HOW GLORIOUS THEY THINK IT IS.
WHAT WOULD PEOPLE SUCH AS THIS KNOW OF GLORY? BEFORE I FOUND THEM, ALL THEY KNEW WAS **VIOLENCE** AND FORNICATION.
I HAVE GIVEN THEIR WRETCHED LIVES PURPOSE HERE. THEY ARE **TOOLS.** JUST LIKE THE HAMMERS AND THE NAILS WE FORGE.
TOOLS I USE TO CARRY OUT **GOD'S WILL.**
GOD'S WILL CAN GO FUCK ITSELF. AND SO CAN **YOU.**
WHERE'S THE GODDAMN GIANT?
I HAVE WALKED WITH GOD ALL MY LIFE AND FOUND GRACE IN HIS EYES. HE TOLD ME WHAT WAS TO COME. THE END OF ALL FLESH.
AND HE TOLD ME WHAT I WAS TO BUILD.
Aaron & rmG.

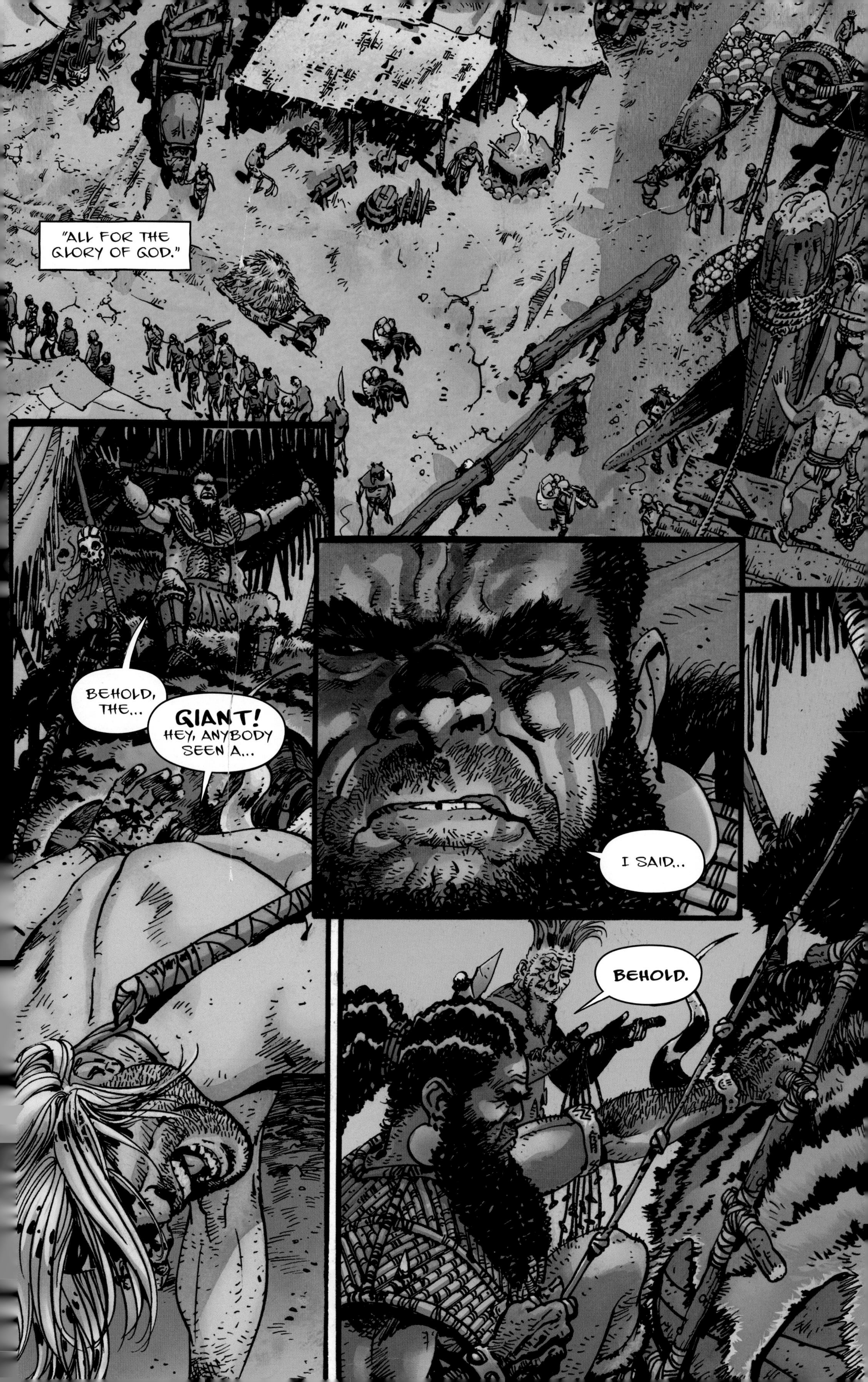

"ALL FOR THE GLORY OF GOD."
BEHOLD, THE...
GIANT! HEY, ANYBODY SEEN A...
I SAID...
BEHOLD.

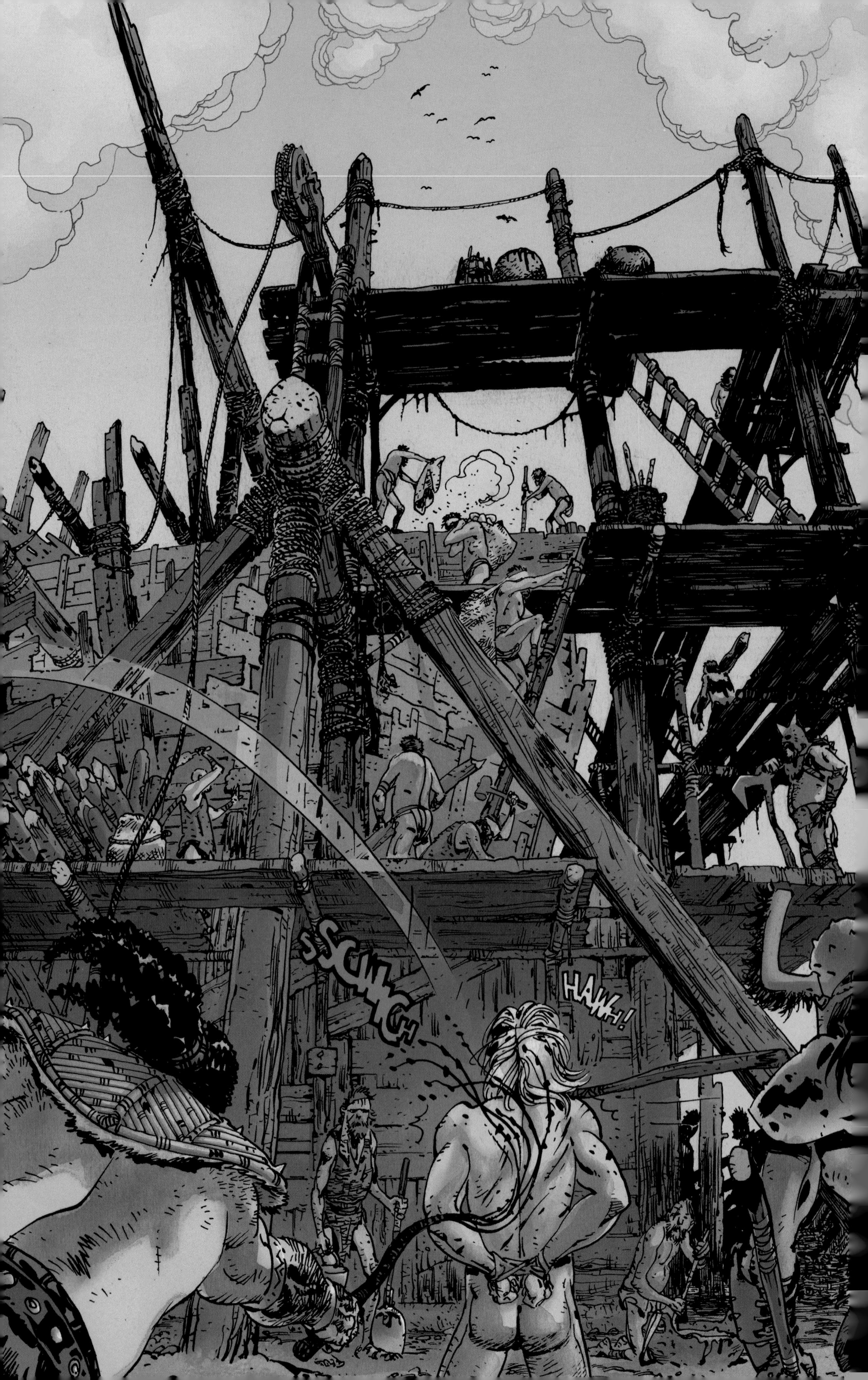
SSCHHCH
HAAHH!

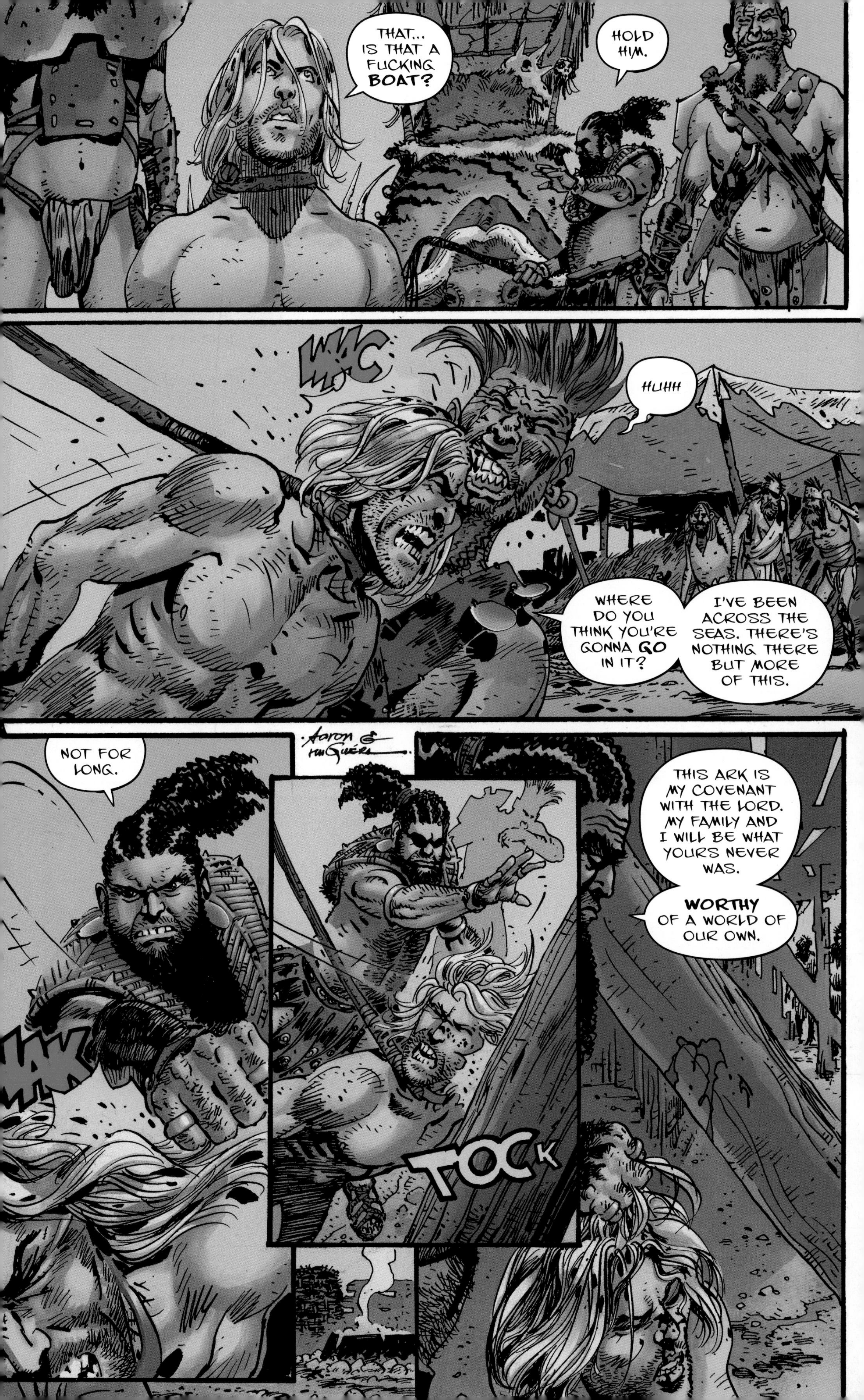

THAT... IS THAT A FUCKING BOAT?
HOLD HIM.
WHAC
HUHH
WHERE DO YOU THINK YOU'RE GONNA GO IN IT?
I'VE BEEN ACROSS THE SEAS. THERE'S NOTHING THERE BUT MORE OF THIS.
NOT FOR LONG.
THIS ARK IS MY COVENANT WITH THE LORD. MY FAMILY AND I WILL BE WHAT YOURS NEVER WAS.
WORTHY OF A WORLD OF OUR OWN.
TOCK

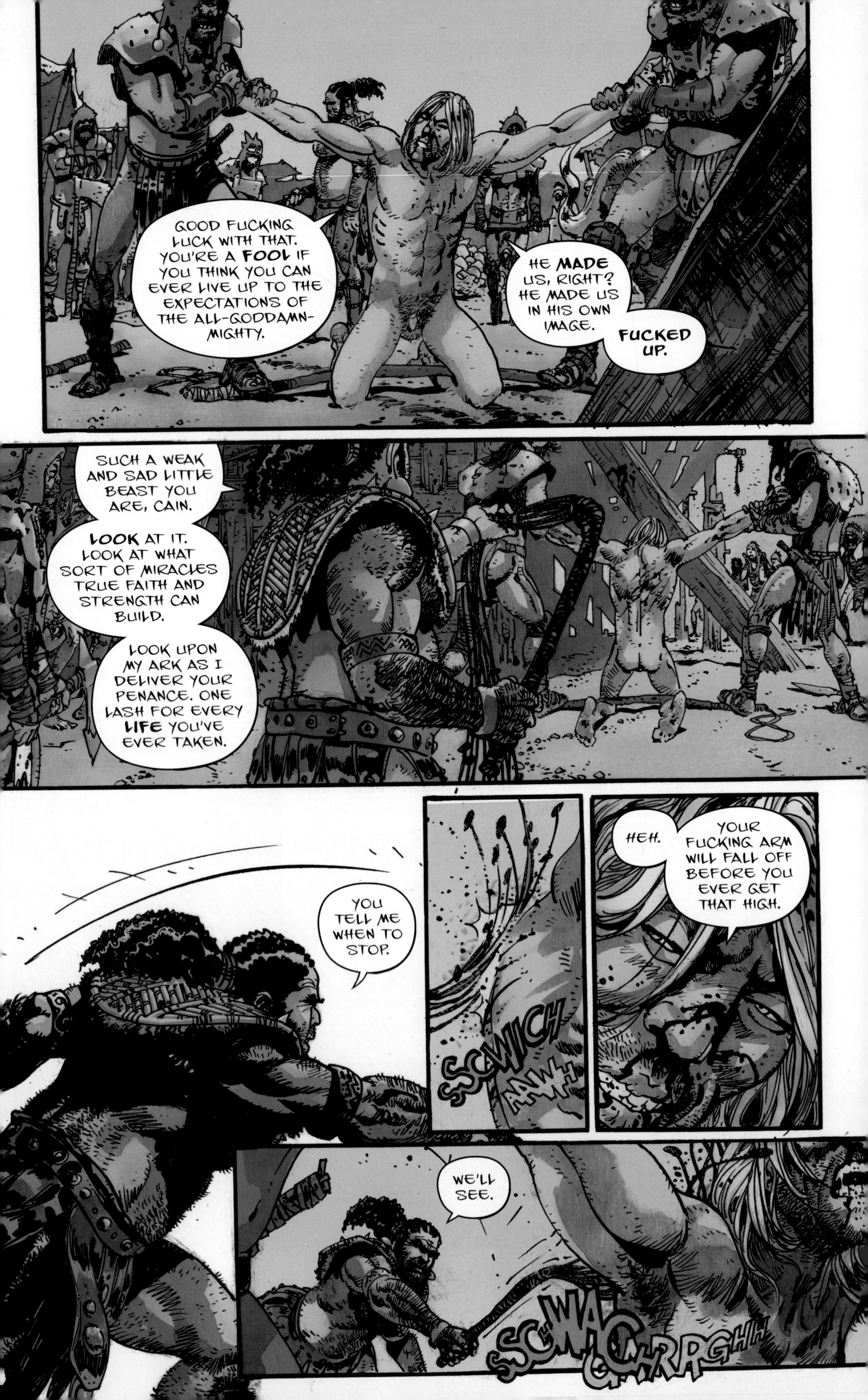
GOOD FUCKING LUCK WITH THAT. YOU'RE A **FOOL** IF YOU THINK YOU CAN EVER LIVE UP TO THE EXPECTATIONS OF THE ALL-GODDAMN-MIGHTY.
HE **MADE** US, RIGHT? HE MADE US IN HIS OWN IMAGE.
FUCKED UP.
SUCH A WEAK AND SAD LITTLE BEAST YOU ARE, CAIN.
LOOK AT IT. LOOK AT WHAT SORT OF MIRACLES TRUE FAITH AND STRENGTH CAN BUILD.
LOOK UPON MY ARK AS I DELIVER YOUR PENANCE. ONE LASH FOR EVERY **LIFE** YOU'VE EVER TAKEN.
YOU TELL ME WHEN TO STOP.
SCWICH
HEH.
YOUR FUCKING ARM WILL FALL OFF BEFORE YOU EVER GET THAT HIGH.
WE'LL SEE.
SCHWAC
CHRRGHH

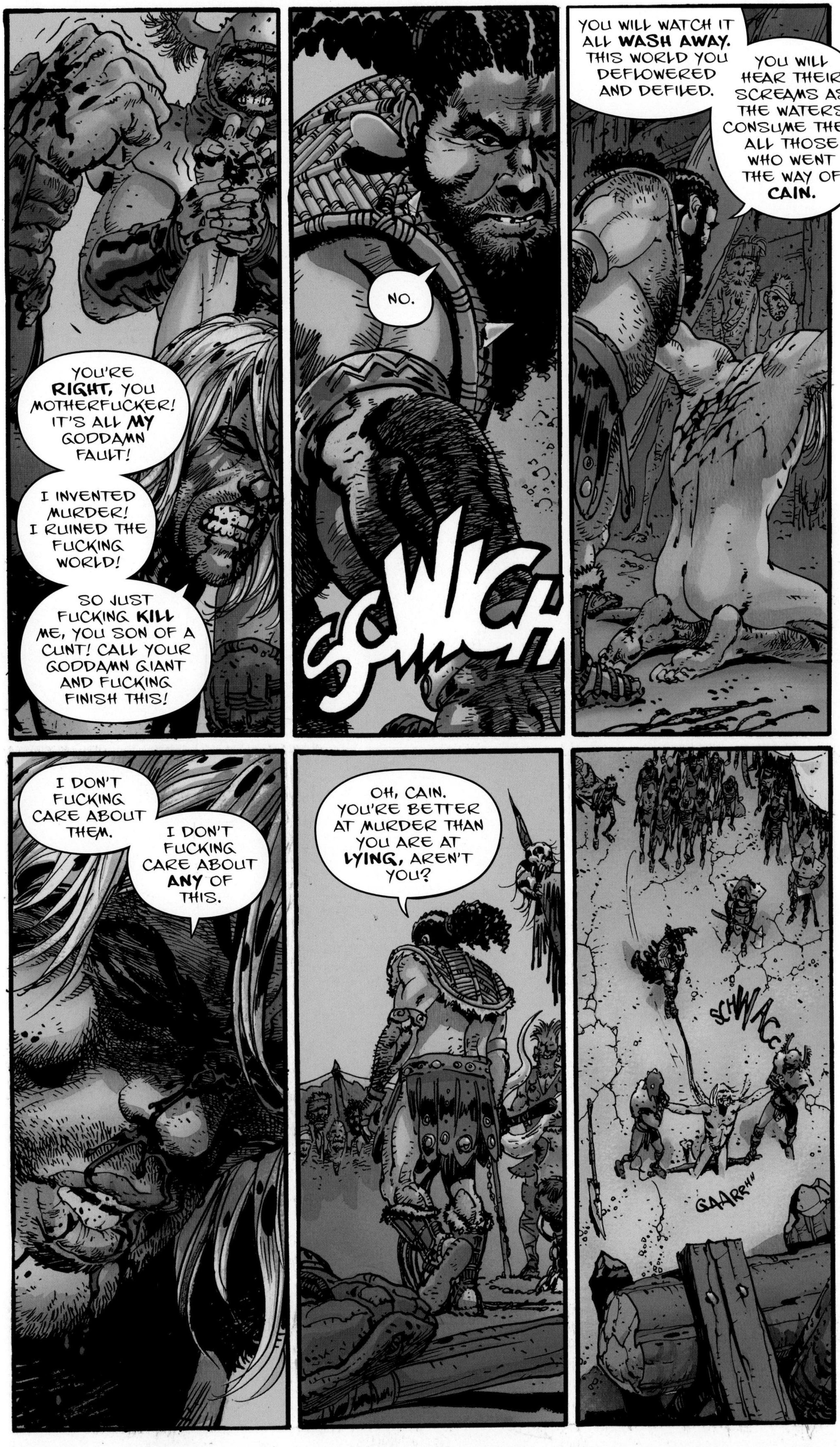
YOU'RE RIGHT, YOU MOTHERFUCKER! IT'S ALL MY GODDAMN FAULT!
I INVENTED MURDER! I RUINED THE FUCKING WORLD!
SO JUST FUCKING KILL ME, YOU SON OF A CUNT! CALL YOUR GODDAMN GIANT AND FUCKING FINISH THIS!
NO.
SCWCH
YOU WILL WATCH IT ALL WASH AWAY. THIS WORLD YOU DEFLOWERED AND DEFILED.
YOU WILL HEAR THEIR SCREAMS AS THE WATERS CONSUME THEM. ALL THOSE WHO WENT THE WAY OF CAIN.
I DON'T FUCKING CARE ABOUT THEM.
I DON'T FUCKING CARE ABOUT ANY OF THIS.
OH, CAIN. YOU'RE BETTER AT MURDER THAN YOU ARE AT LYING, AREN'T YOU?
SCHWACC
GAARRHH

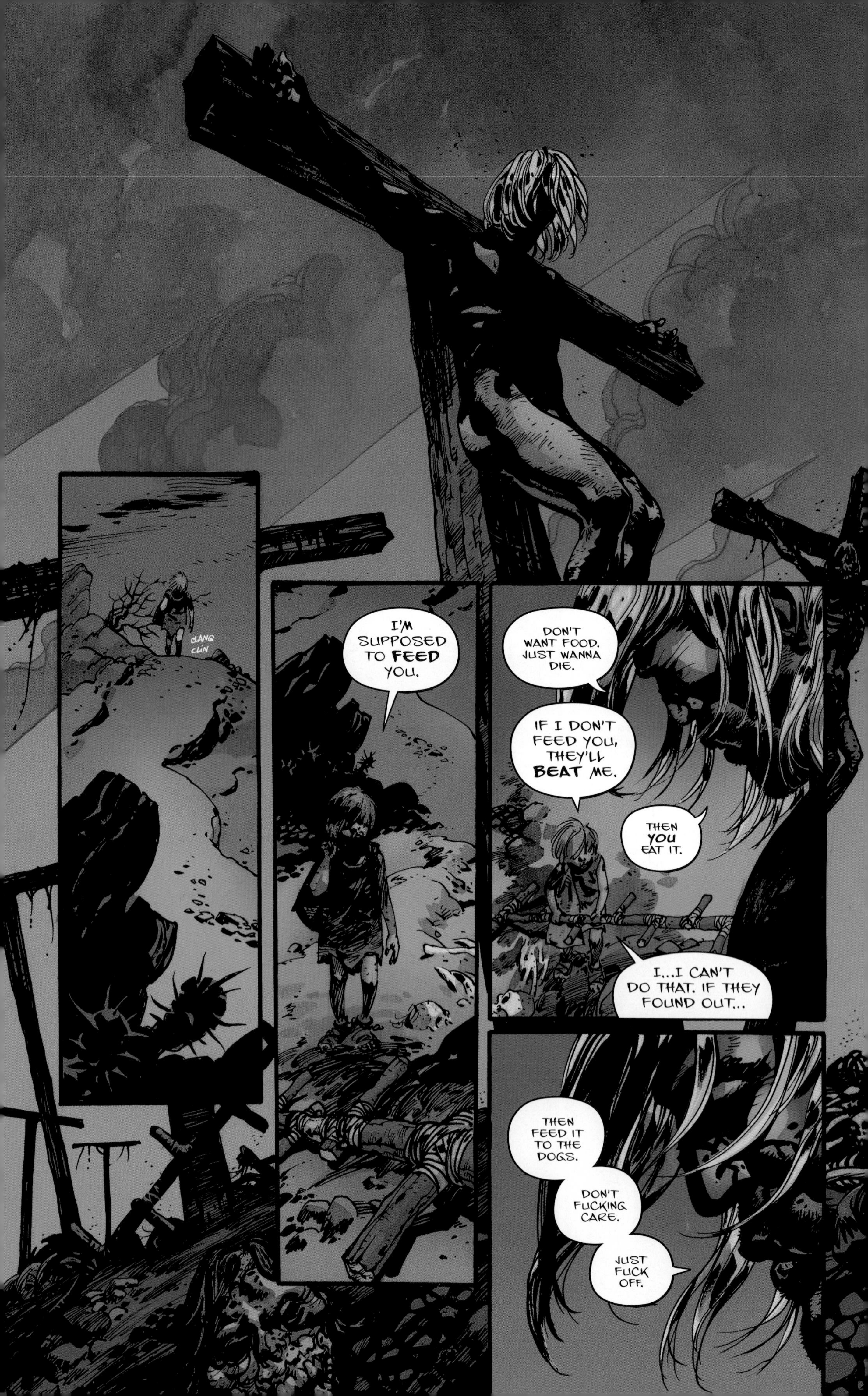
CLANG
CLIN
I'M SUPPOSED TO FEED YOU.
DON'T WANT FOOD. JUST WANNA DIE.
IF I DON'T FEED YOU, THEY'LL BEAT ME.
THEN YOU EAT IT.
I...I CAN'T DO THAT. IF THEY FOUND OUT...
THEN FEED IT TO THE DOGS.
DON'T FUCKING CARE.
JUST FUCK OFF.

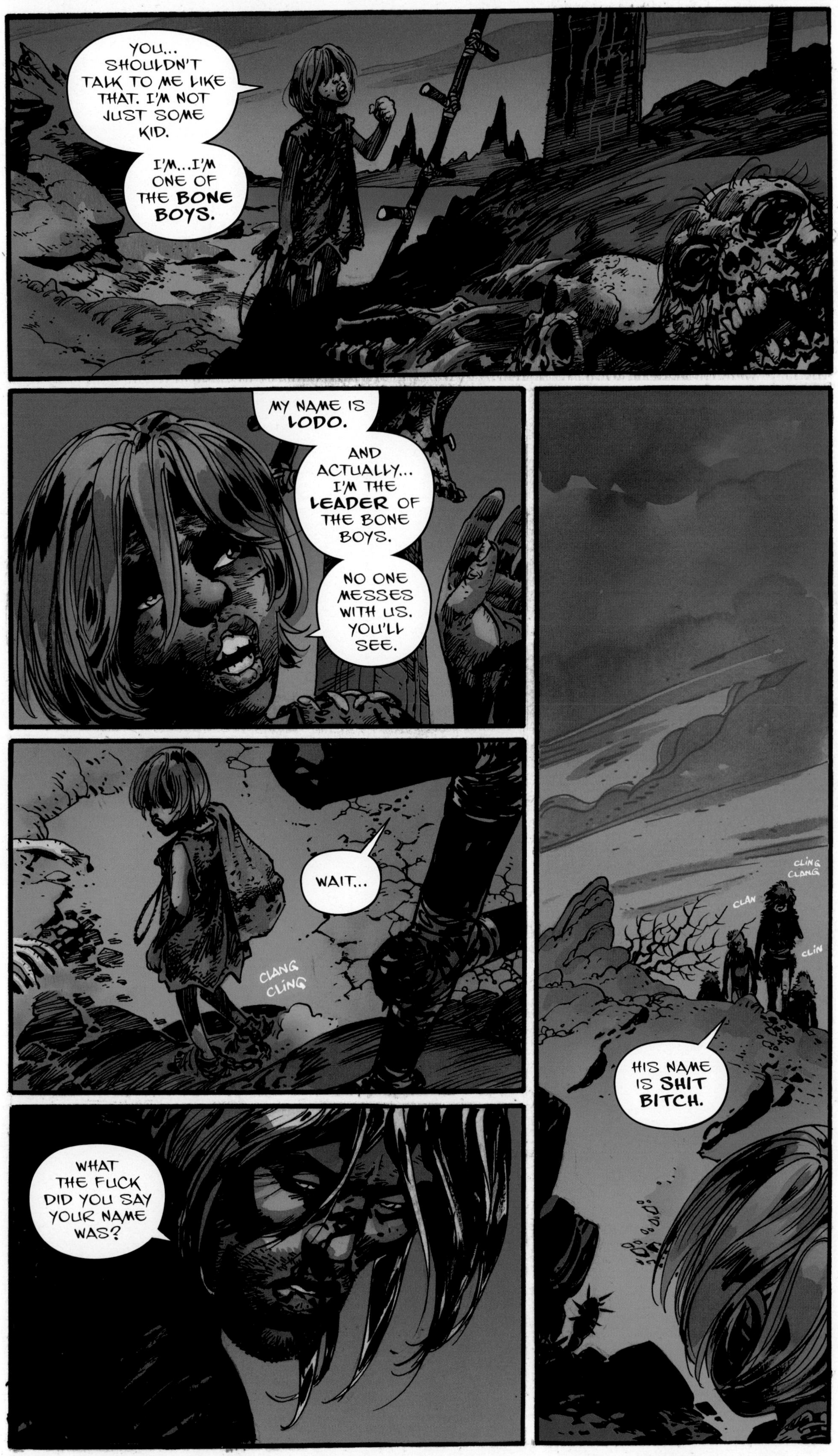

YOU... SHOULDN'T TALK TO ME LIKE THAT. I'M NOT JUST SOME KID.
I'M...I'M ONE OF THE BONE BOYS.
MY NAME IS LODO.
AND ACTUALLY... I'M THE LEADER OF THE BONE BOYS.
NO ONE MESSES WITH US. YOU'LL SEE.
WAIT...
CLANG CLING
WHAT THE FUCK DID YOU SAY YOUR NAME WAS?
CLING CLANG
CLAN
CLIN
HIS NAME IS SHIT BITCH.

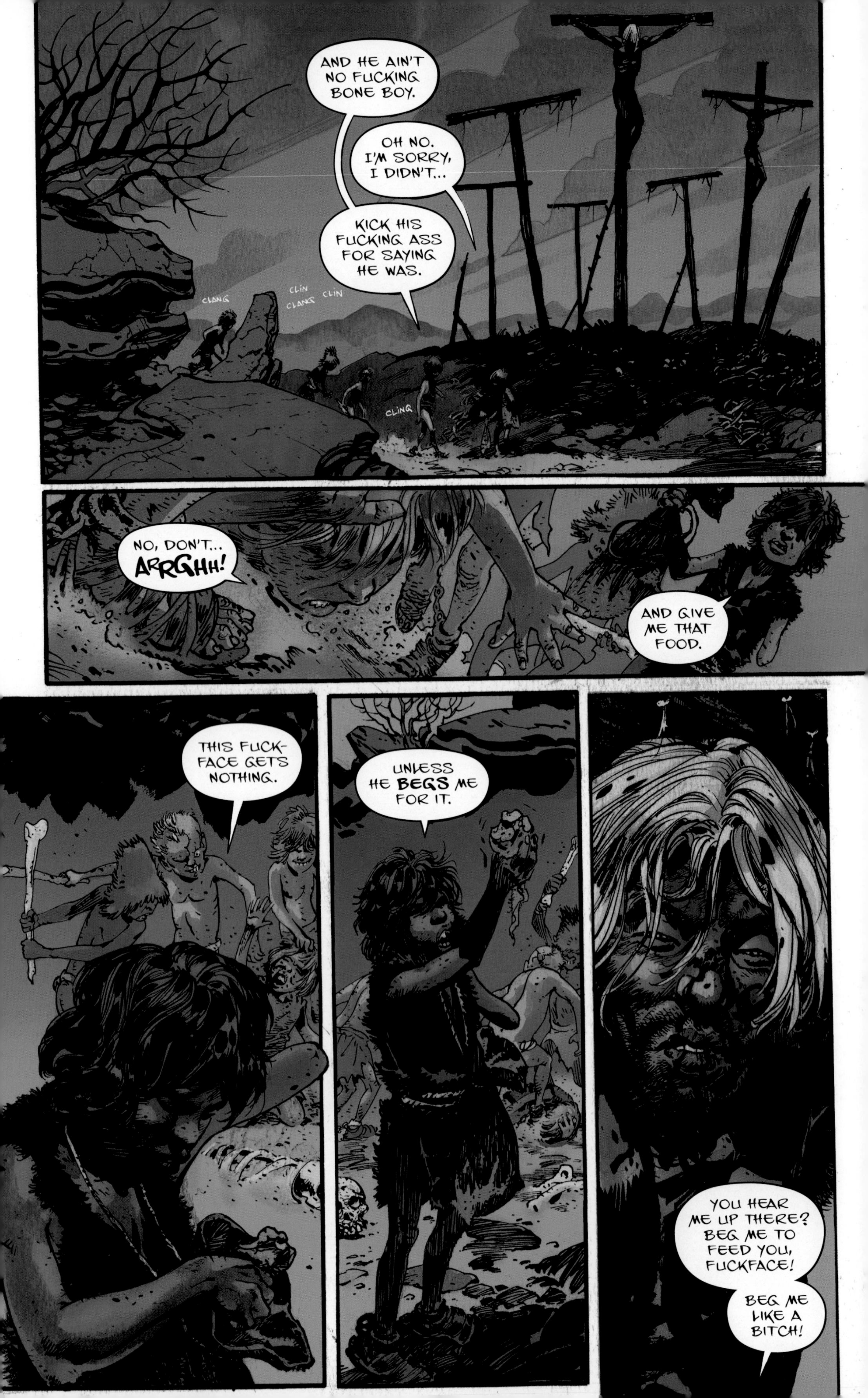
AND HE AIN'T NO FUCKING BONE BOY.
OH NO. I'M SORRY, I DIDN'T...
KICK HIS FUCKING ASS FOR SAYING HE WAS.
CLANG
CLIN
CLANG
CLIN
CLING
NO, DON'T... ARRGHH!
AND GIVE ME THAT FOOD.
THIS FUCK-FACE GETS NOTHING.
UNLESS HE BEGS ME FOR IT.
YOU HEAR ME UP THERE? BEG ME TO FEED YOU, FUCKFACE!
BEG ME LIKE A BITCH!

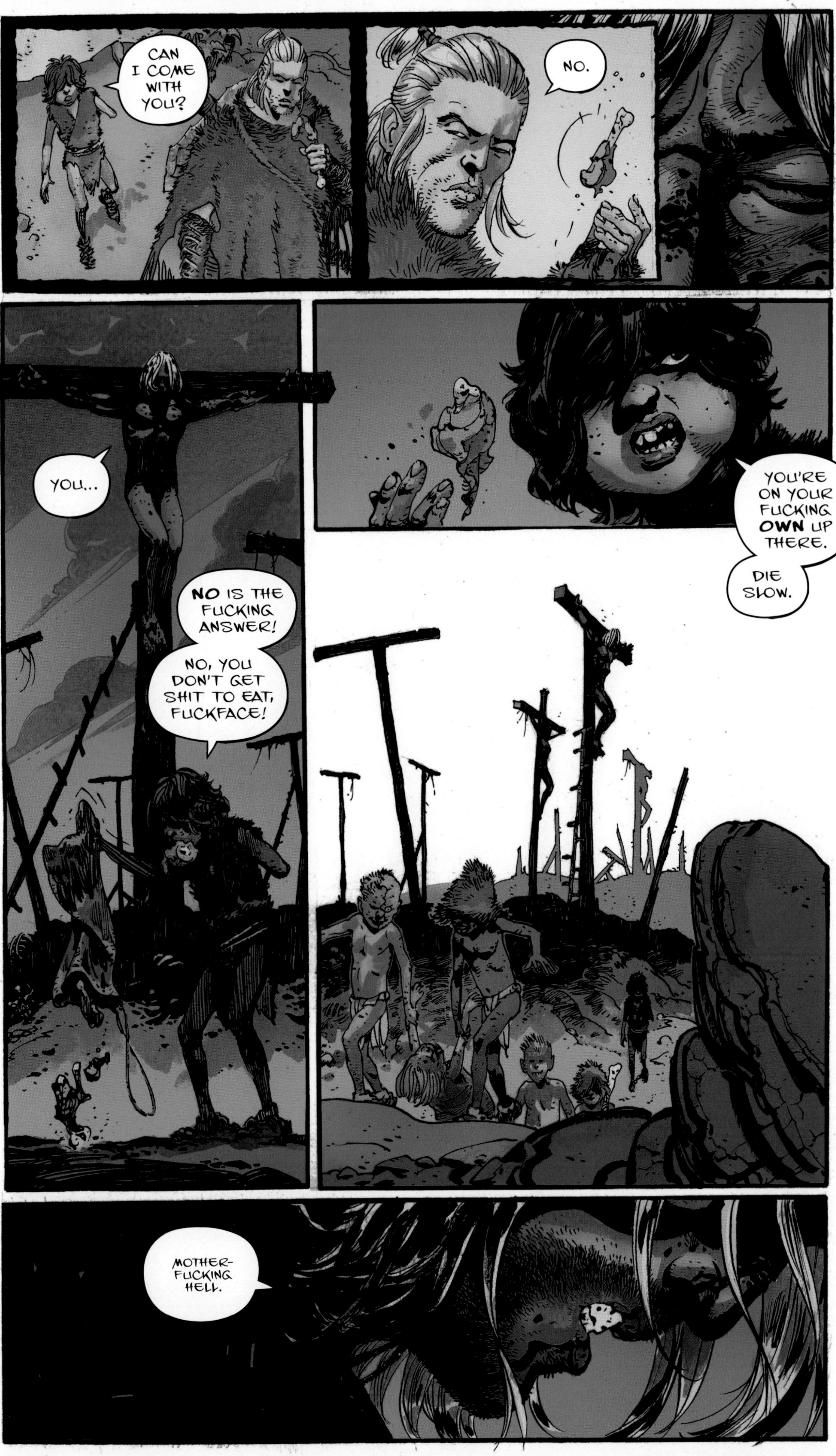
CAN I COME WITH YOU?
NO.
YOU...
YOU'RE ON YOUR FUCKING OWN UP THERE.
DIE SLOW.
NO IS THE FUCKING ANSWER!
NO, YOU DON'T GET SHIT TO EAT, FUCKFACE!
MOTHER-FUCKING HELL.

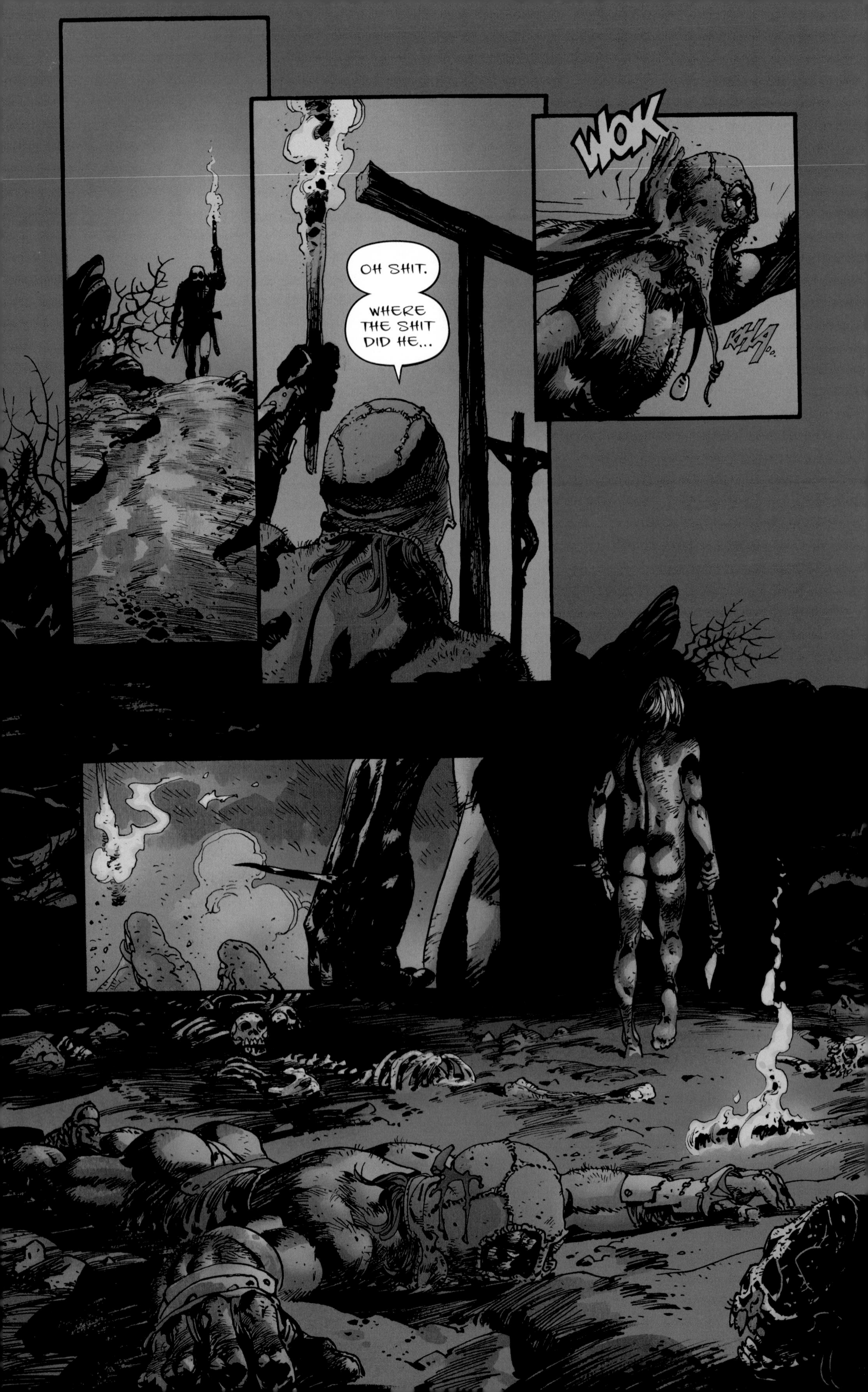
OH SHIT.
WHERE THE SHIT DID HE...
WOK

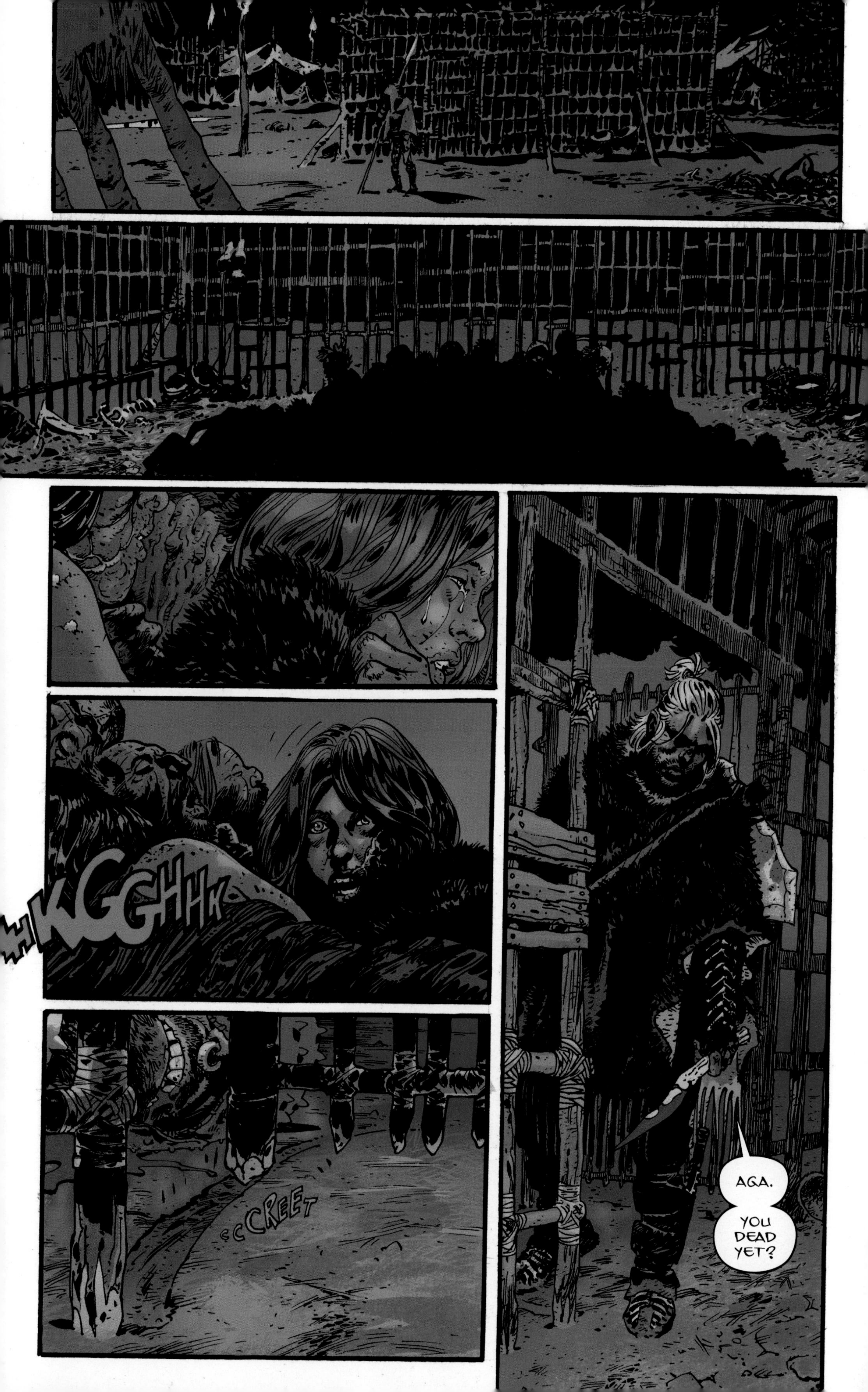
HKGGHHK
CCCREET
AGA.
YOU DEAD YET?

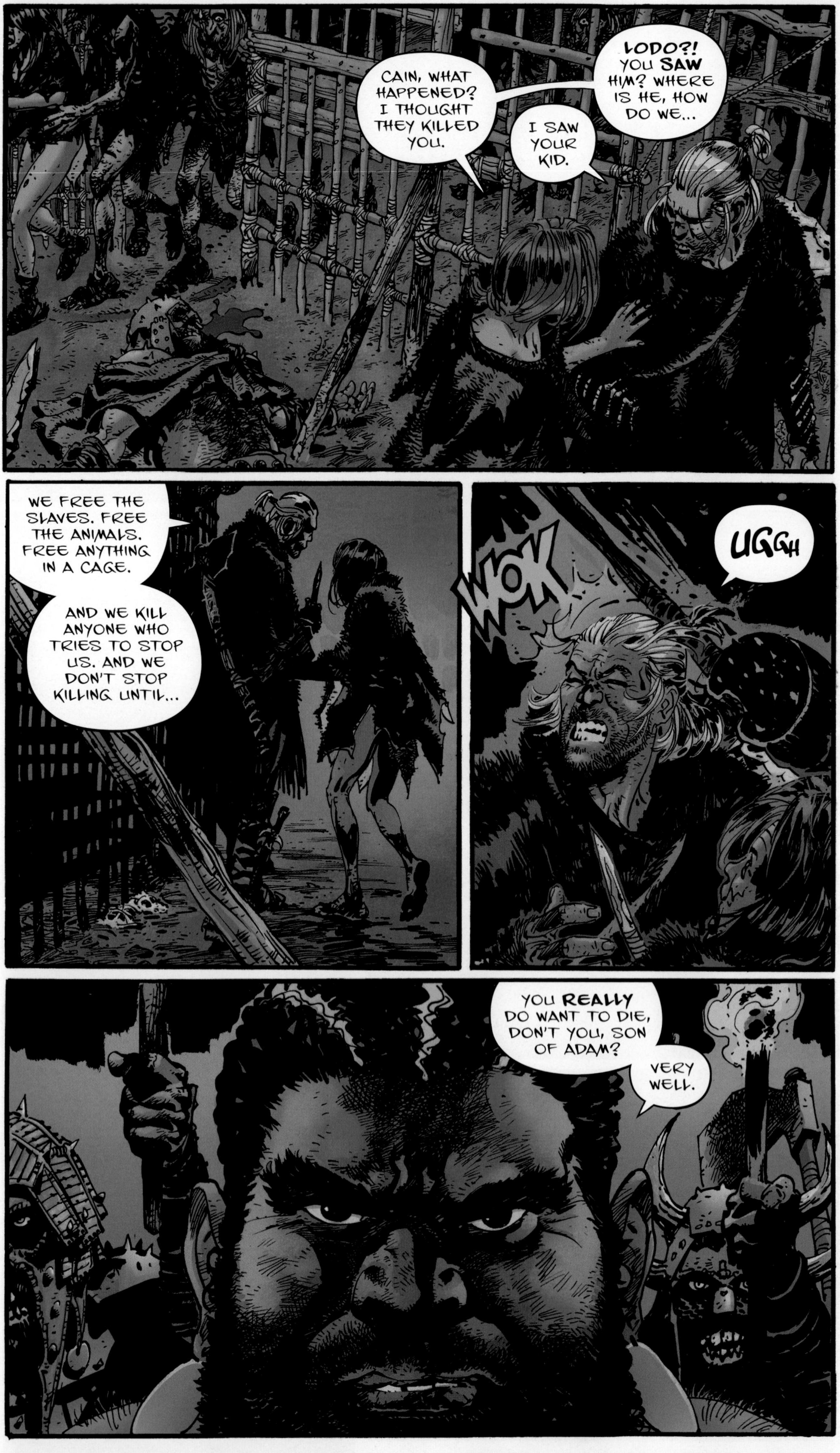
CAIN, WHAT HAPPENED? I THOUGHT THEY KILLED YOU.
I SAW YOUR KID.
LODO?! YOU SAW HIM? WHERE IS HE, HOW DO WE...
WE FREE THE SLAVES. FREE THE ANIMALS. FREE ANYTHING IN A CAGE.
AND WE KILL ANYONE WHO TRIES TO STOP US. AND WE DON'T STOP KILLING UNTIL...
WOK
UGGH
YOU REALLY DO WANT TO DIE, DON'T YOU, SON OF ADAM?
VERY WELL.

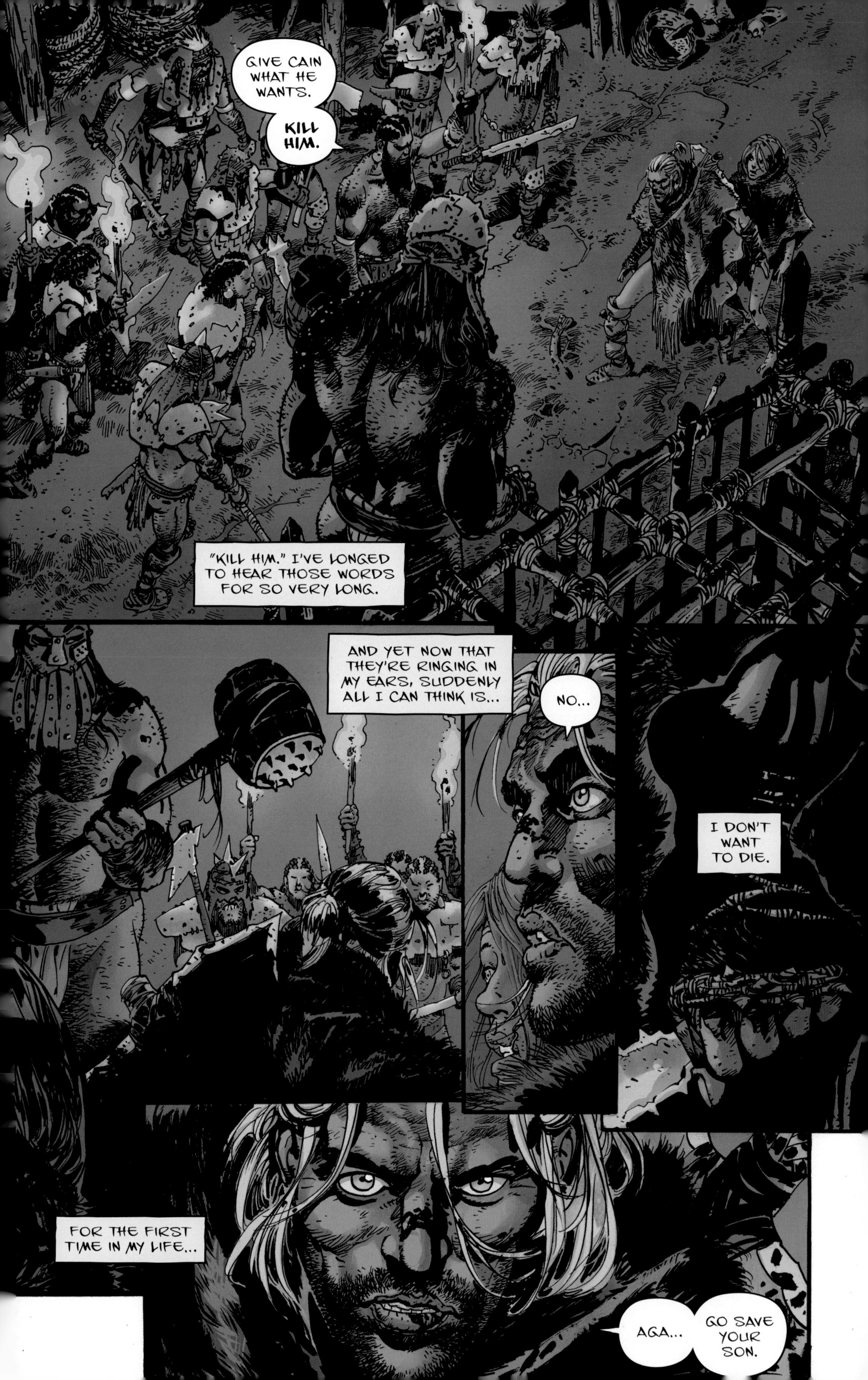

GIVE CAIN WHAT HE WANTS.
KILL HIM.
"KILL HIM." I'VE LONGED TO HEAR THOSE WORDS FOR SO VERY LONG.
AND YET NOW THAT THEY'RE RINGING IN MY EARS, SUDDENLY ALL I CAN THINK IS...
NO...
I DON'T WANT TO DIE.
FOR THE FIRST TIME IN MY LIFE...
AGA...
GO SAVE YOUR SON.

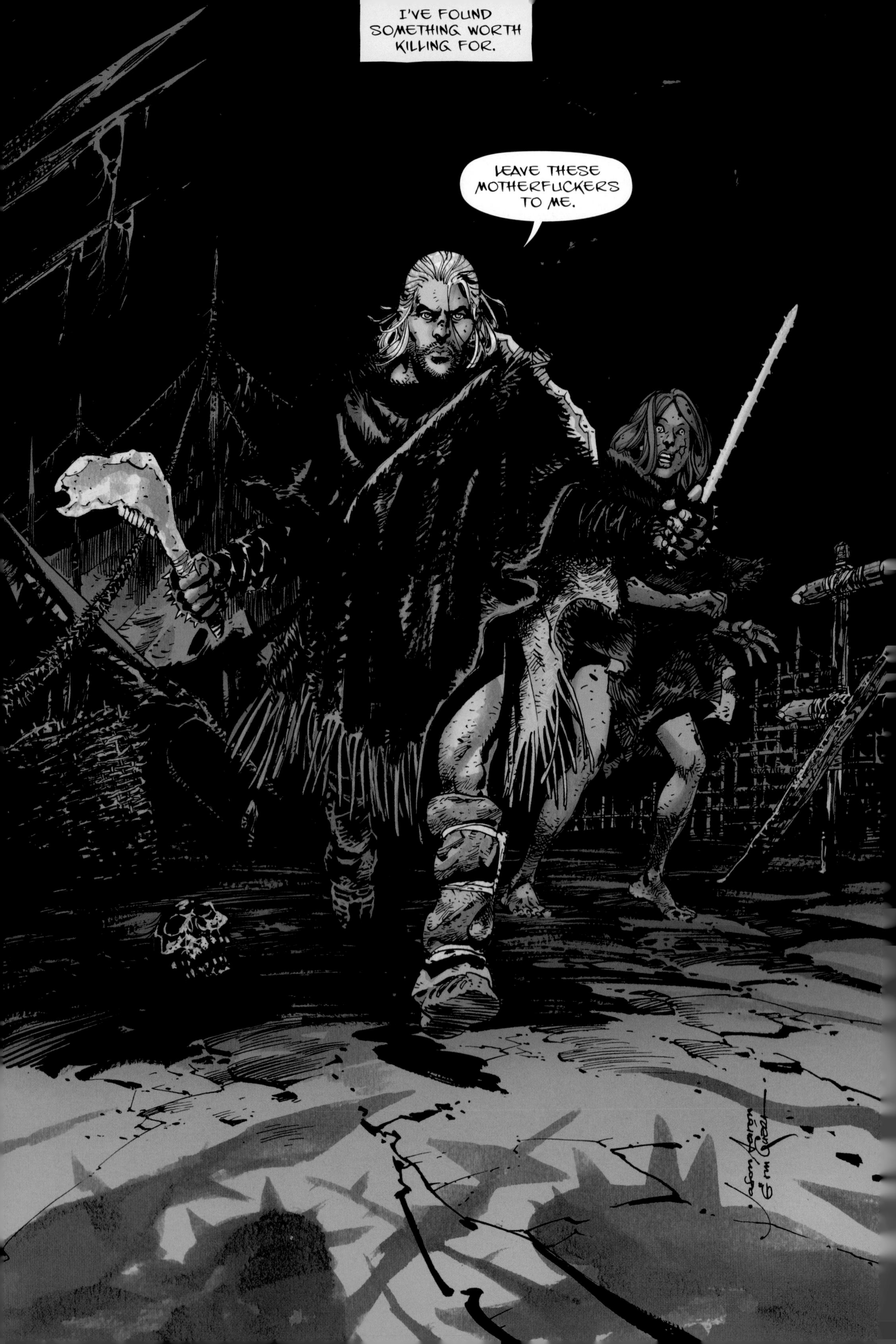
I'VE FOUND SOMETHING WORTH KILLING FOR.
LEAVE THESE MOTHERFUCKERS TO ME.

chapter five

God's Monsters

And the Lord said, I will destroy
man whom I have created from
the face of the earth.

Both man, and beast, and the
creeping thing, and the fowls
of the air.

For it repenteth me that I have
made them.

Genesis 6:7

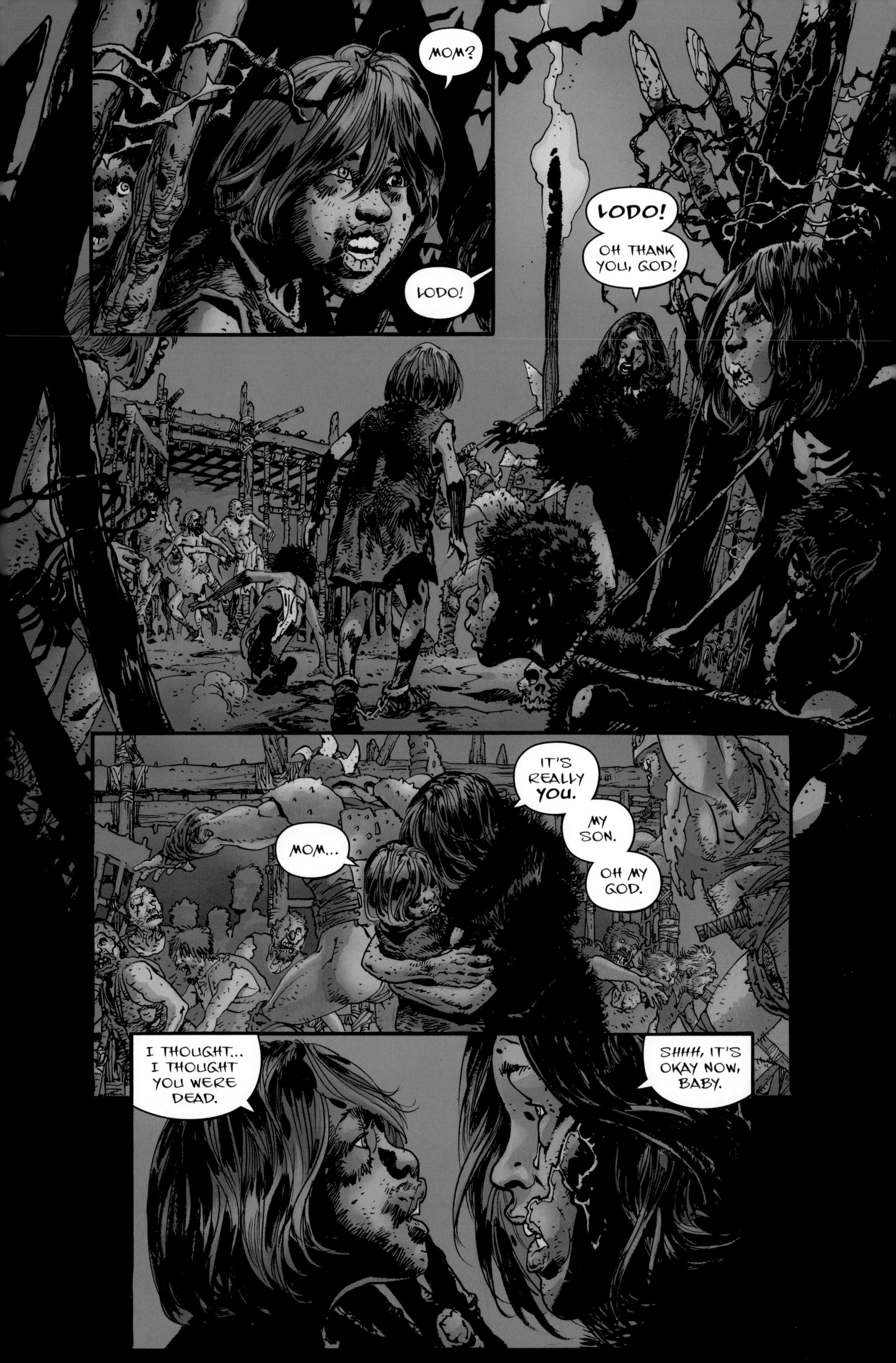
MOM?
LODO!
LODO!
OH THANK YOU, GOD!
IT'S REALLY YOU.
MY SON.
OH MY GOD.
MOM...
I THOUGHT... I THOUGHT YOU WERE DEAD.
SHHH, IT'S OKAY NOW, BABY.

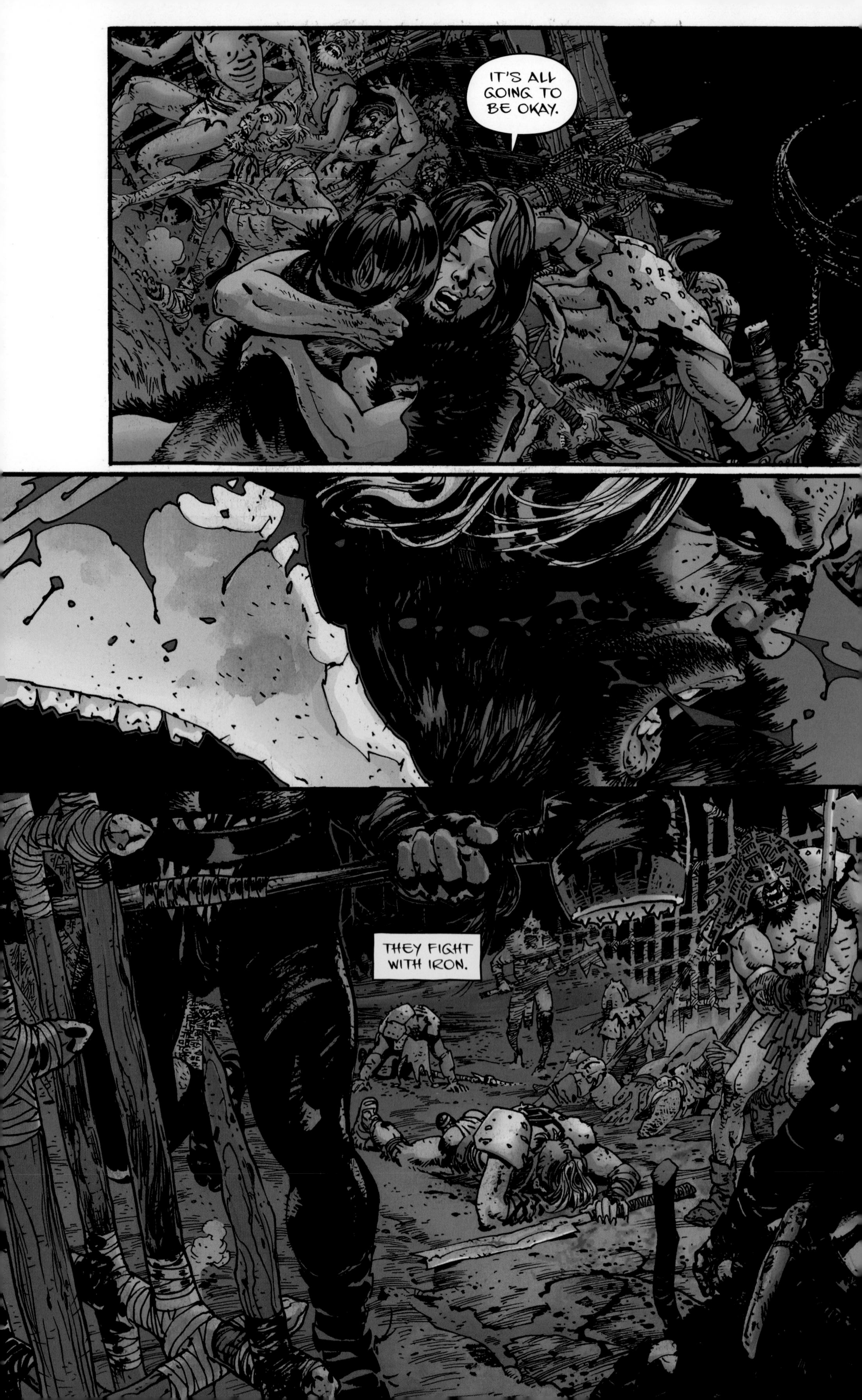
IT'S ALL GOING TO BE OKAY.
THEY FIGHT WITH IRON.

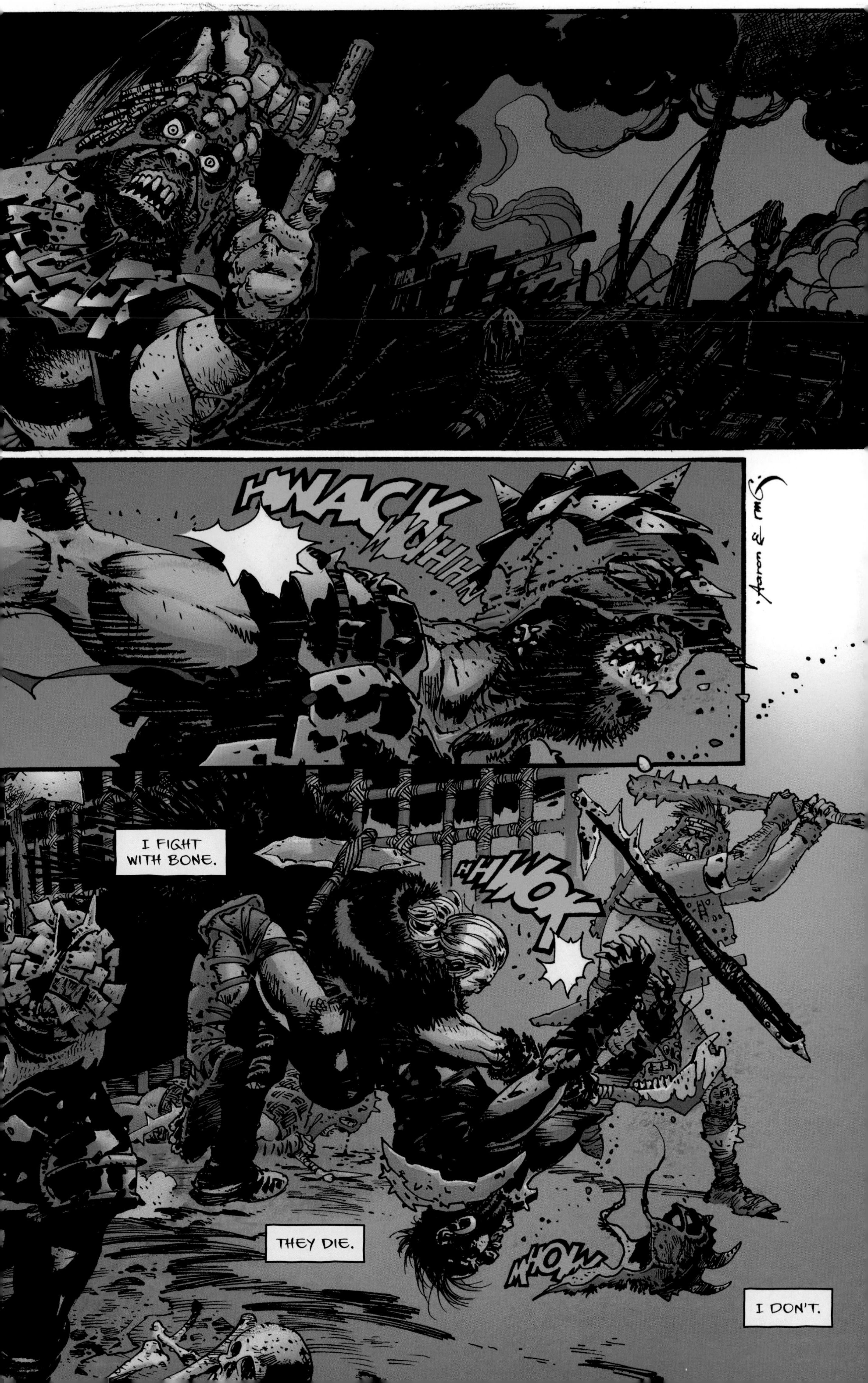
HWACK
I FIGHT WITH BONE.
HWOK
THEY DIE.
I DON'T.

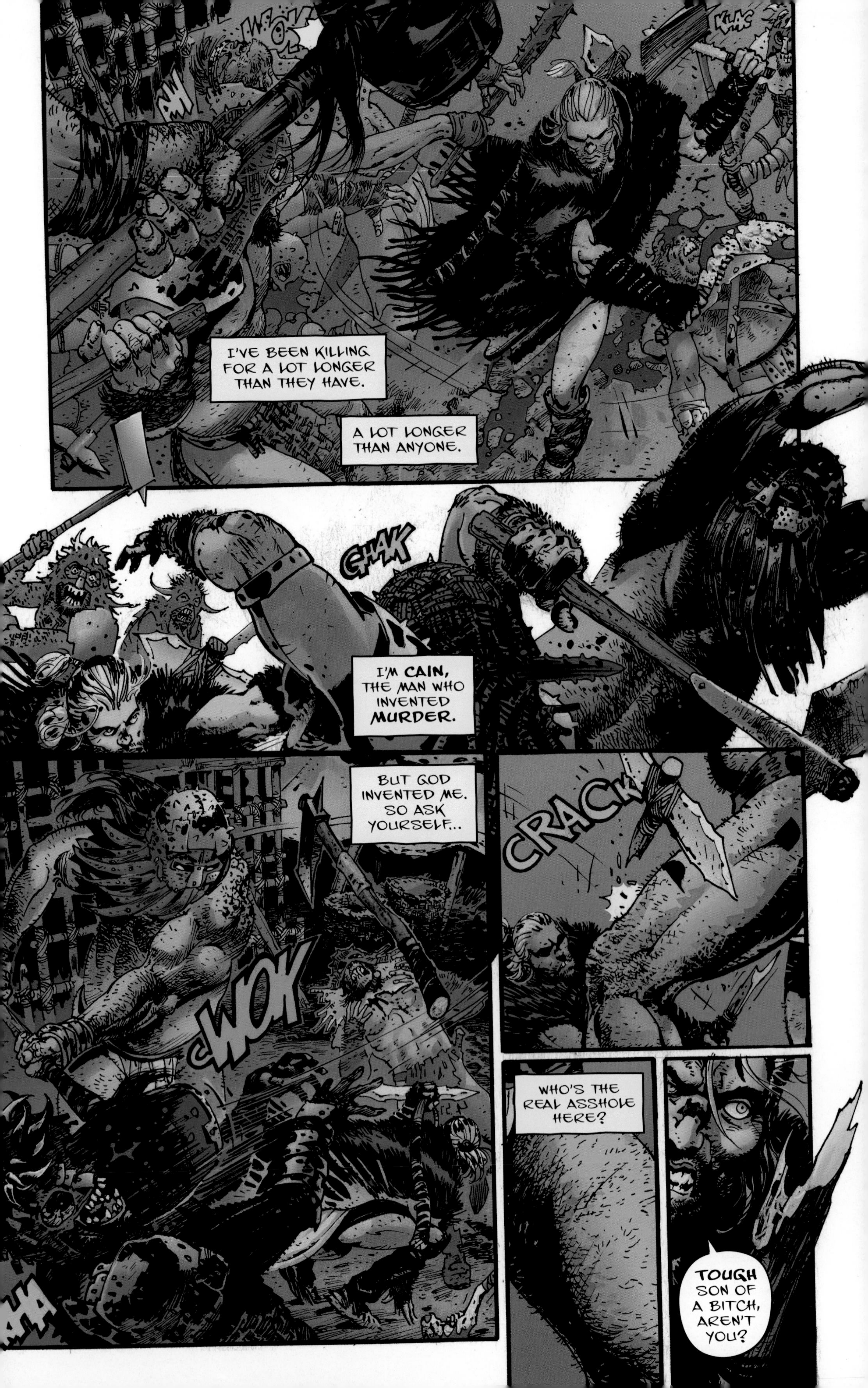
I'VE BEEN KILLING FOR A LOT LONGER THAN THEY HAVE.
A LOT LONGER THAN ANYONE.
CHAK
I'M CAIN, THE MAN WHO INVENTED MURDER.
BUT GOD INVENTED ME. SO ASK YOURSELF...
CRACK
WHO'S THE REAL ASSHOLE HERE?
TOUGH SON OF A BITCH, AREN'T YOU?

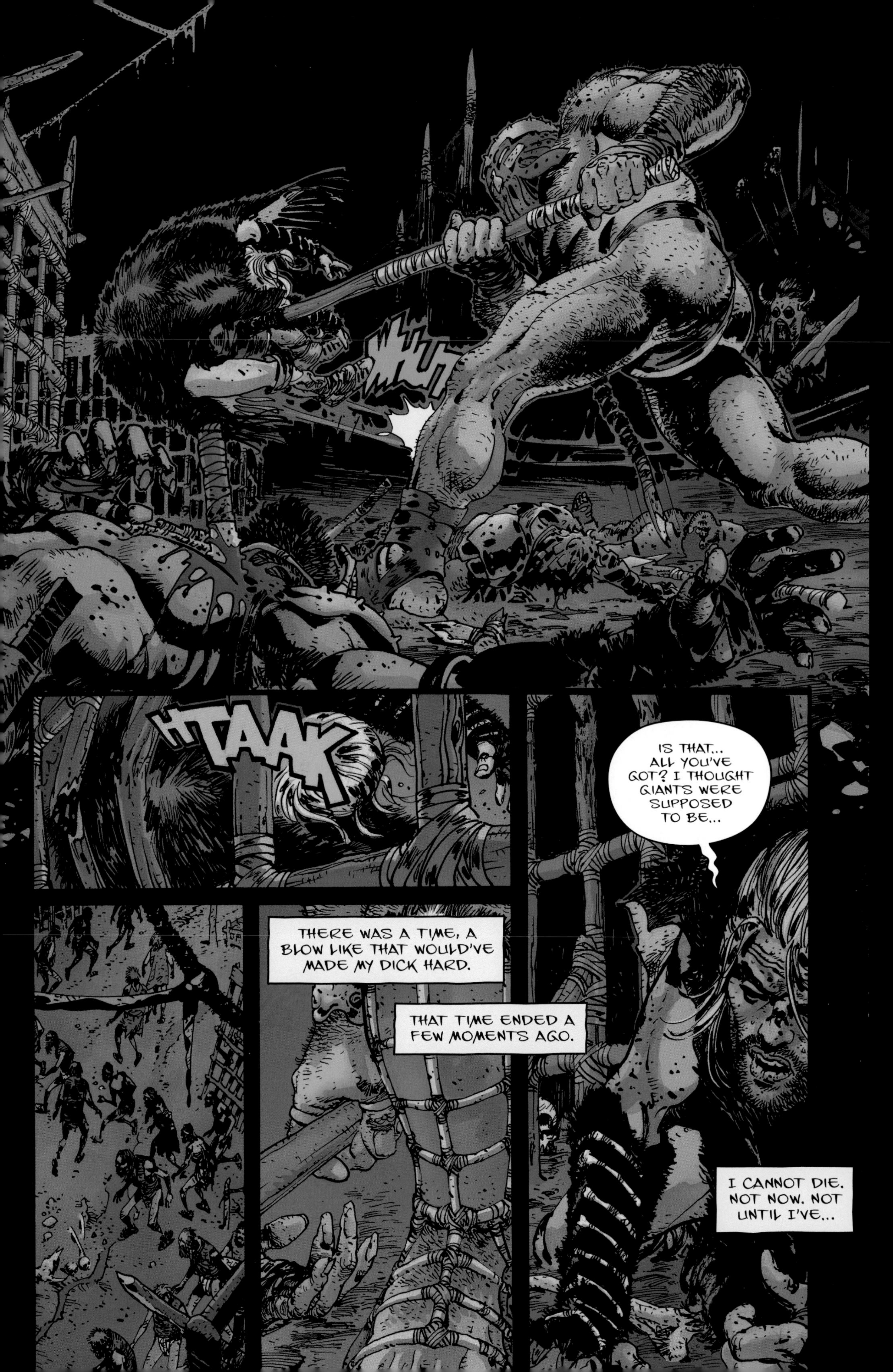
WHUT
TAAK
IS THAT... ALL YOU'VE GOT? I THOUGHT GIANTS WERE SUPPOSED TO BE...
THERE WAS A TIME, A BLOW LIKE THAT WOULD'VE MADE MY DICK HARD.
THAT TIME ENDED A FEW MOMENTS AGO.
I CANNOT DIE. NOT NOW. NOT UNTIL I'VE...

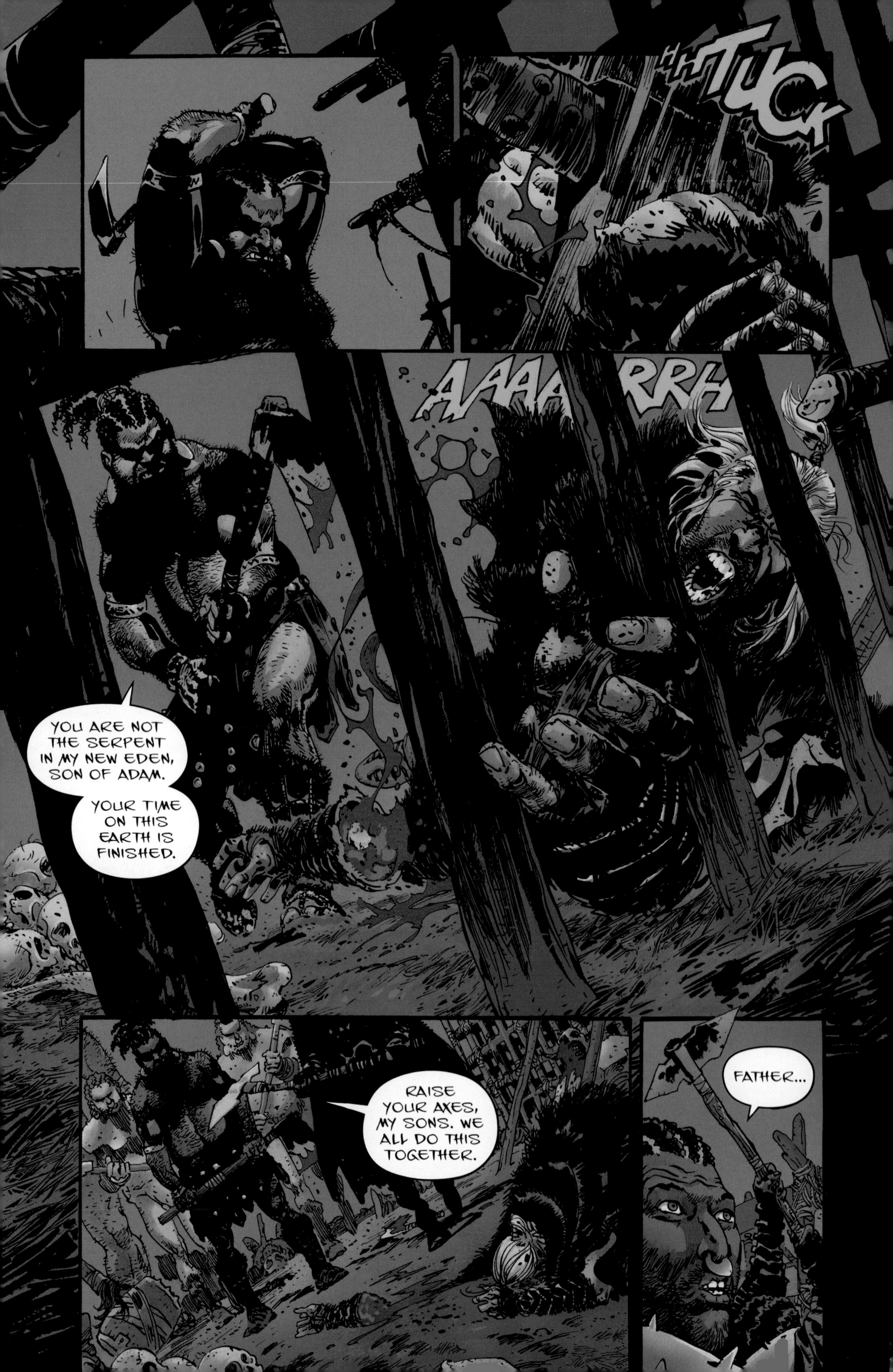
THTUCK
AAAARRRH
YOU ARE NOT THE SERPENT IN MY NEW EDEN, SON OF ADAM.
YOUR TIME ON THIS EARTH IS FINISHED.
RAISE YOUR AXES, MY SONS. WE ALL DO THIS TOGETHER.
FATHER...

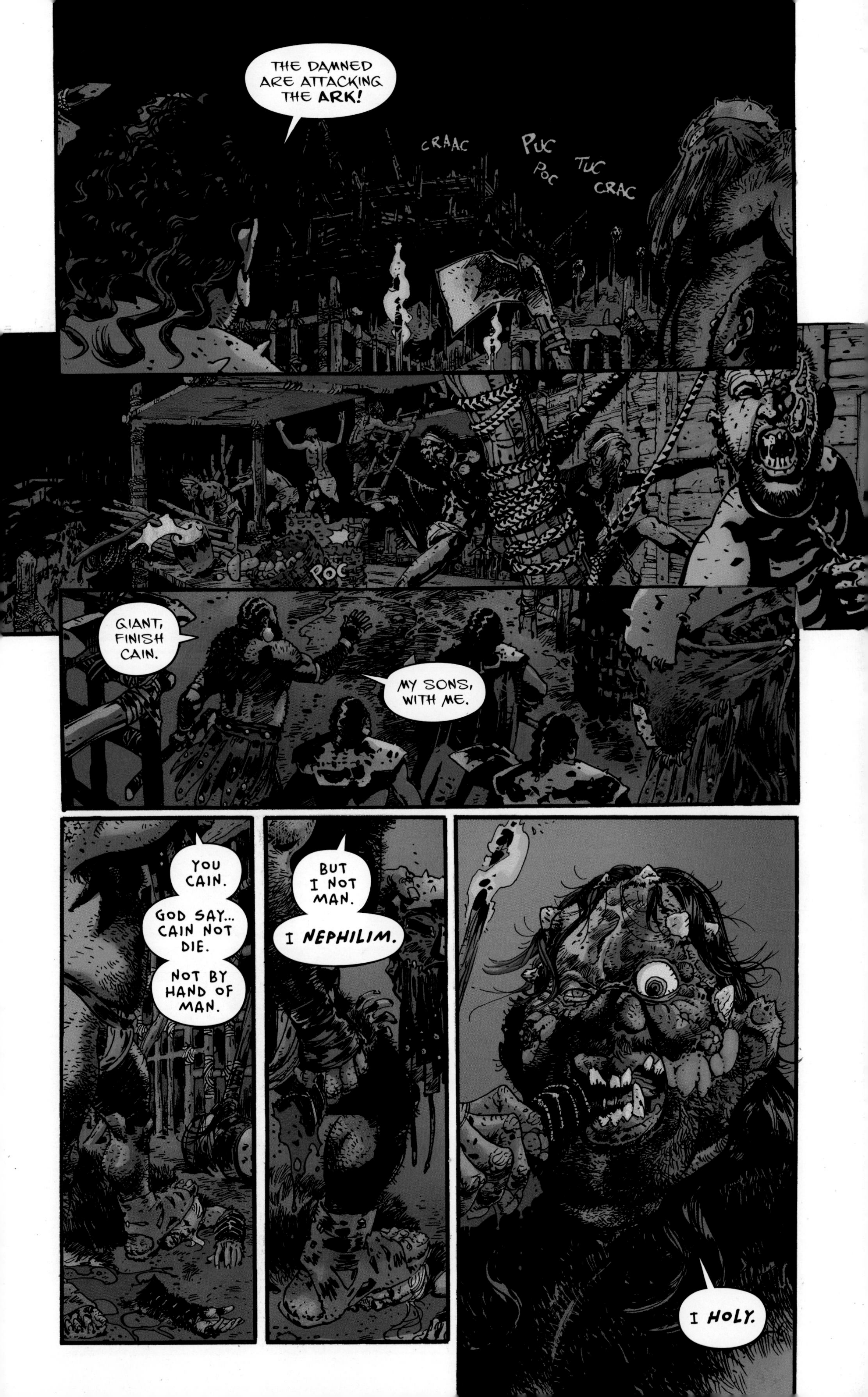
THE DAMNED ARE ATTACKING THE ARK!
CRAAC
PUC
POC
TUC
CRAC
POC
GIANT, FINISH CAIN.
MY SONS, WITH ME.
YOU CAIN.
GOD SAY... CAIN NOT DIE.
NOT BY HAND OF MAN.
BUT I NOT MAN.
I NEPHILIM.
I HOLY.

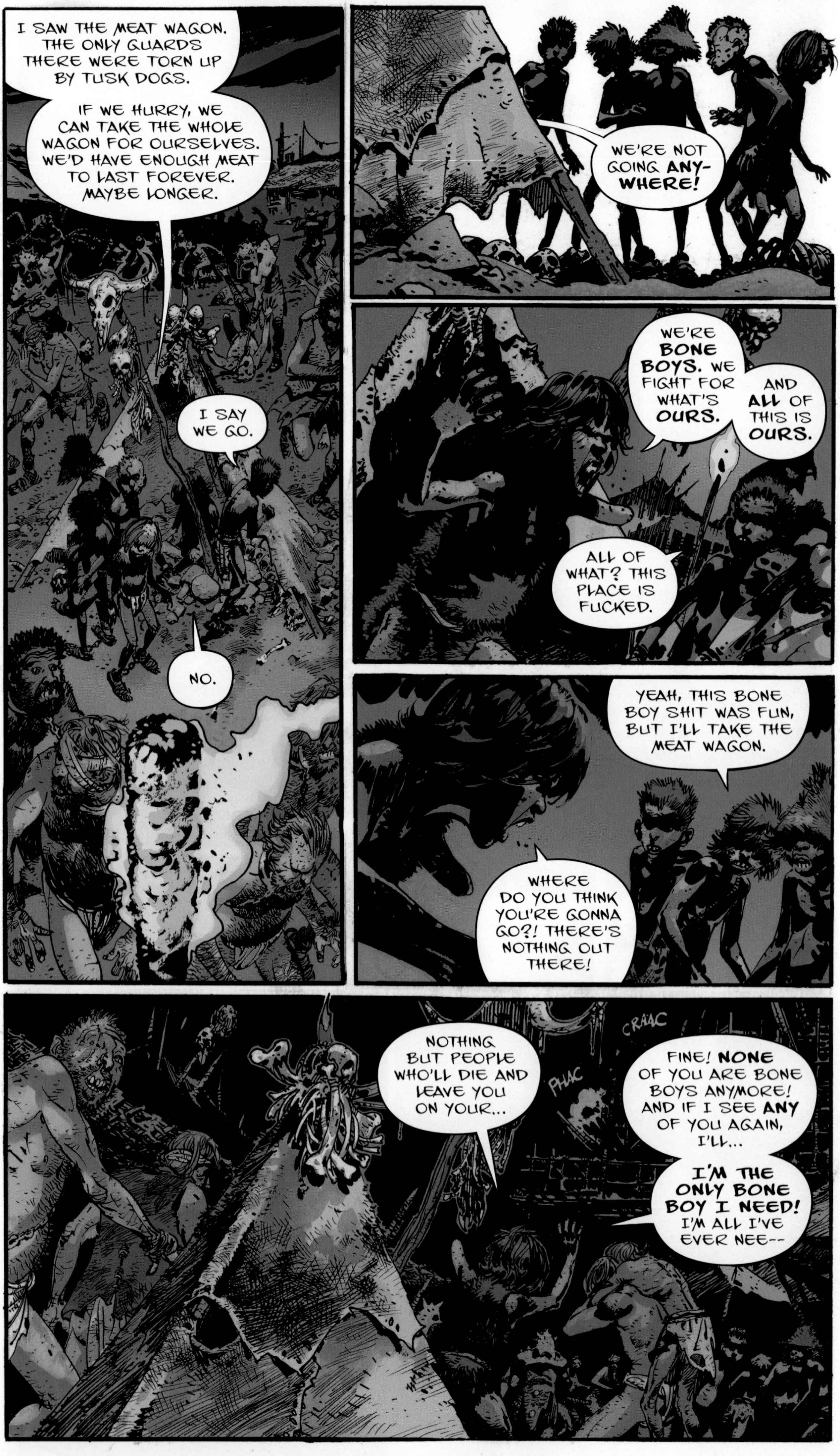
I SAW THE MEAT WAGON. THE ONLY GUARDS THERE WERE TORN UP BY TUSK DOGS.
IF WE HURRY, WE CAN TAKE THE WHOLE WAGON FOR OURSELVES. WE'D HAVE ENOUGH MEAT TO LAST FOREVER. MAYBE LONGER.
WE'RE NOT GOING **ANYWHERE!**
I SAY WE GO.
NO.
WE'RE **BONE BOYS.** WE FIGHT FOR WHAT'S **OURS.**
AND **ALL** OF THIS IS **OURS.**
ALL OF WHAT? THIS PLACE IS FUCKED.
YEAH, THIS BONE BOY SHIT WAS FUN, BUT I'LL TAKE THE MEAT WAGON.
WHERE DO YOU THINK YOU'RE GONNA GO?! THERE'S NOTHING OUT THERE!
NOTHING BUT PEOPLE WHO'LL DIE AND LEAVE YOU ON YOUR...
CRAAC
PHAC
FINE! **NONE** OF YOU ARE BONE BOYS ANYMORE! AND IF I SEE **ANY** OF YOU AGAIN, I'LL...
I'M THE ONLY BONE BOY I NEED! I'M ALL I'VE EVER NEE--

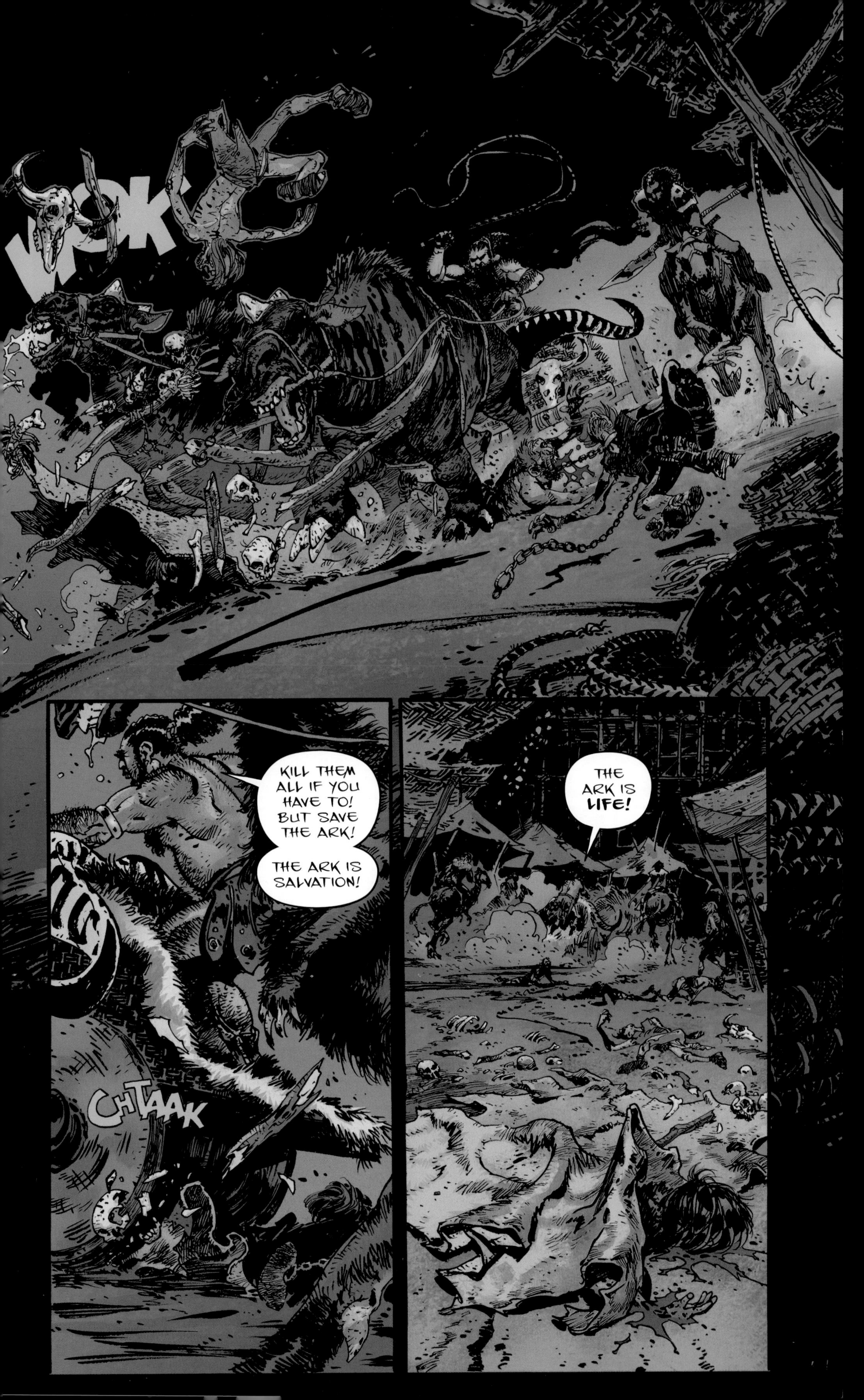
WOK
KILL THEM ALL IF YOU HAVE TO! BUT SAVE THE ARK!
THE ARK IS SALVATION!
CHTAAK
THE ARK IS LIFE!

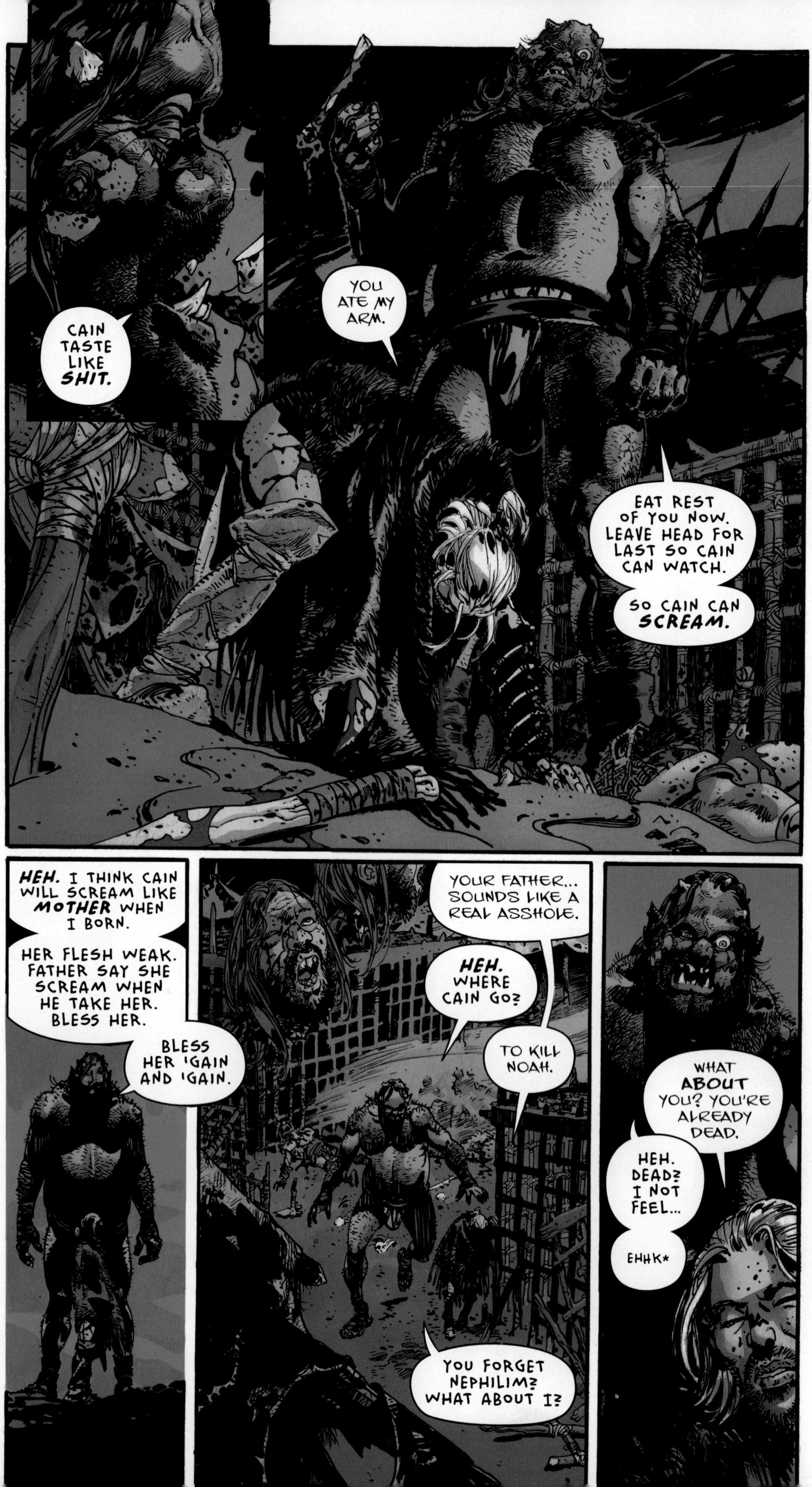
CAIN TASTE LIKE SHIT.
YOU ATE MY ARM.
EAT REST OF YOU NOW. LEAVE HEAD FOR LAST SO CAIN CAN WATCH.
SO CAIN CAN SCREAM.
HEH. I THINK CAIN WILL SCREAM LIKE MOTHER WHEN I BORN.
HER FLESH WEAK. FATHER SAY SHE SCREAM WHEN HE TAKE HER. BLESS HER.
BLESS HER 'GAIN AND 'GAIN.
YOUR FATHER... SOUNDS LIKE A REAL ASSHOLE.
HEH. WHERE CAIN GO?
TO KILL NOAH.
YOU FORGET NEPHILIM? WHAT ABOUT I?
WHAT ABOUT YOU? YOU'RE ALREADY DEAD.
HEH. DEAD? I NOT FEEL...
EHHK*

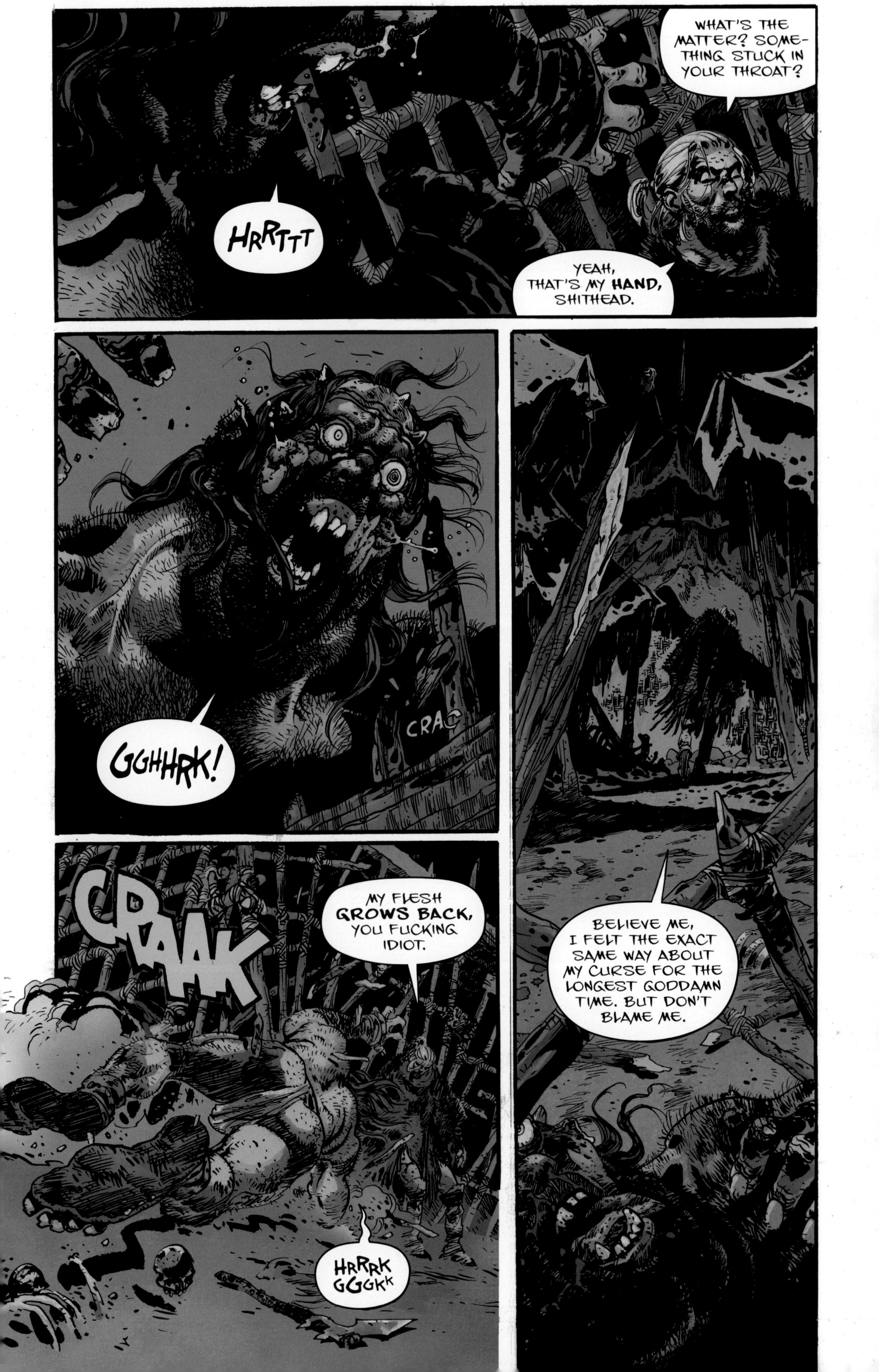
WHAT'S THE MATTER? SOMETHING STUCK IN YOUR THROAT?
HRRTTT
YEAH, THAT'S MY HAND, SHITHEAD.
GGHHRK!
CRAC
CRAAK
MY FLESH GROWS BACK, YOU FUCKING IDIOT.
HRRRK GGGKK
BELIEVE ME, I FELT THE EXACT SAME WAY ABOUT MY CURSE FOR THE LONGEST GODDAMN TIME. BUT DON'T BLAME ME.

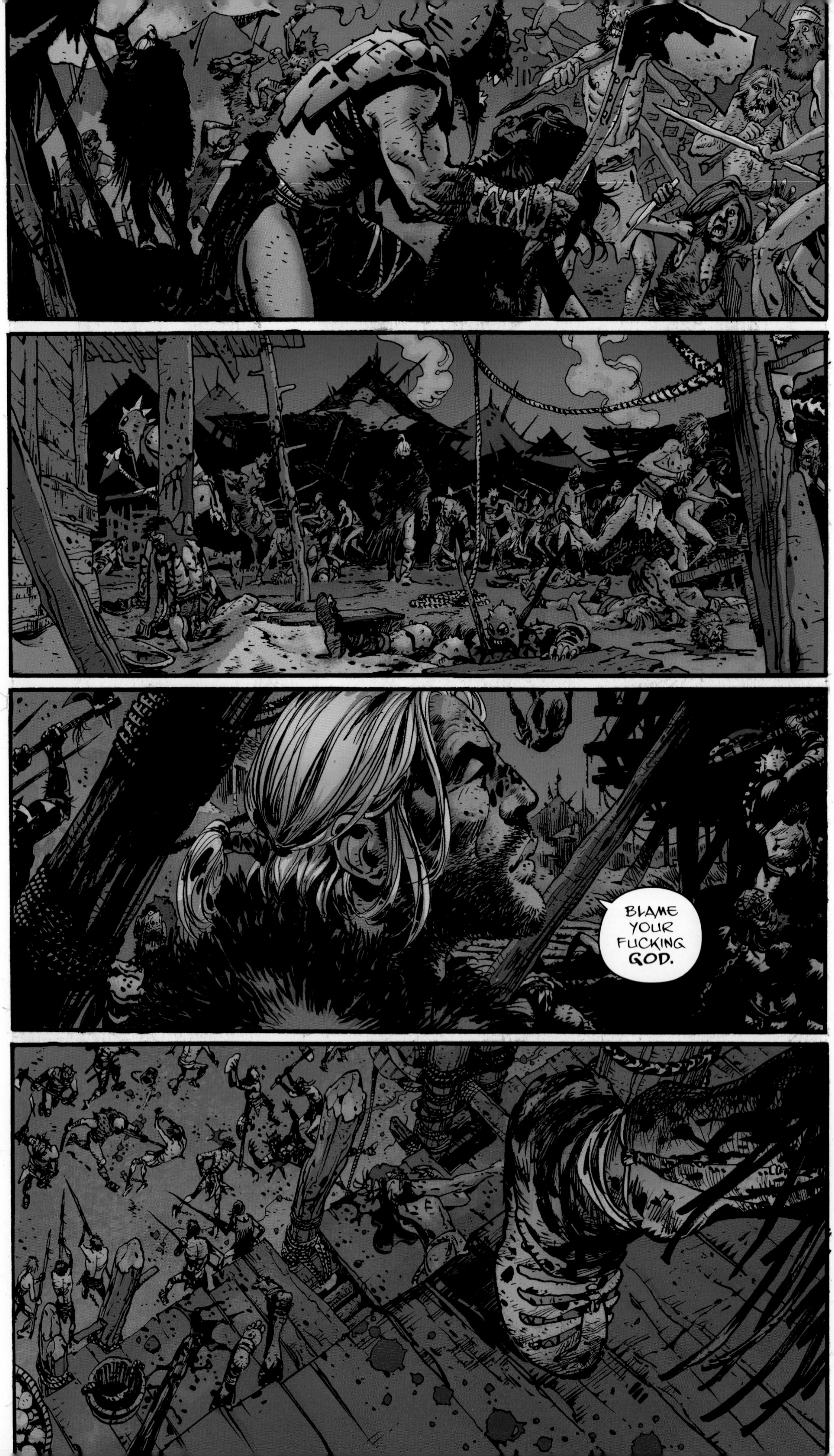
BLAME YOUR FUCKING GOD.

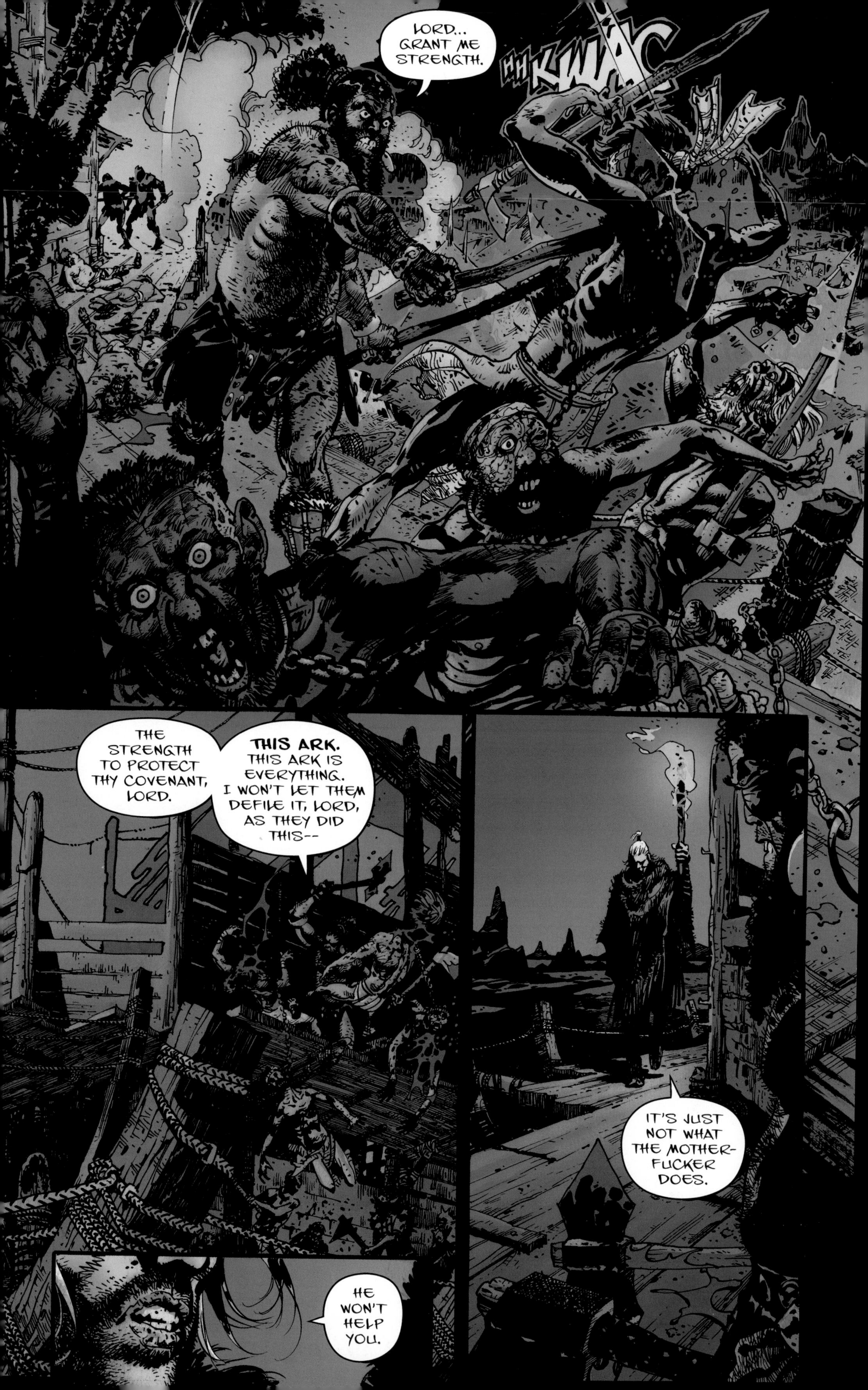
LORD... GRANT ME STRENGTH.
HHKWAC
THE STRENGTH TO PROTECT THY COVENANT, LORD.
THIS ARK. THIS ARK IS EVERYTHING. I WON'T LET THEM DEFILE IT, LORD, AS THEY DID THIS--
IT'S JUST NOT WHAT THE MOTHER-FUCKER DOES.
HE WON'T HELP YOU.

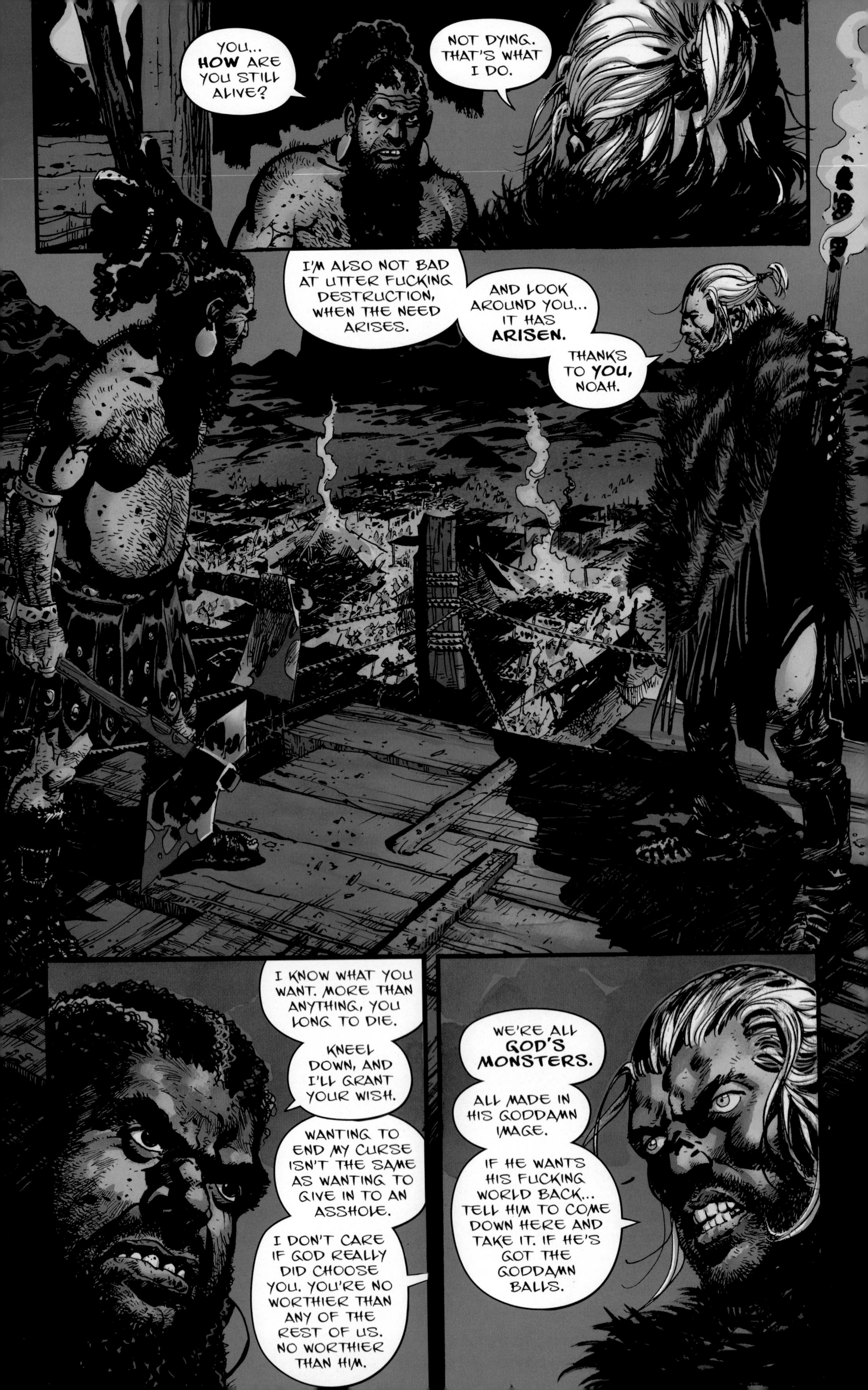
YOU... HOW ARE YOU STILL ALIVE?
NOT DYING. THAT'S WHAT I DO.
I'M ALSO NOT BAD AT UTTER FUCKING DESTRUCTION, WHEN THE NEED ARISES.
AND LOOK AROUND YOU... IT HAS ARISEN.
THANKS TO YOU, NOAH.
I KNOW WHAT YOU WANT. MORE THAN ANYTHING, YOU LONG TO DIE.
KNEEL DOWN, AND I'LL GRANT YOUR WISH.
WANTING TO END MY CURSE ISN'T THE SAME AS WANTING TO GIVE IN TO AN ASSHOLE.
I DON'T CARE IF GOD REALLY DID CHOOSE YOU. YOU'RE NO WORTHIER THAN ANY OF THE REST OF US. NO WORTHIER THAN HIM.
WE'RE ALL GOD'S MONSTERS.
ALL MADE IN HIS GODDAMN IMAGE.
IF HE WANTS HIS FUCKING WORLD BACK... TELL HIM TO COME DOWN HERE AND TAKE IT. IF HE'S GOT THE GODDAMN BALLS.

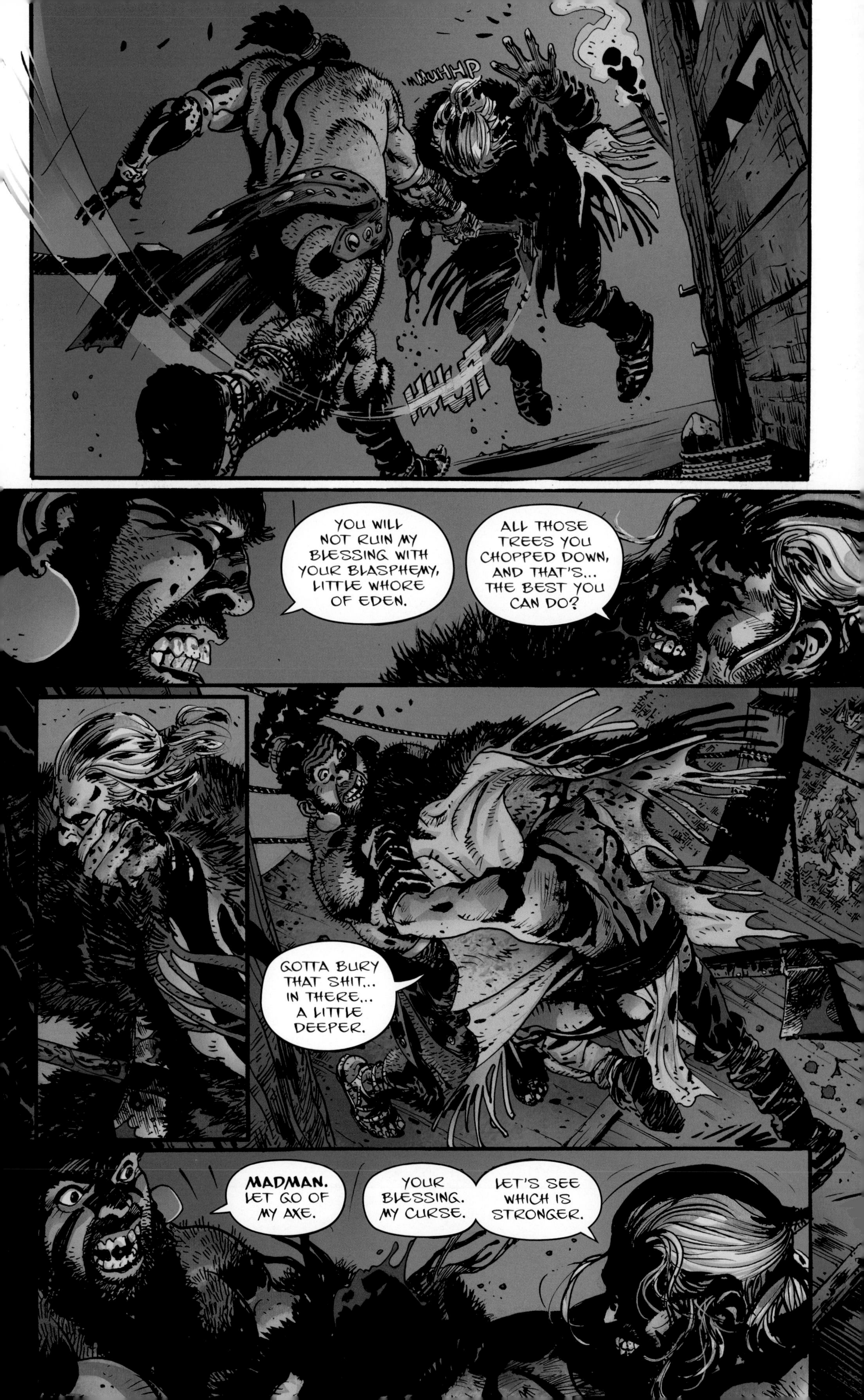
MUHHP
YOU WILL NOT RUIN MY BLESSING WITH YOUR BLASPHEMY, LITTLE WHORE OF EDEN.
ALL THOSE TREES YOU CHOPPED DOWN, AND THAT'S... THE BEST YOU CAN DO?
GOTTA BURY THAT SHIT... IN THERE... A LITTLE DEEPER.
MADMAN. LET GO OF MY AXE.
YOUR BLESSING. MY CURSE.
LET'S SEE WHICH IS STRONGER.

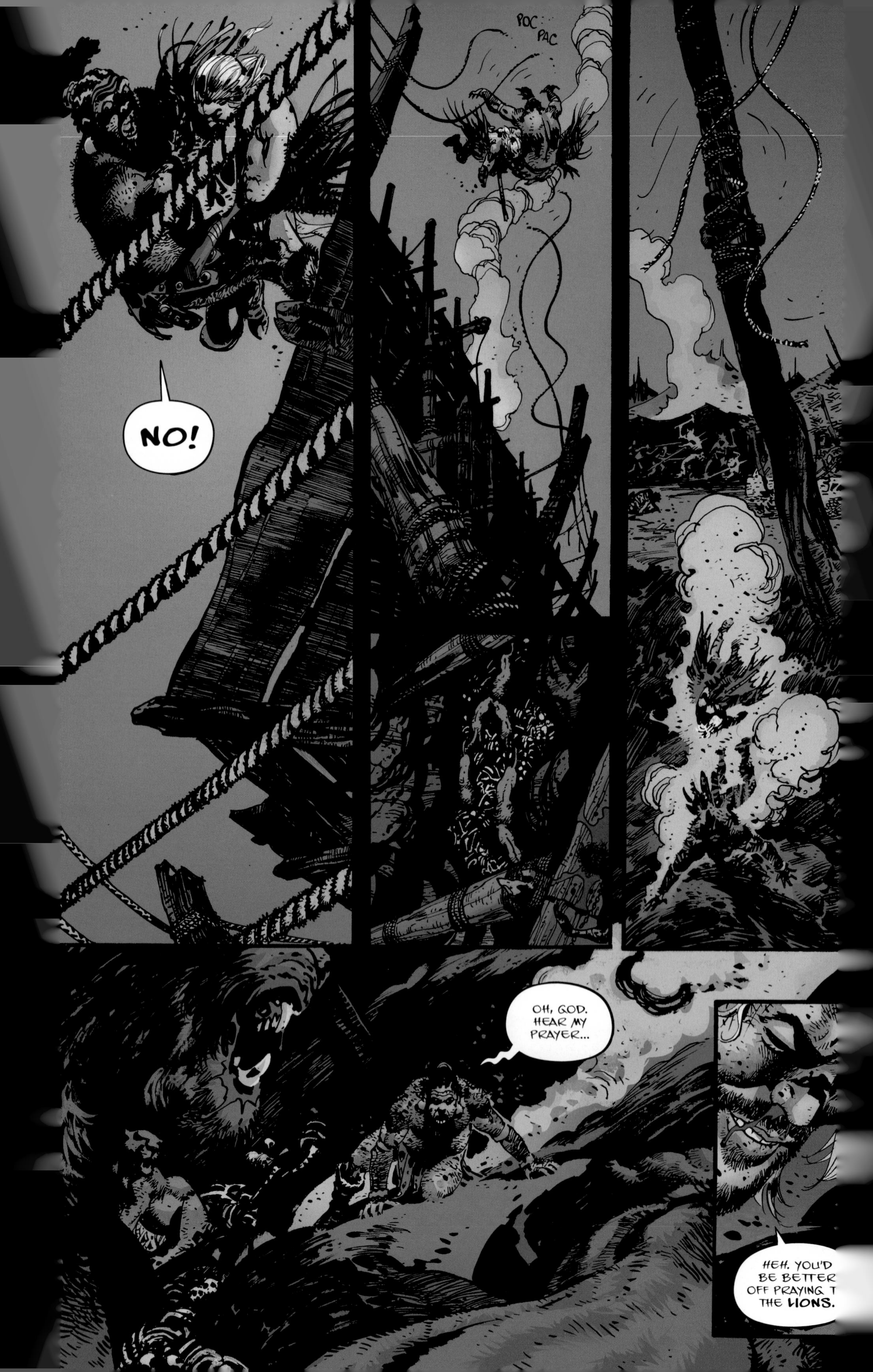
NO!
POC
PAC
OH, GOD. HEAR MY PRAYER...
HEH. YOU'D BE BETTER OFF PRAYING T THE LIONS.

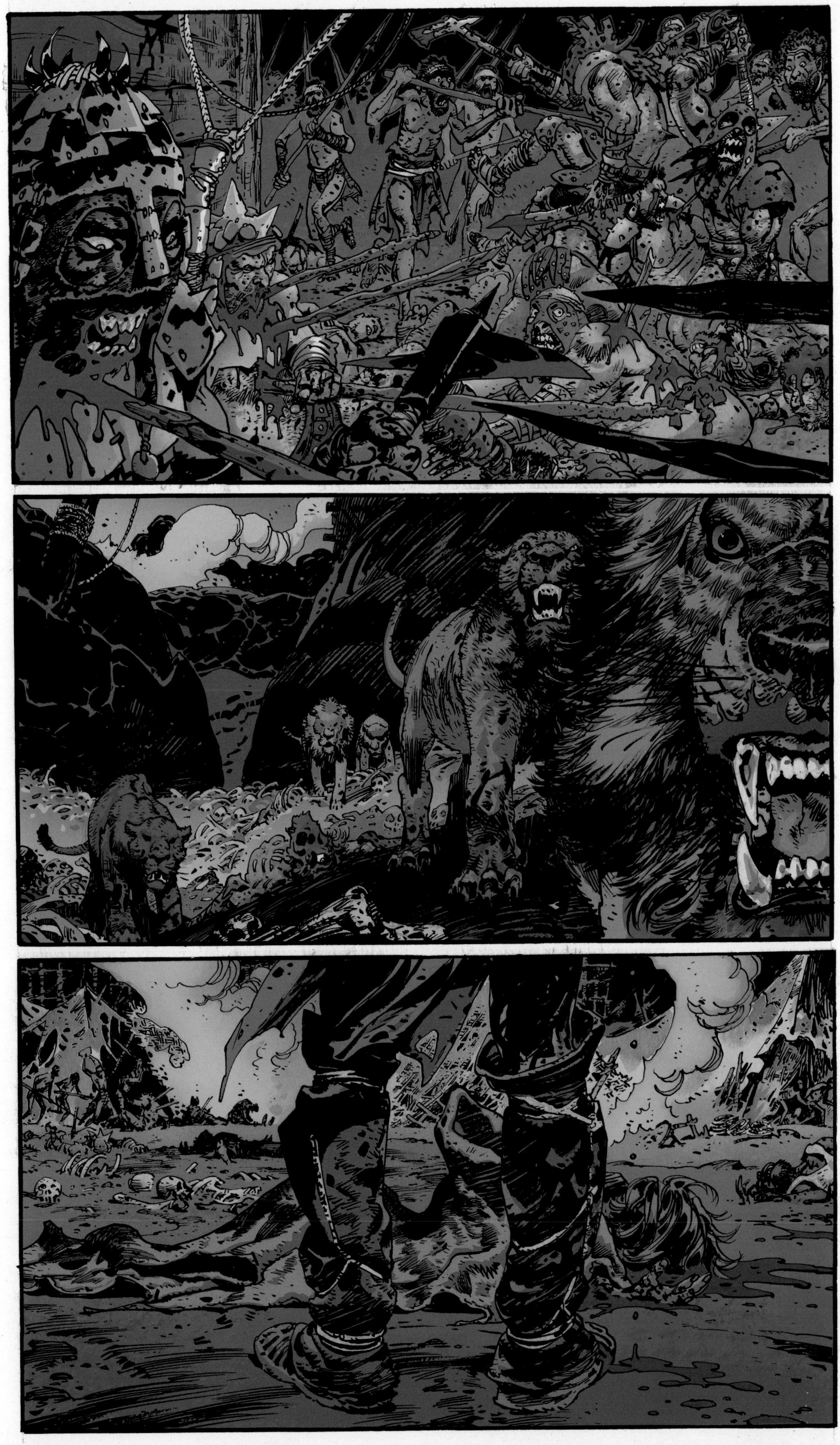

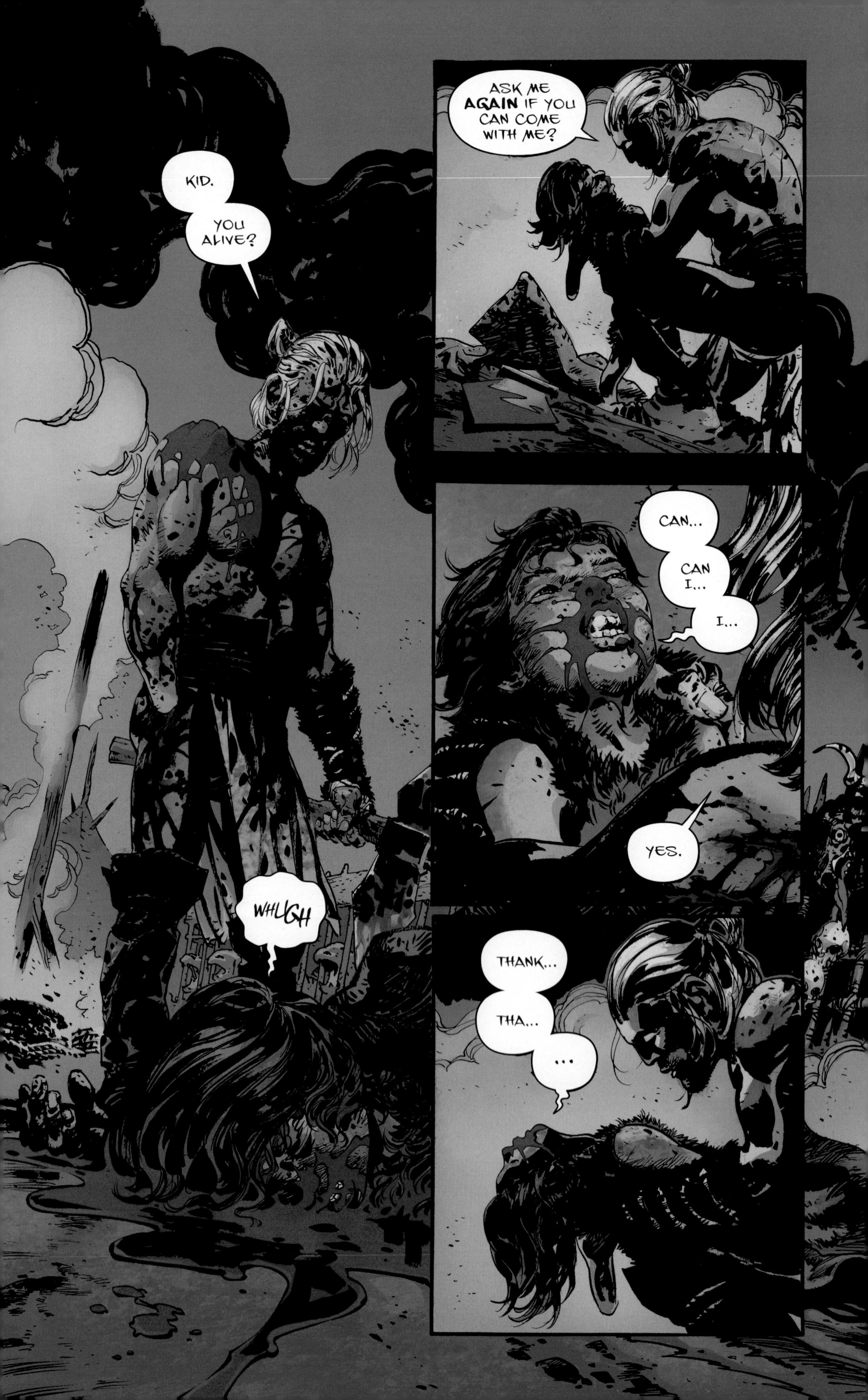
KID.
YOU ALIVE?
WHUGH
ASK ME AGAIN IF YOU CAN COME WITH ME?
CAN...
CAN I...
I...
YES.
THANK...
THA...
...

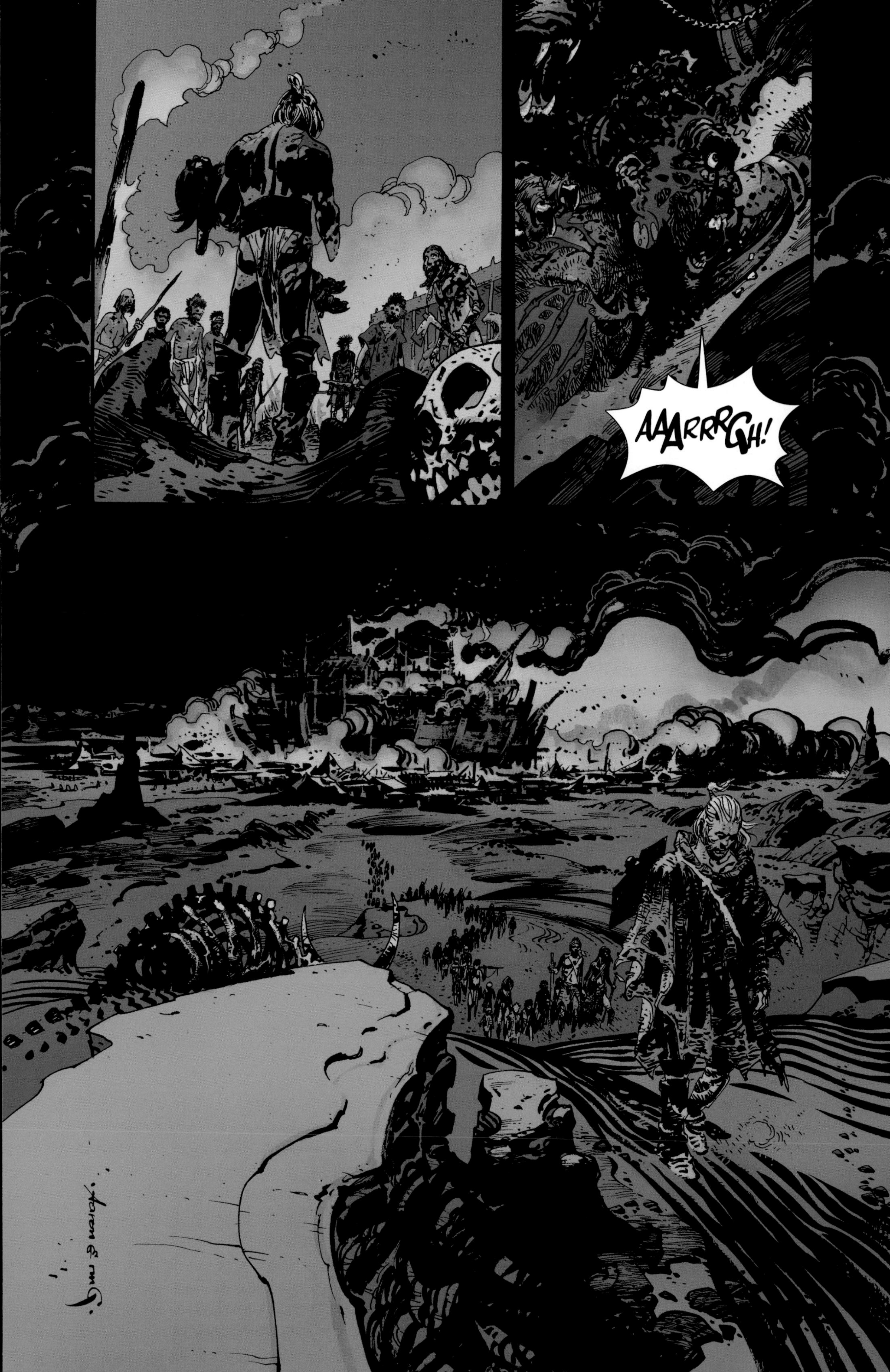
AAARRRGH!

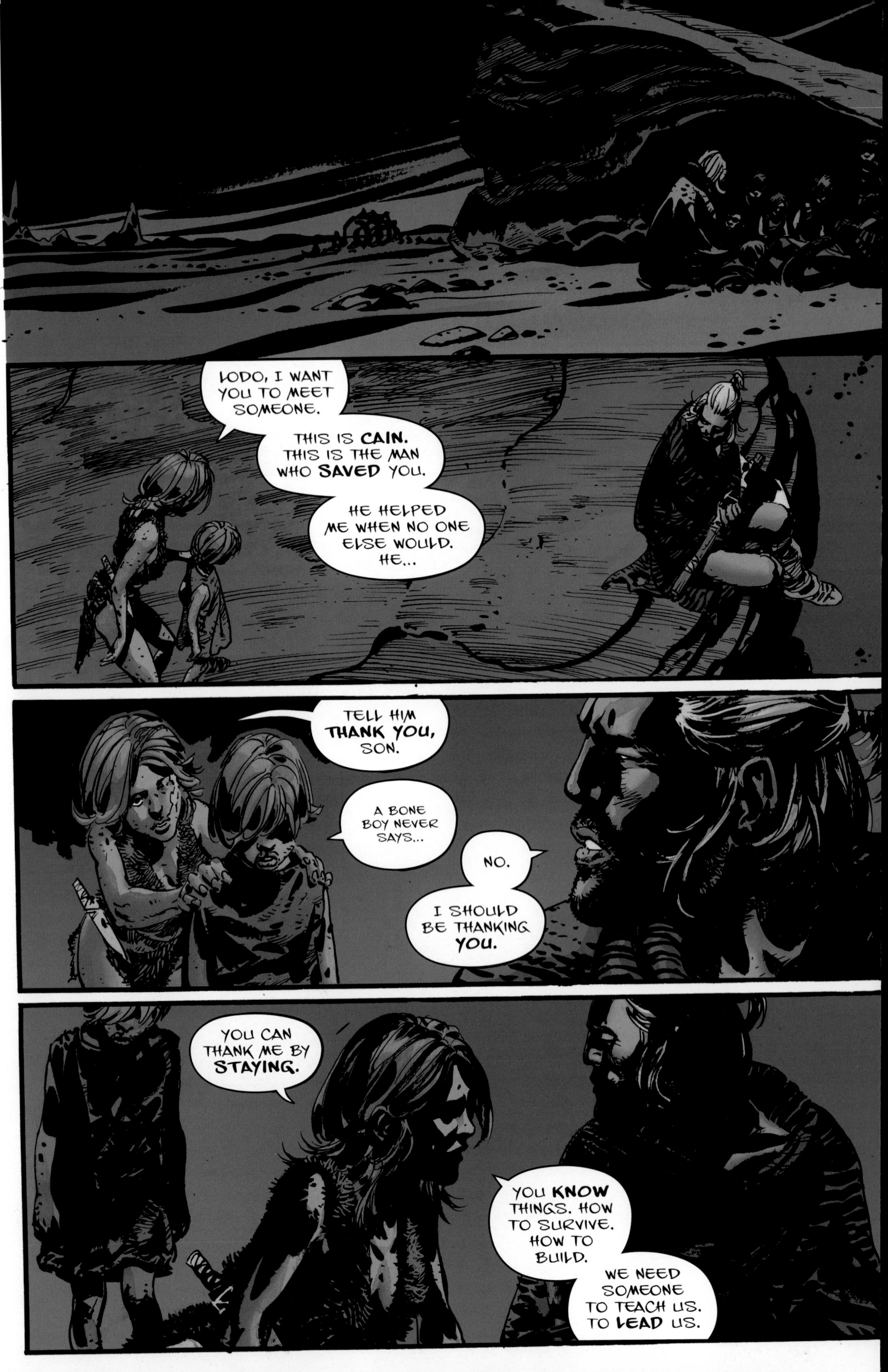
LODO, I WANT YOU TO MEET SOMEONE.
THIS IS CAIN. THIS IS THE MAN WHO SAVED YOU.
HE HELPED ME WHEN NO ONE ELSE WOULD. HE...
TELL HIM THANK YOU, SON.
A BONE BOY NEVER SAYS...
NO.
I SHOULD BE THANKING YOU.
YOU CAN THANK ME BY STAYING.
YOU KNOW THINGS. HOW TO SURVIVE. HOW TO BUILD.
WE NEED SOMEONE TO TEACH US. TO LEAD US.

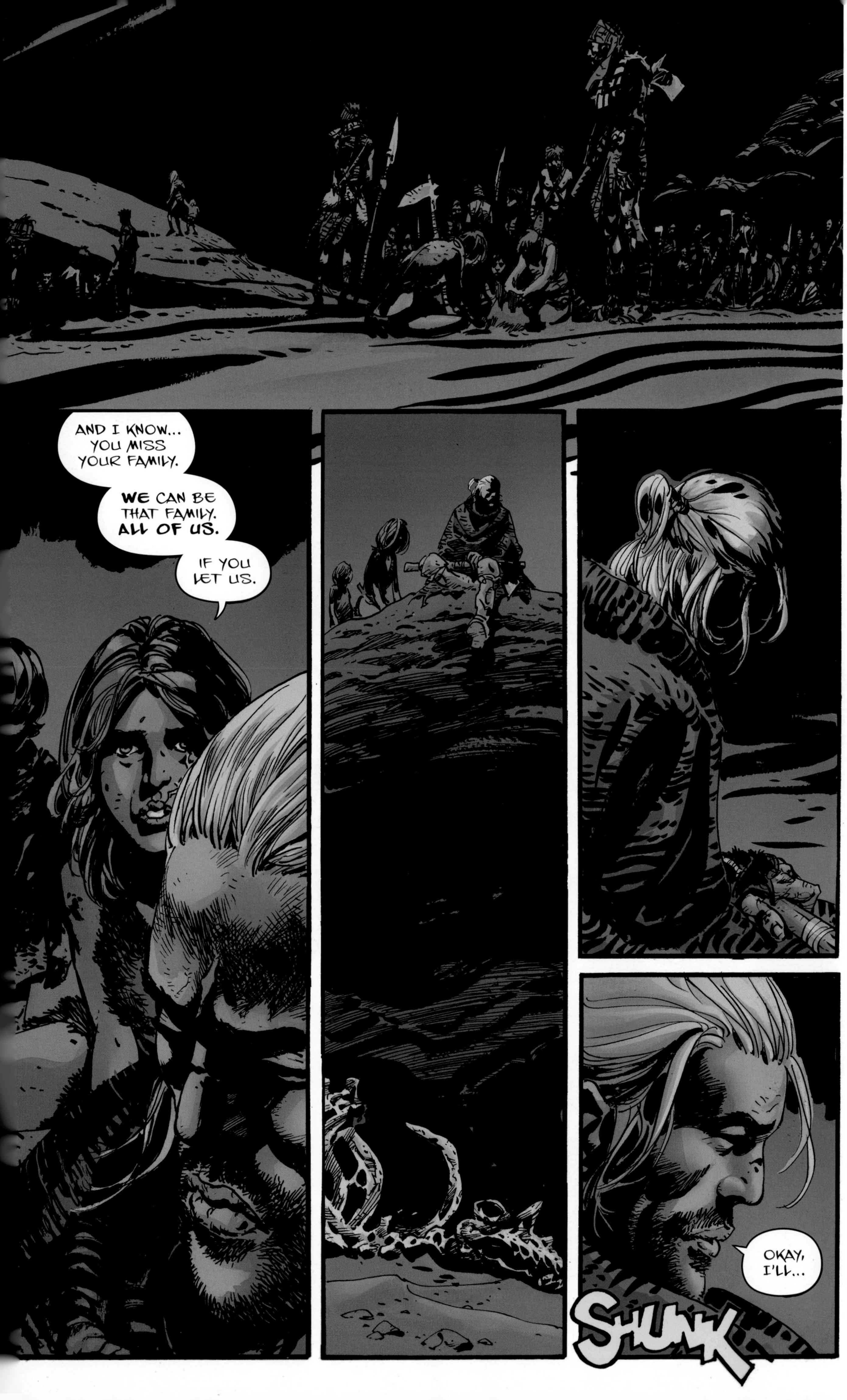
AND I KNOW... YOU MISS YOUR FAMILY.
WE CAN BE THAT FAMILY. **ALL OF US.**
IF YOU LET US.
OKAY, I'LL...
SHUNK

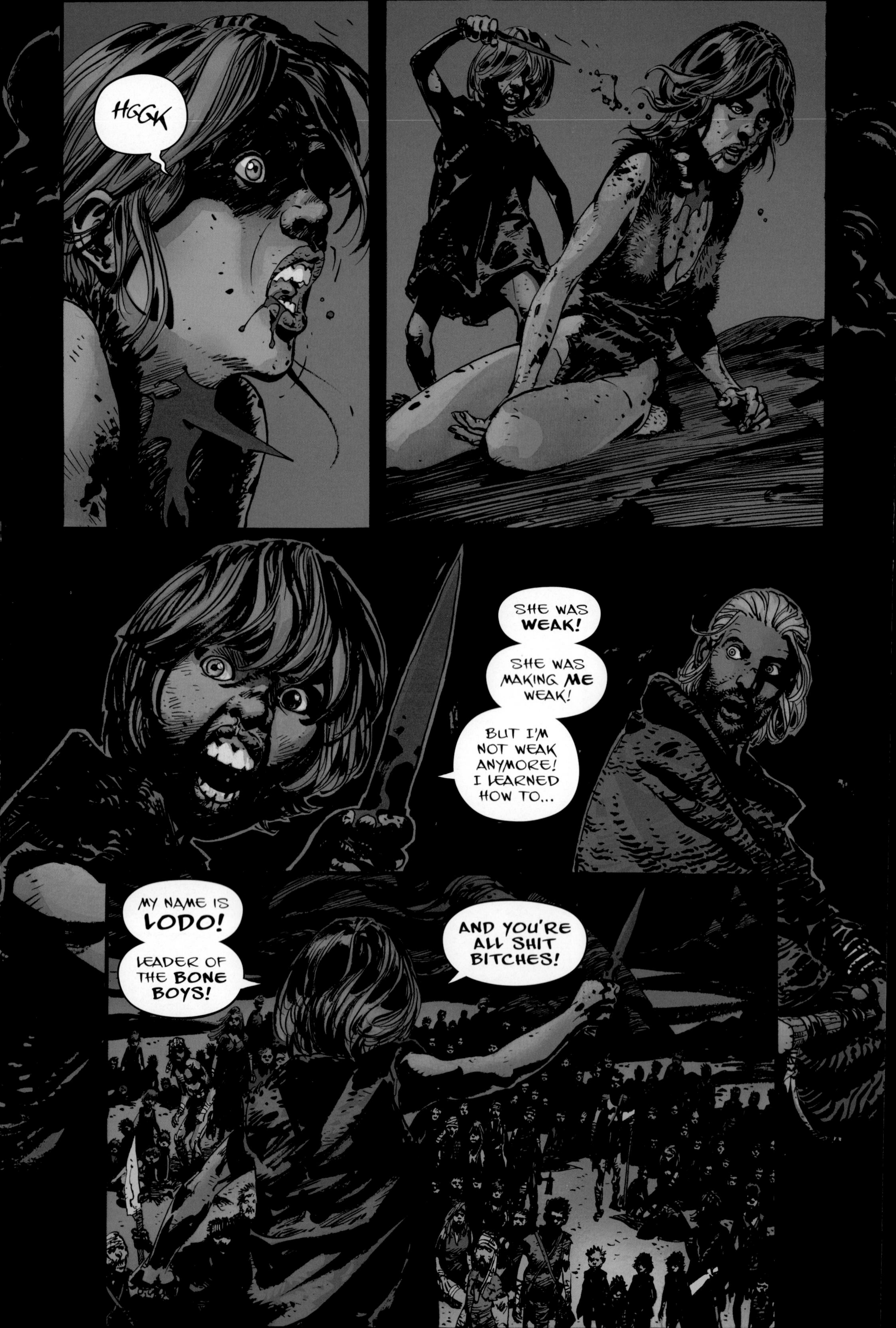
HGGK
SHE WAS WEAK!
SHE WAS MAKING ME WEAK!
BUT I'M NOT WEAK ANYMORE! I LEARNED HOW TO...
MY NAME IS LODO!
LEADER OF THE BONE BOYS!
AND YOU'RE ALL SHIT BITCHES!

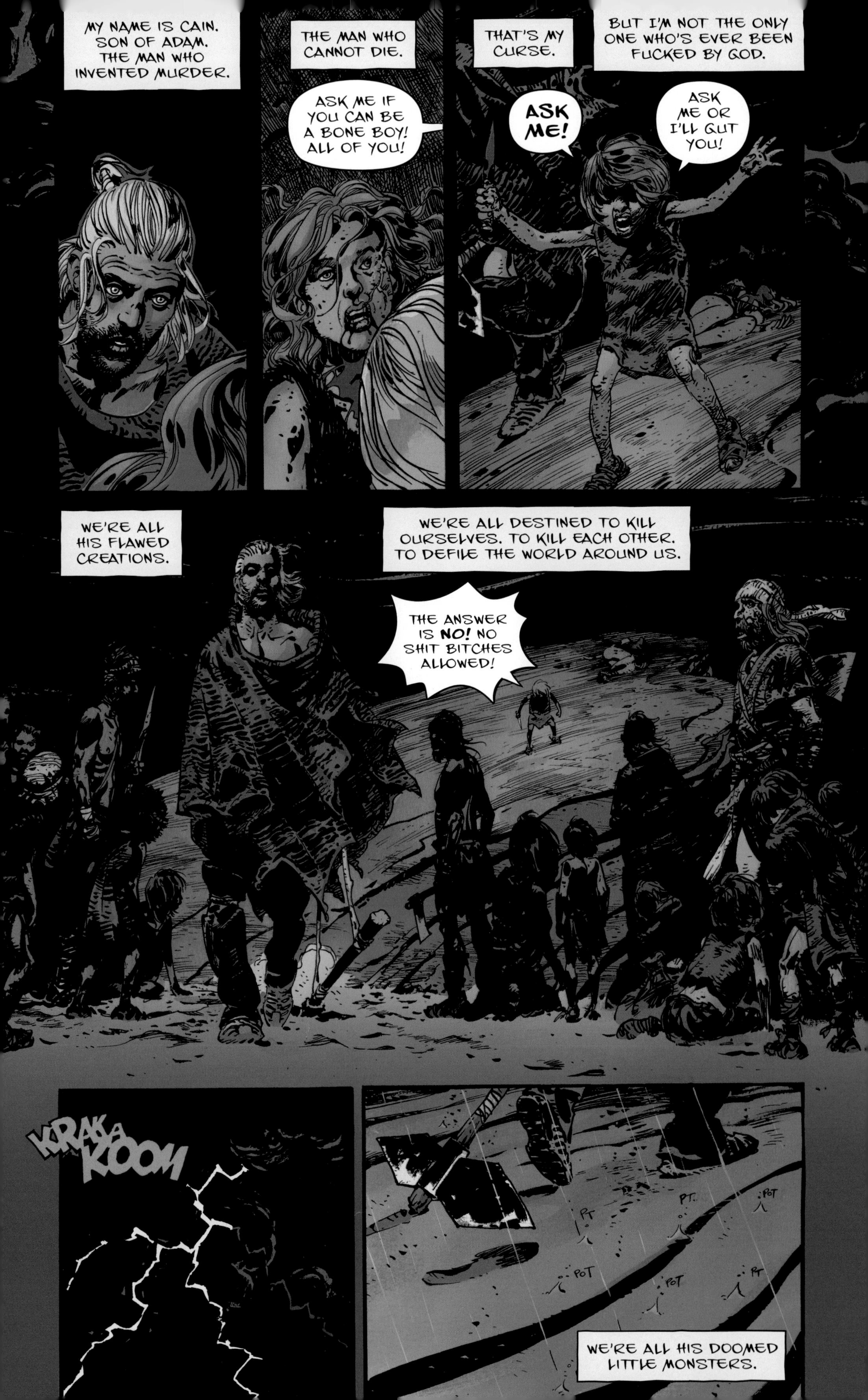
MY NAME IS CAIN. SON OF ADAM. THE MAN WHO INVENTED MURDER.
THE MAN WHO CANNOT DIE.
ASK ME IF YOU CAN BE A BONE BOY! ALL OF YOU!
THAT'S MY CURSE.
BUT I'M NOT THE ONLY ONE WHO'S EVER BEEN FUCKED BY GOD.
ASK ME!
ASK ME OR I'LL GUT YOU!
WE'RE ALL HIS FLAWED CREATIONS.
WE'RE ALL DESTINED TO KILL OURSELVES. TO KILL EACH OTHER. TO DEFILE THE WORLD AROUND US.
THE ANSWER IS NO! NO SHIT BITCHES ALLOWED!
KRAKA KOOM
PT
PT
POT
POT
POT
PT
WE'RE ALL HIS DOOMED LITTLE MONSTERS.

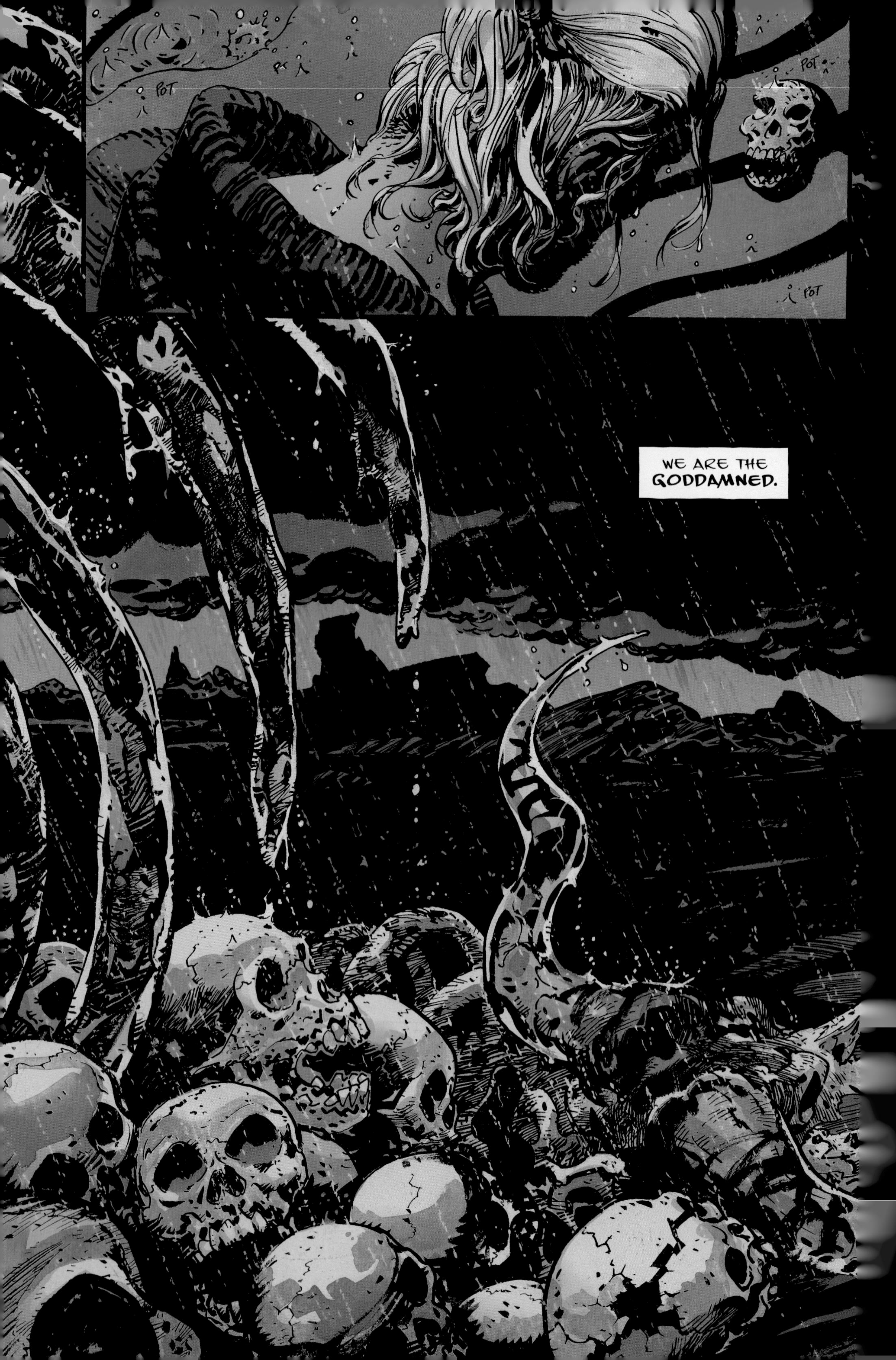
POT
PK
POT
POT
WE ARE THE
GODDAMNED.

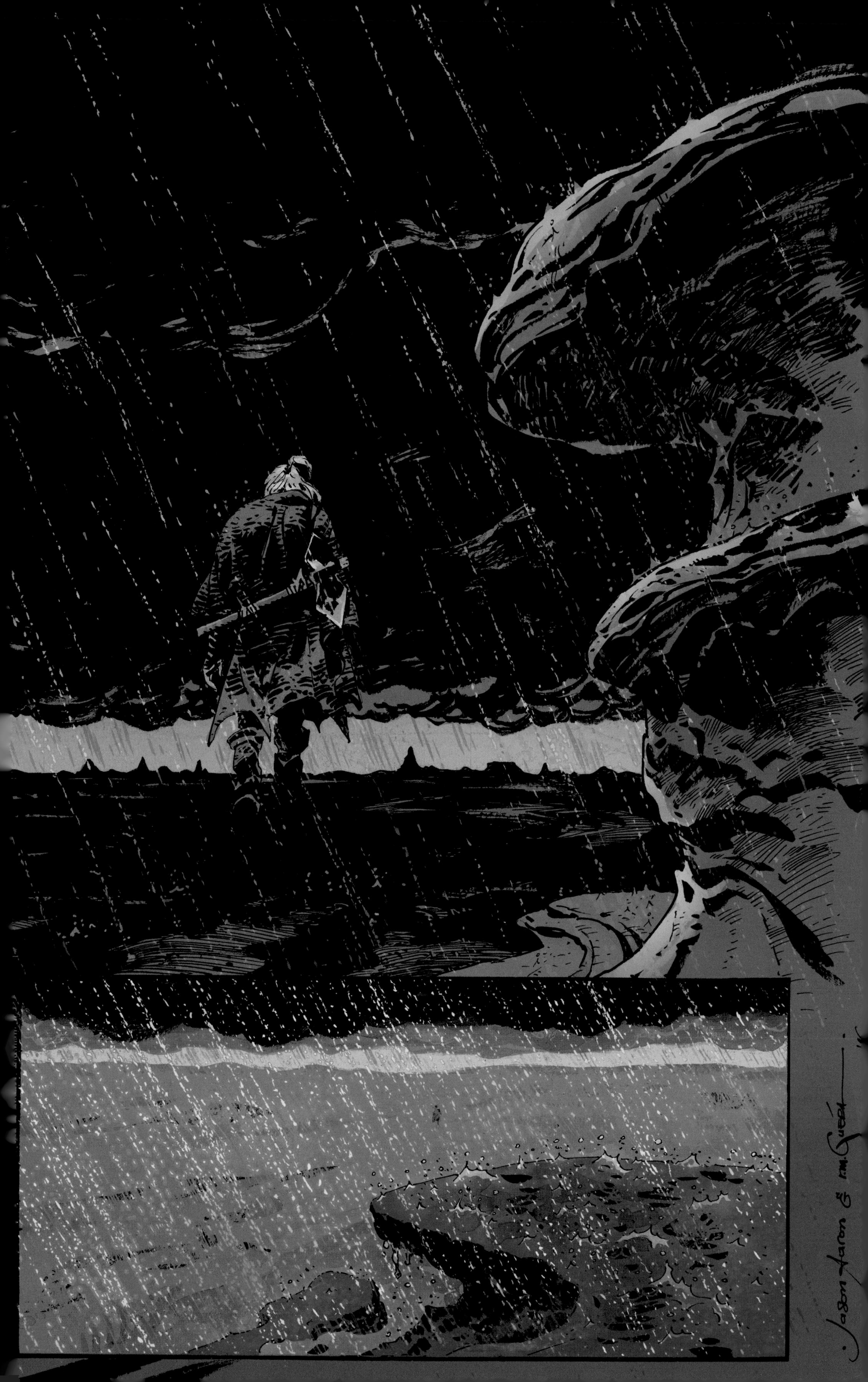
Jason Aaron & R.M. Guéra

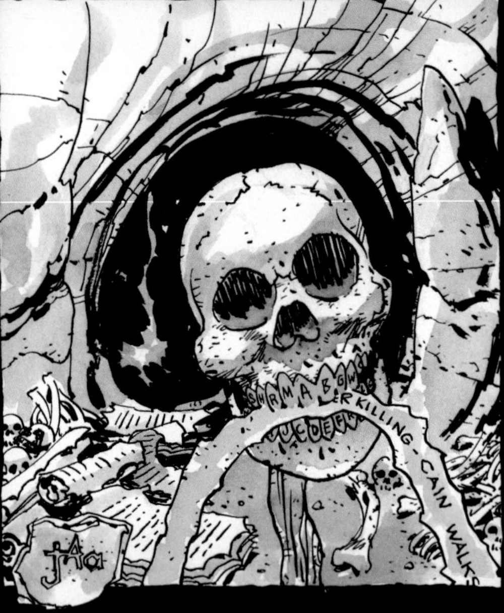
KILLING CAIN WALKS

Jason Aaron is a comic book writer best known for his work on the *New York Times* best-selling crime series SCALPED for Vertigo Comics and the Eisner Award-winning SOUTHERN BASTARDS from Image Comics, as well as for various projects with Marvel Comics. Aaron's current work for Marvel includes the creation of the headline-grabbing female version of THOR and the launch of an all-new STAR WARS series, the first issue of which sold over one million copies to become the best-selling American comic book in more than 20 years. Aaron was born in Alabama but currently resides in Kansas City.

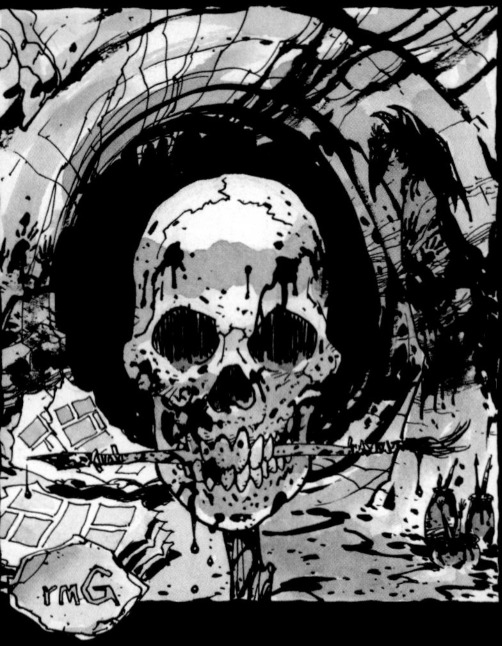
rmG

Rajko Milosevic, known as **r.m.Guéra** is a Serbian artist, living in Spain. He reached early fame and academic awards during 80s in former Yugoslavia. After moving to Barcelona, and after a decade of working in publicity and animation through works for museums and theaters, he published his first comic albums in France, through publishers Glénat and Delcourt. His worldwide breakthrough came with the crime series SCALPED, also written by Jason Aaron and published by Vertigo, DC Comics which garnered worldwide critical acclaim.

Guéra has worked with Quentin Tarantino on a comic book version of *Django Unchained*; continues to publish in France for Jour J, in the UK for Judge Dredd, as well as for all US mainstream editorials including Marvel, DC, Dark Horse, on many one-shots, promotional posters, and covers.

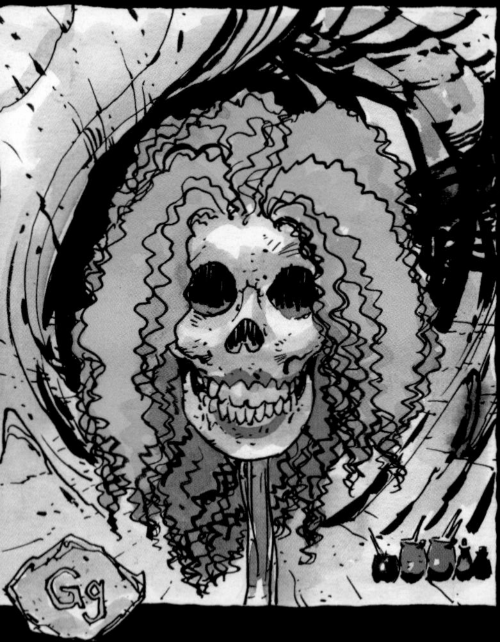
Gg

Giulia Brusco loves colours and ice cream, and she dreams of holidays that never materialise. She obtained a degree in Foreign Languages and Literature at the University of Bologna, writing her final dissertation on Kandinsky's poems *Klänge* (yes, he was a figurative artist, but he also wrote poems about sounds...) and the synesthesia approach to art. This contributes to her understanding of colours as evocative instruments in storytelling. Brusco has been colouring comic books since 2001, working on numerous titles and for various companies. She's best known for her years long collaboration with r.m.Guéra and for her heavy Italian accent while speaking English despite 23 years of life in London, England.

Cover Gallery
+
Sketchbook

r.m. Guéra

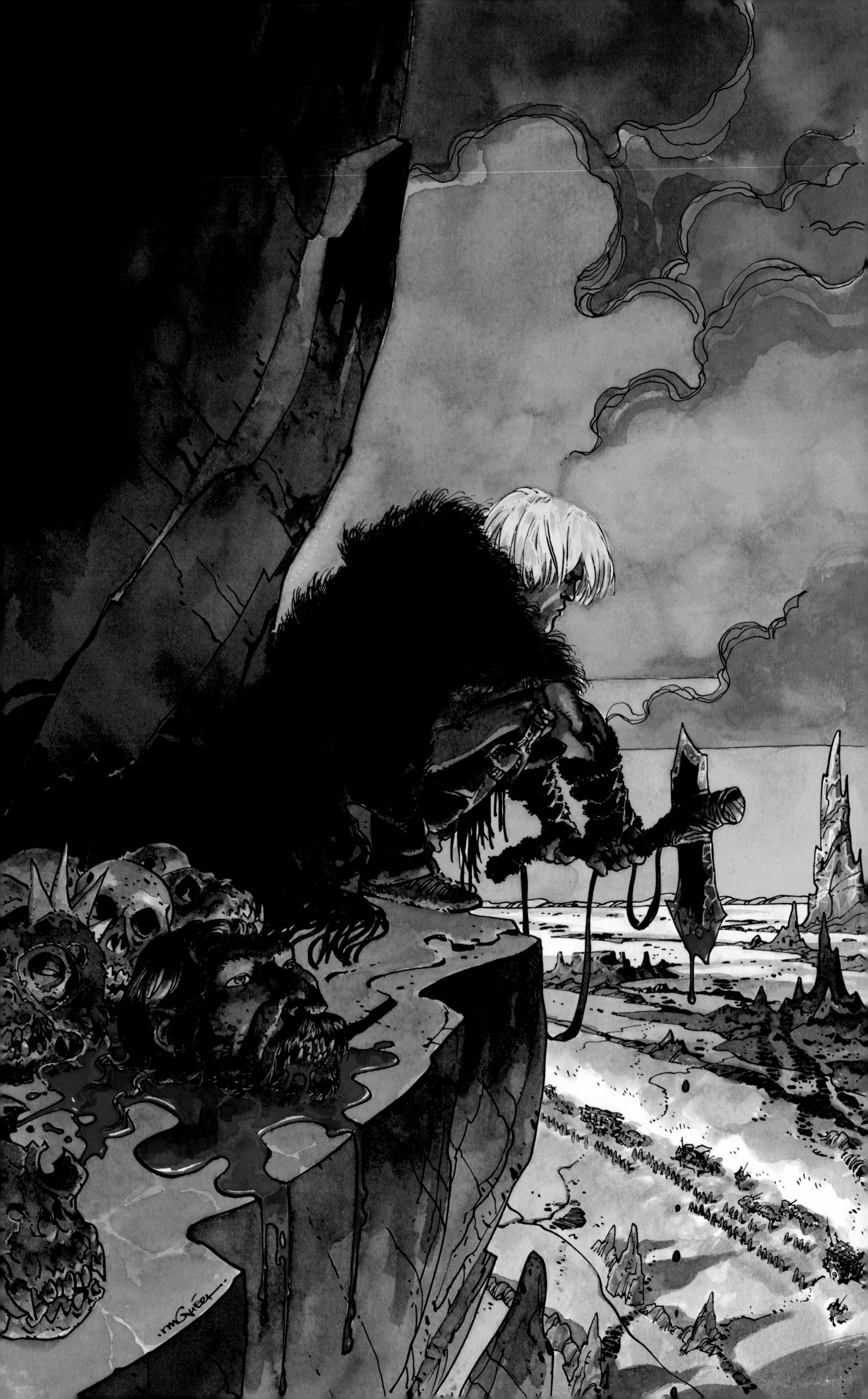

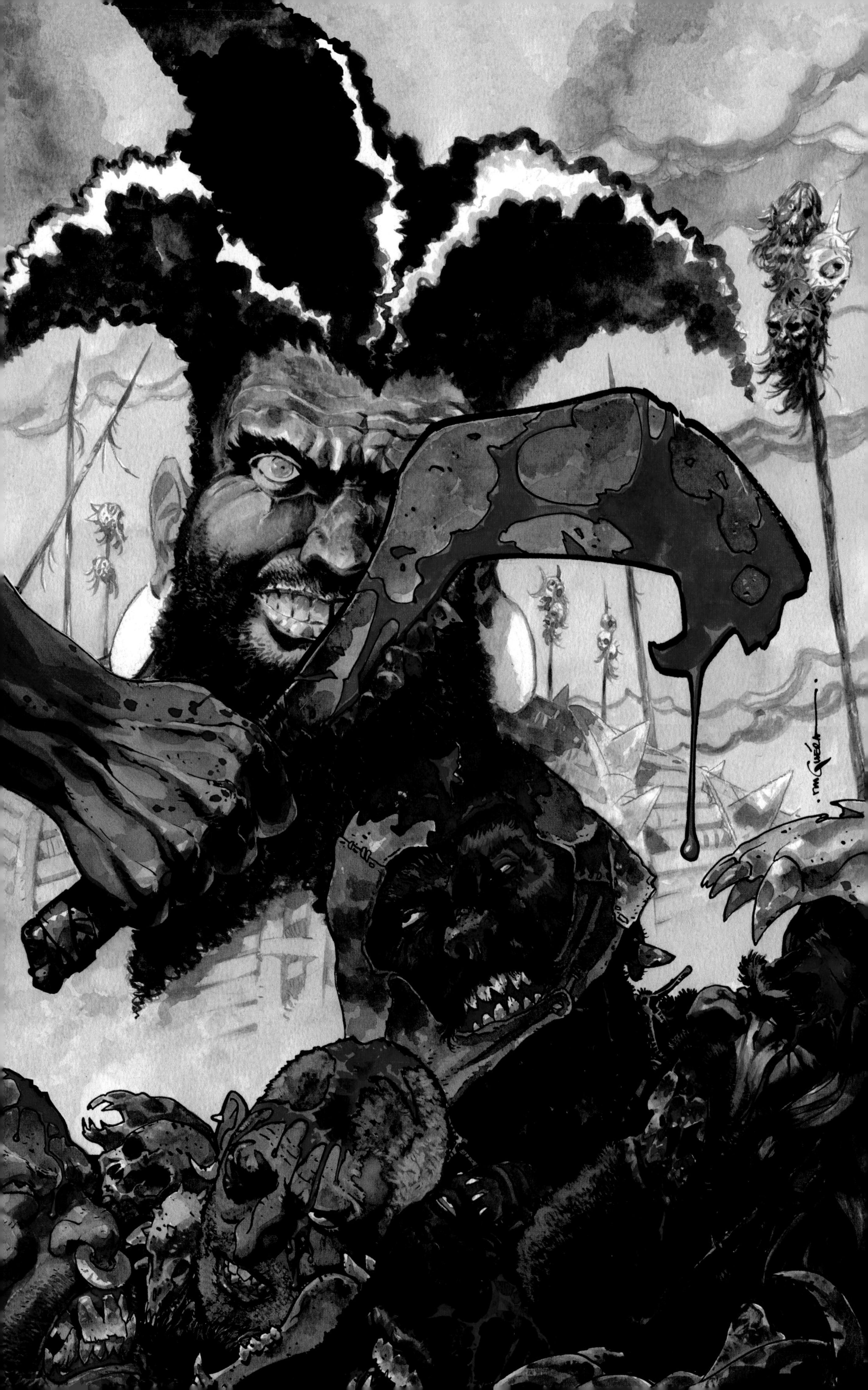

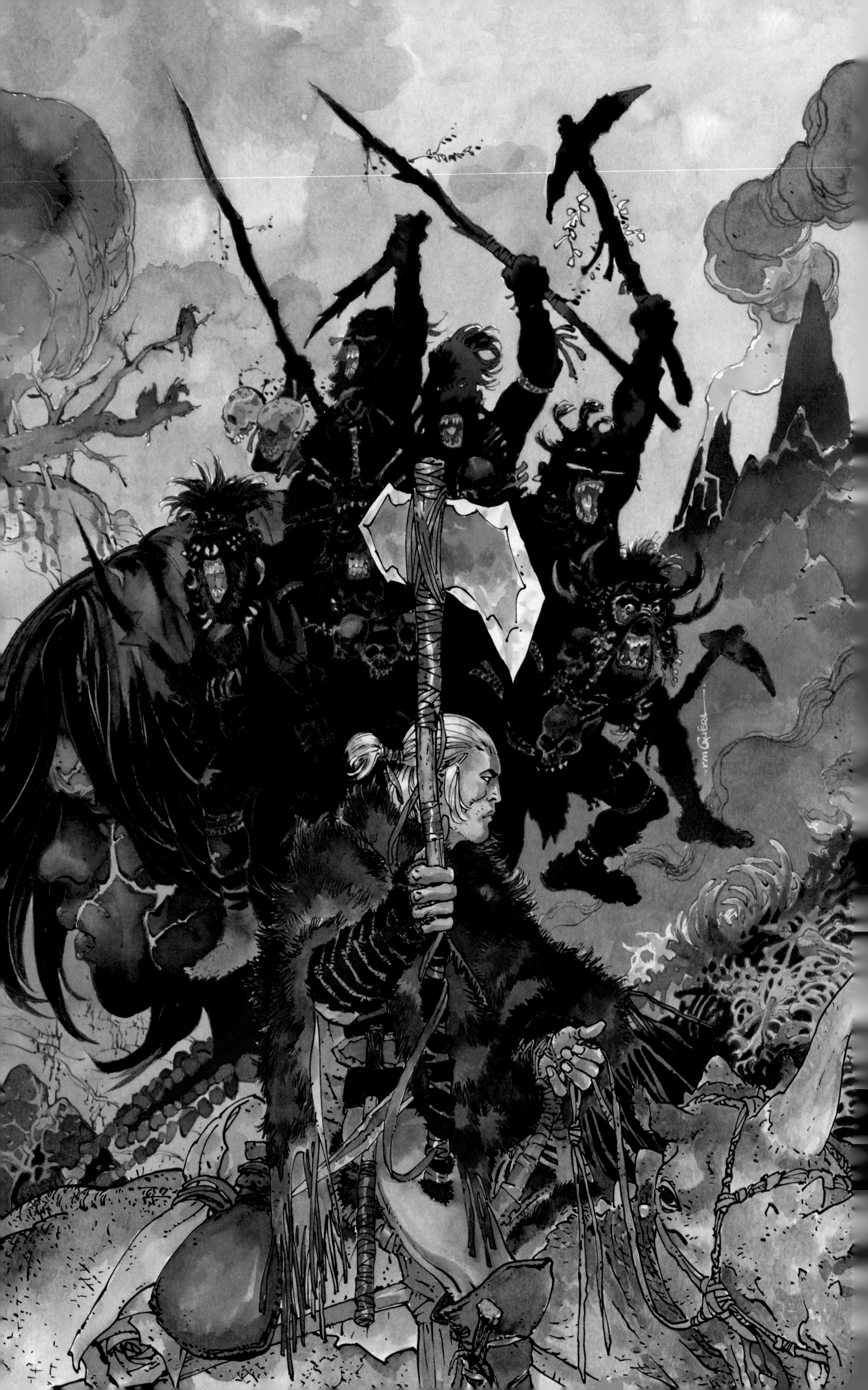

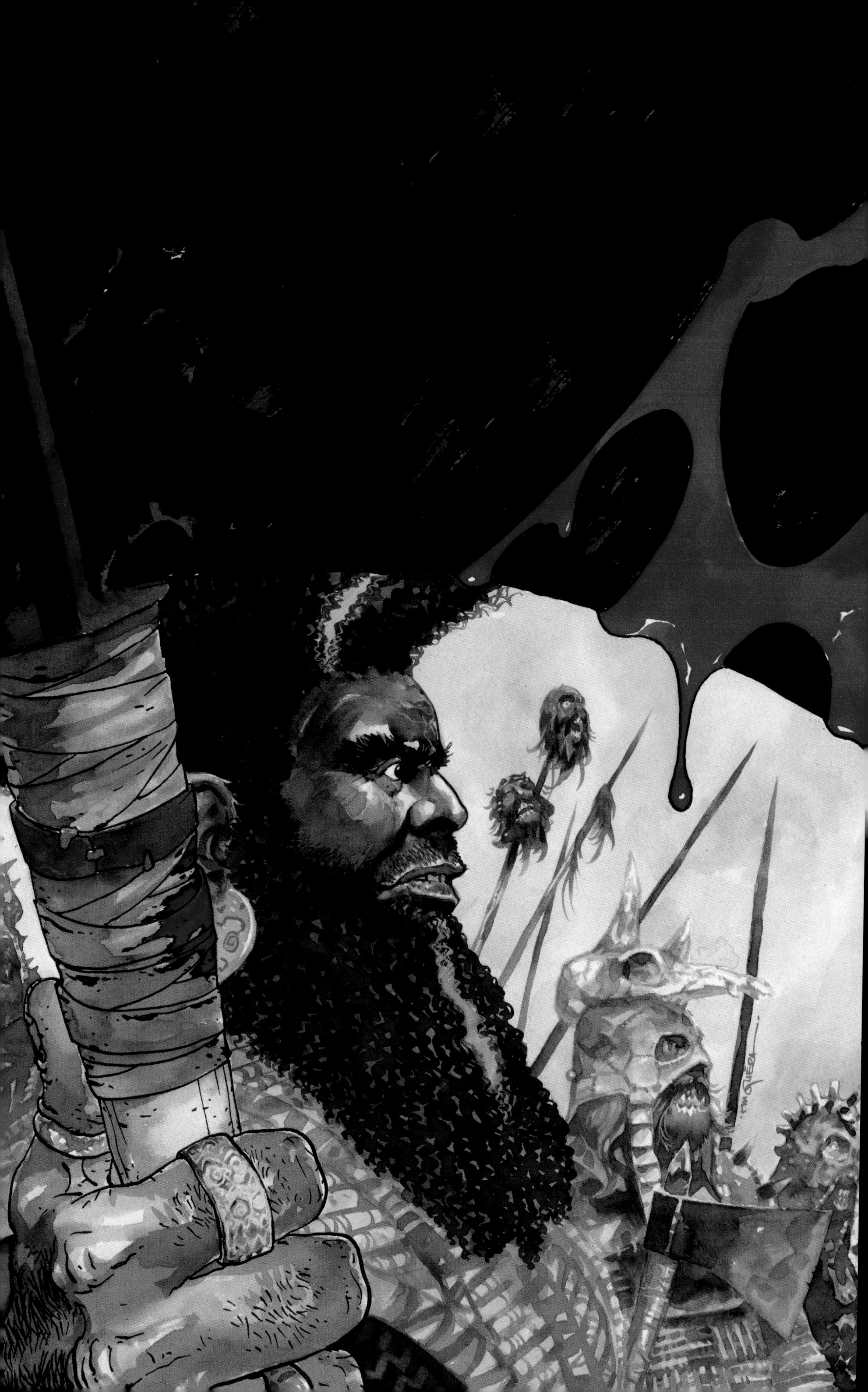

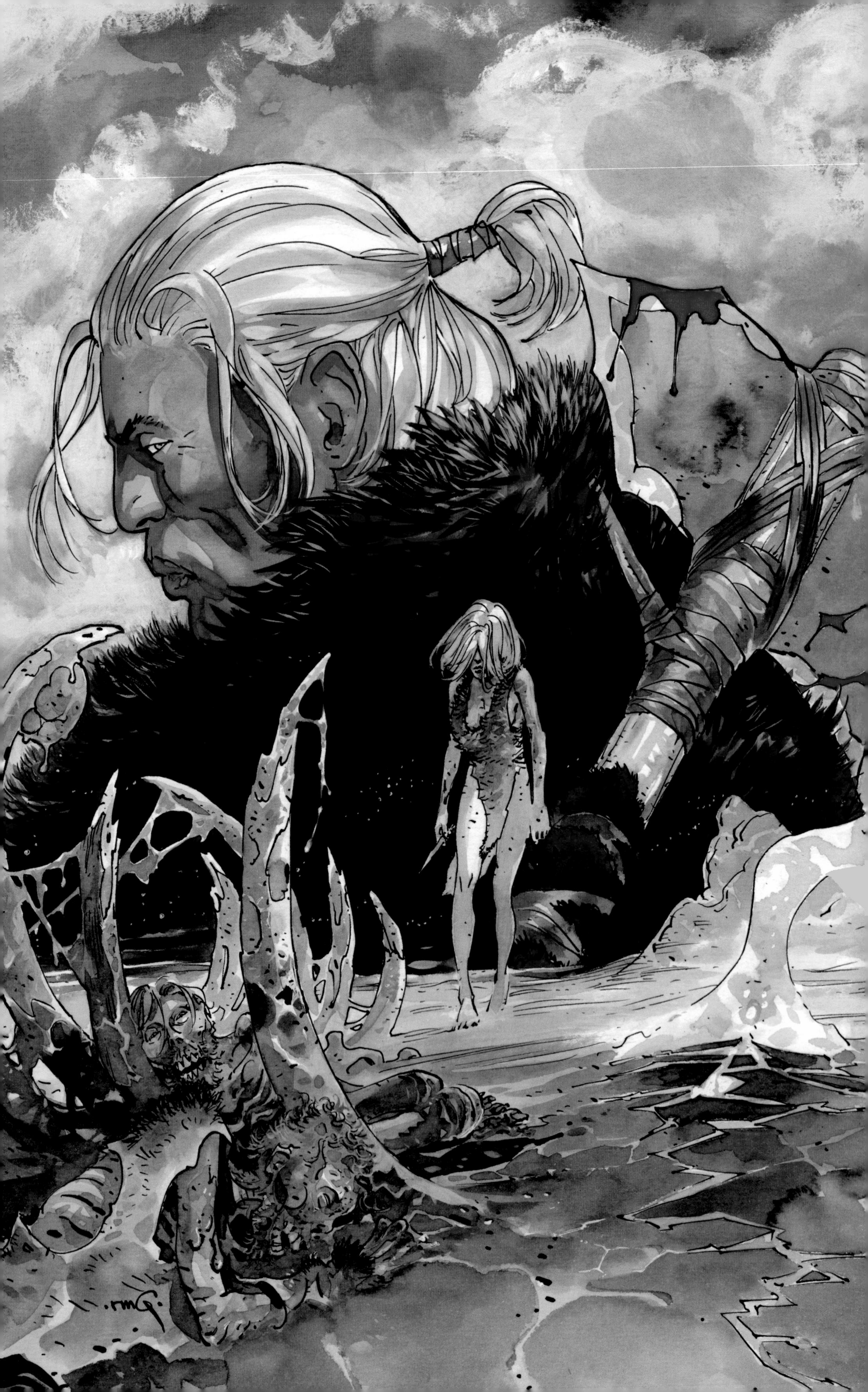

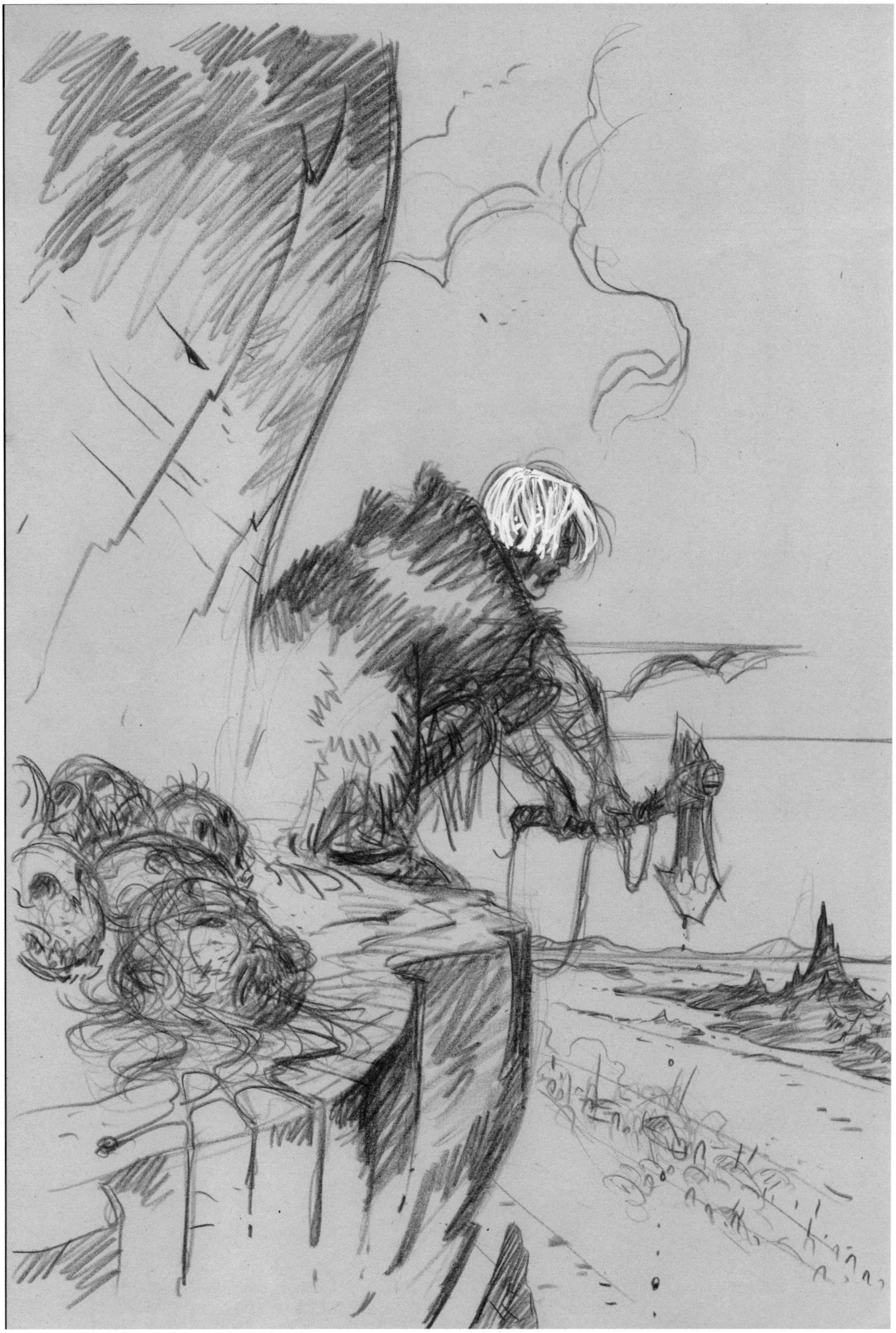

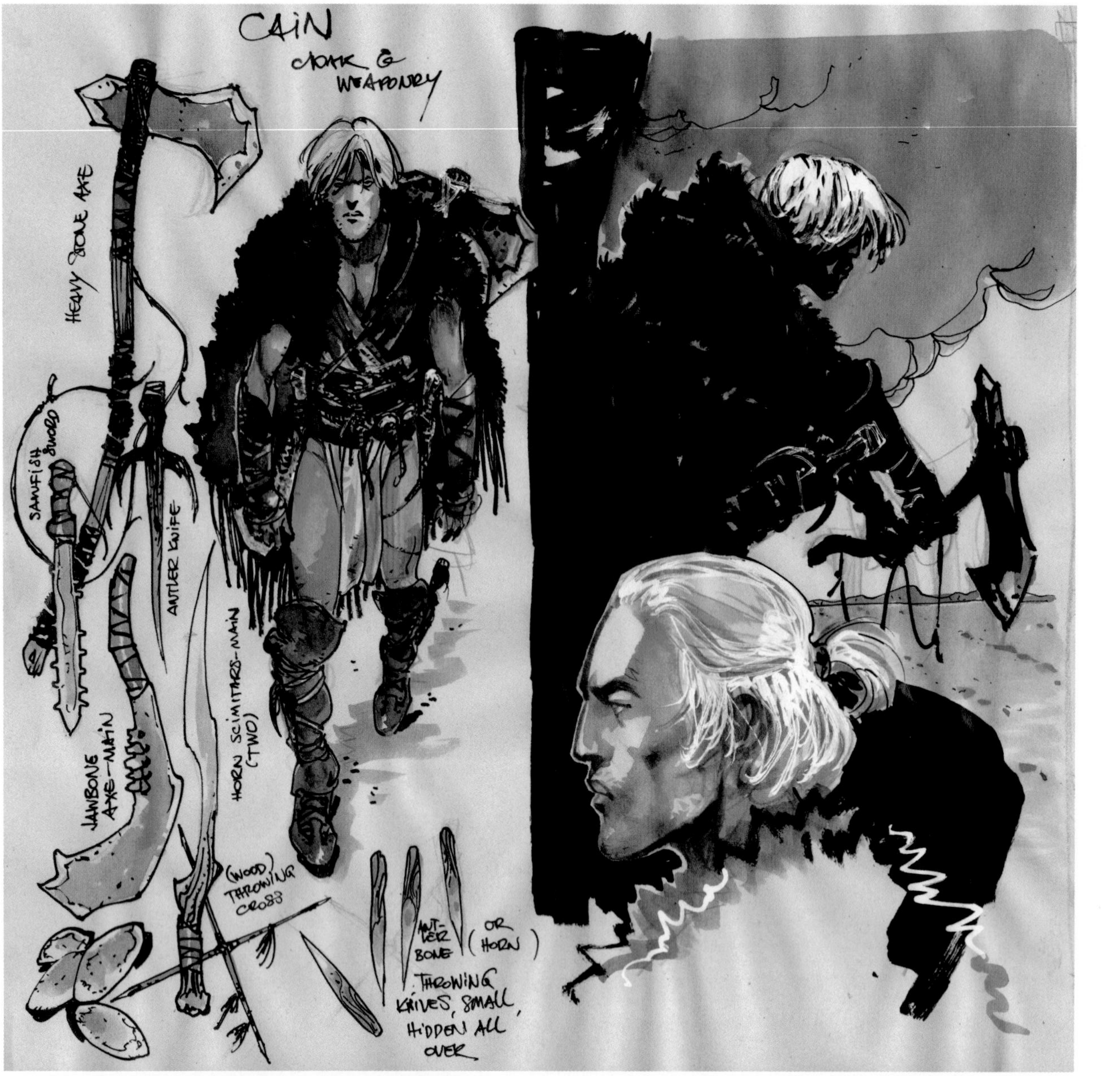
CAIN
CLOAK & WEAPONRY
HEAVY STONE AXE
ANTLER KNIFE
JAWBONE AXE-MAIN
HORN SCIMITARS-MAIN (TWO)
(WOOD) THROWING CROSS
ANT-LER BONE (OR HORN)
THROWING KNIVES, SMALL, HIDDEN ALL OVER

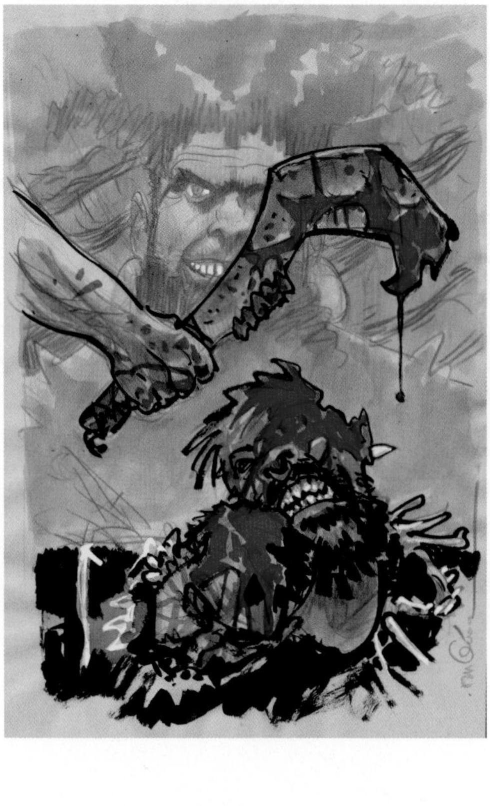

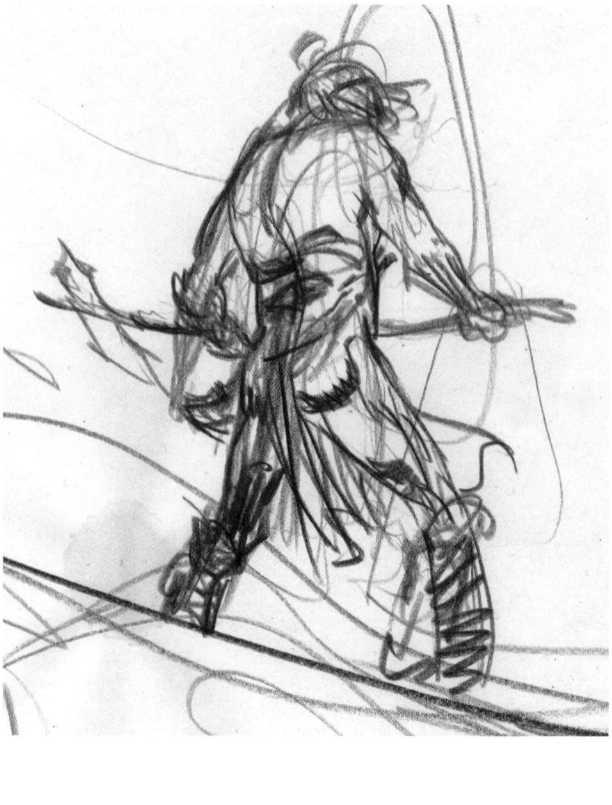

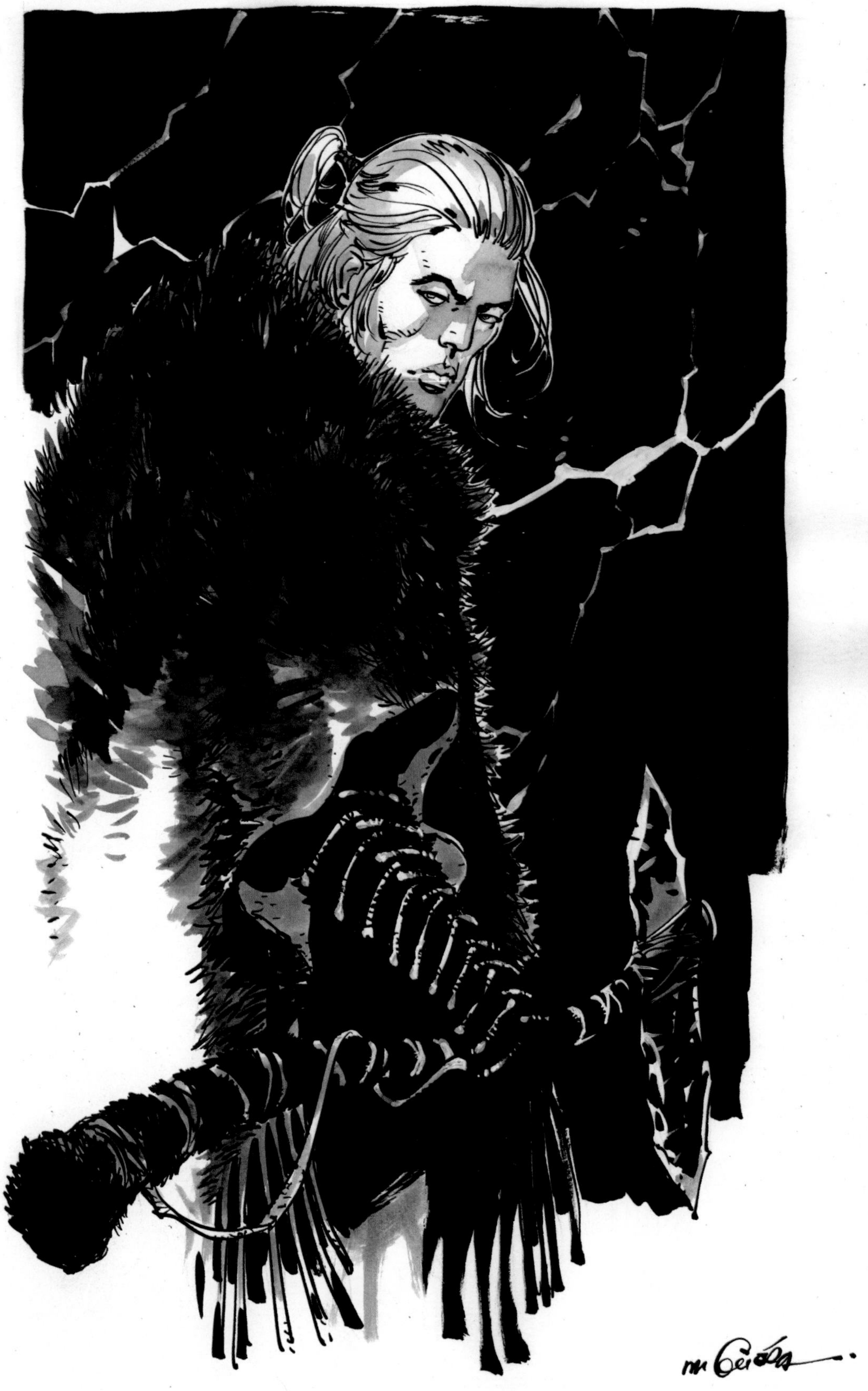

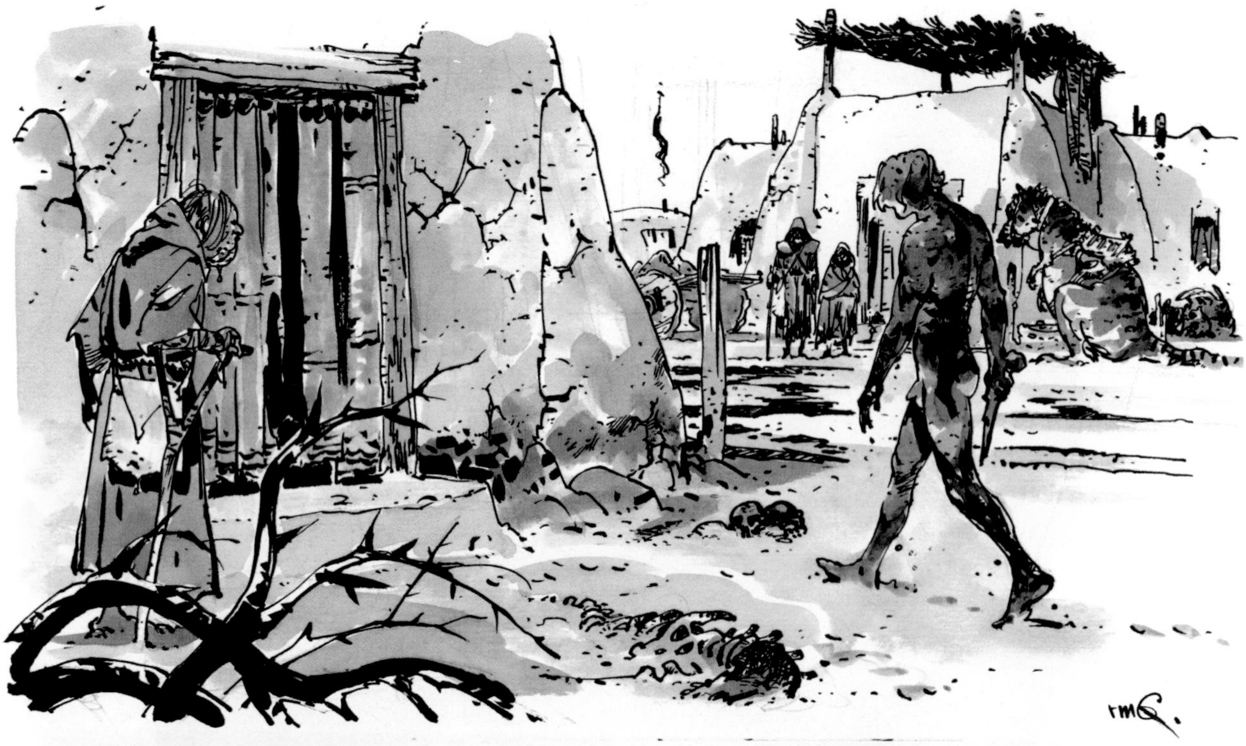

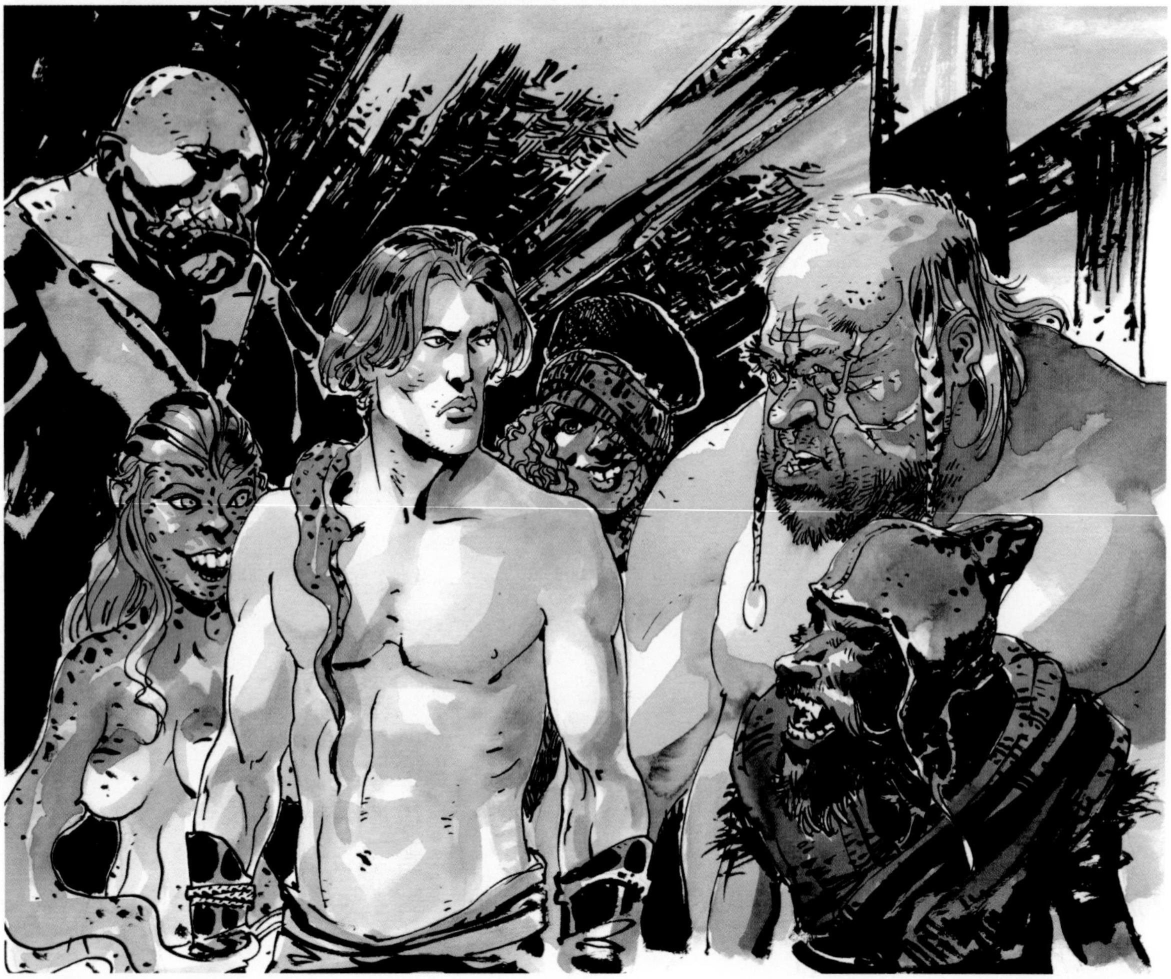

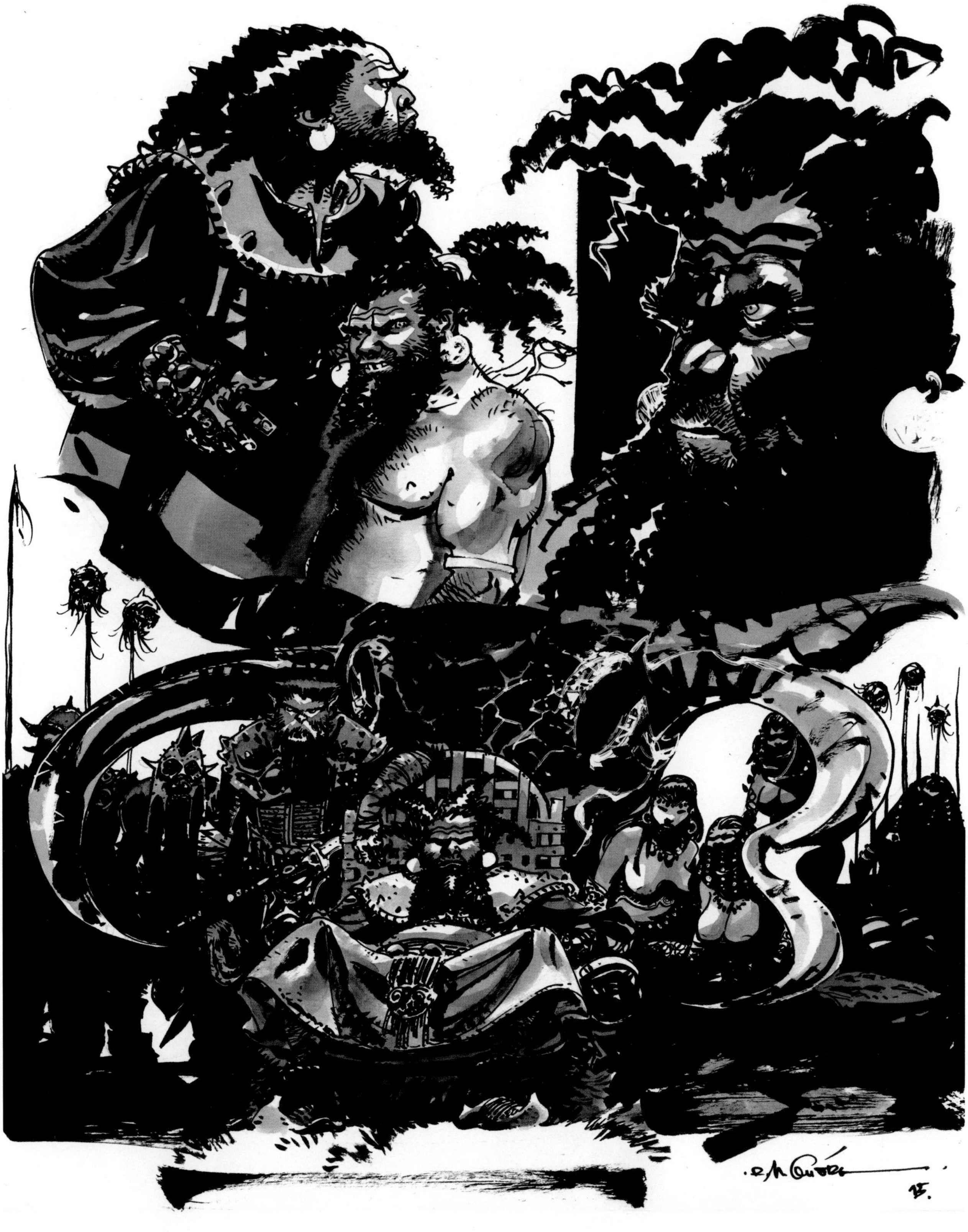

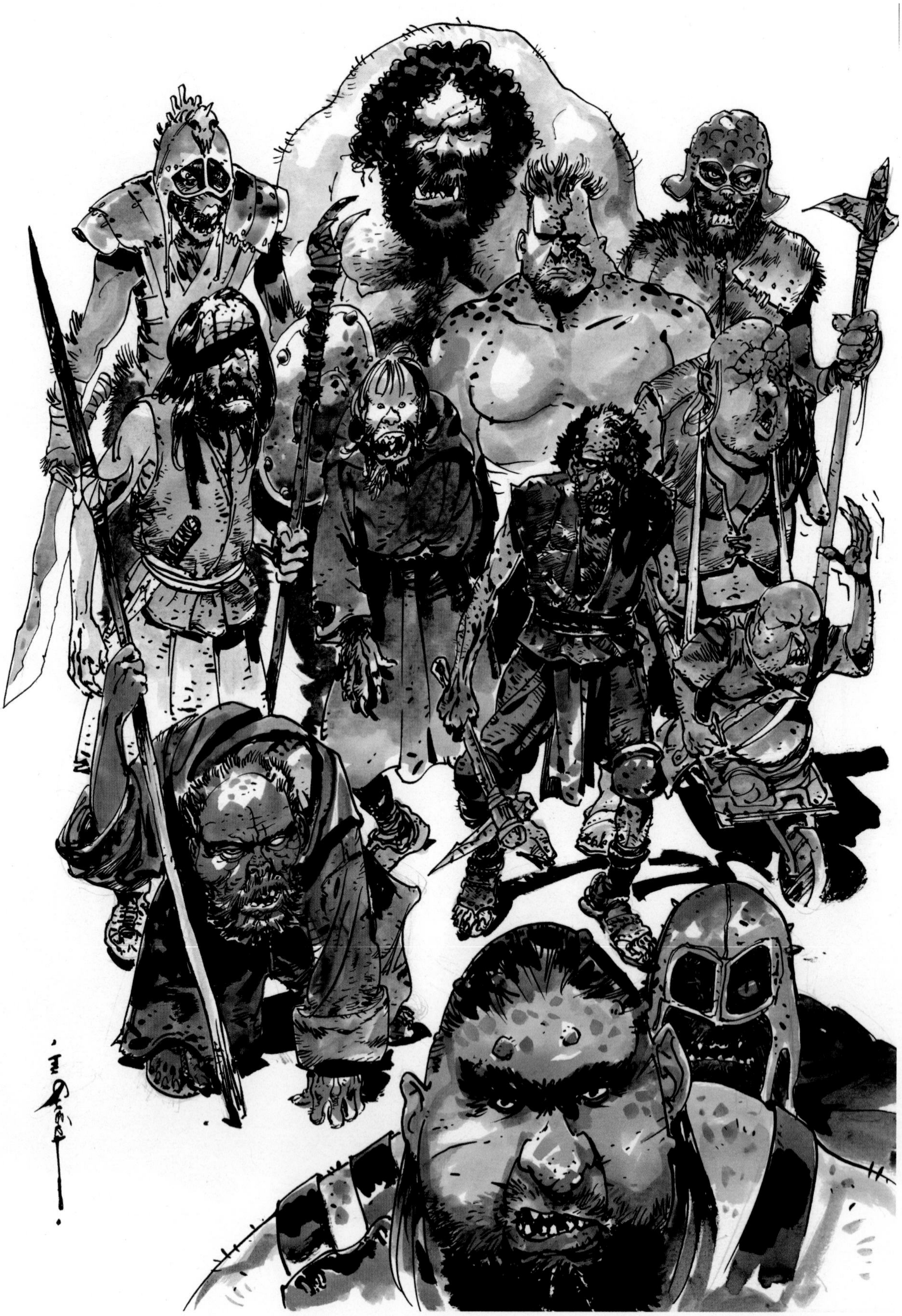

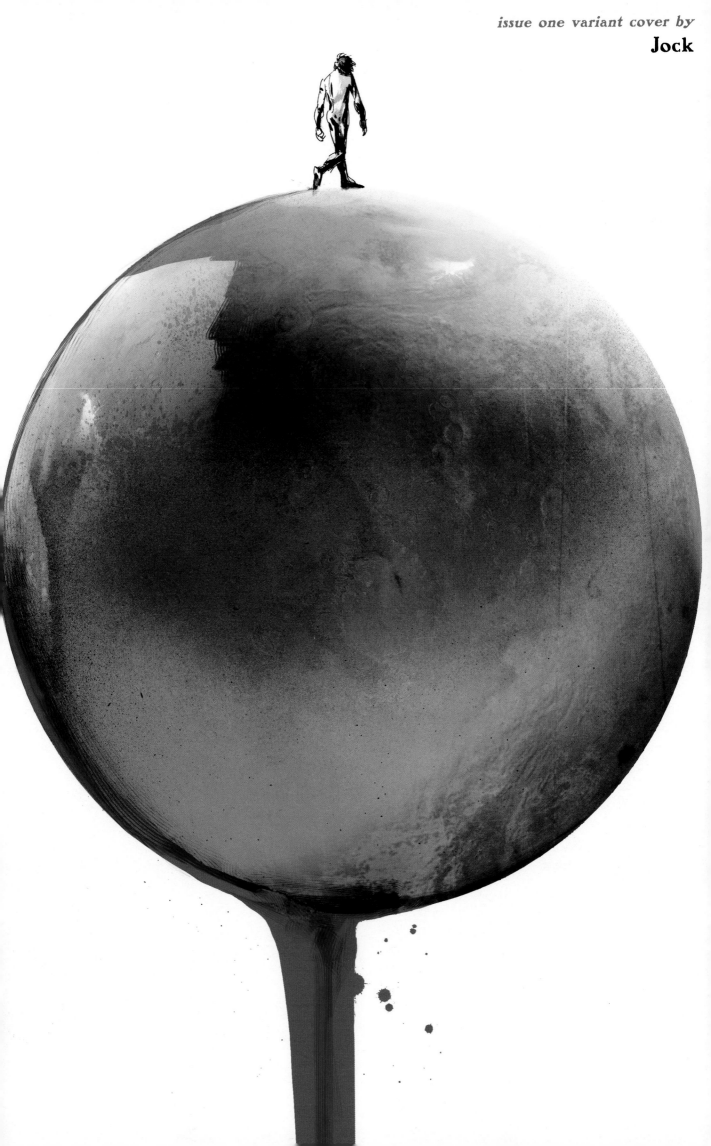

issue one variant cover by
Jock

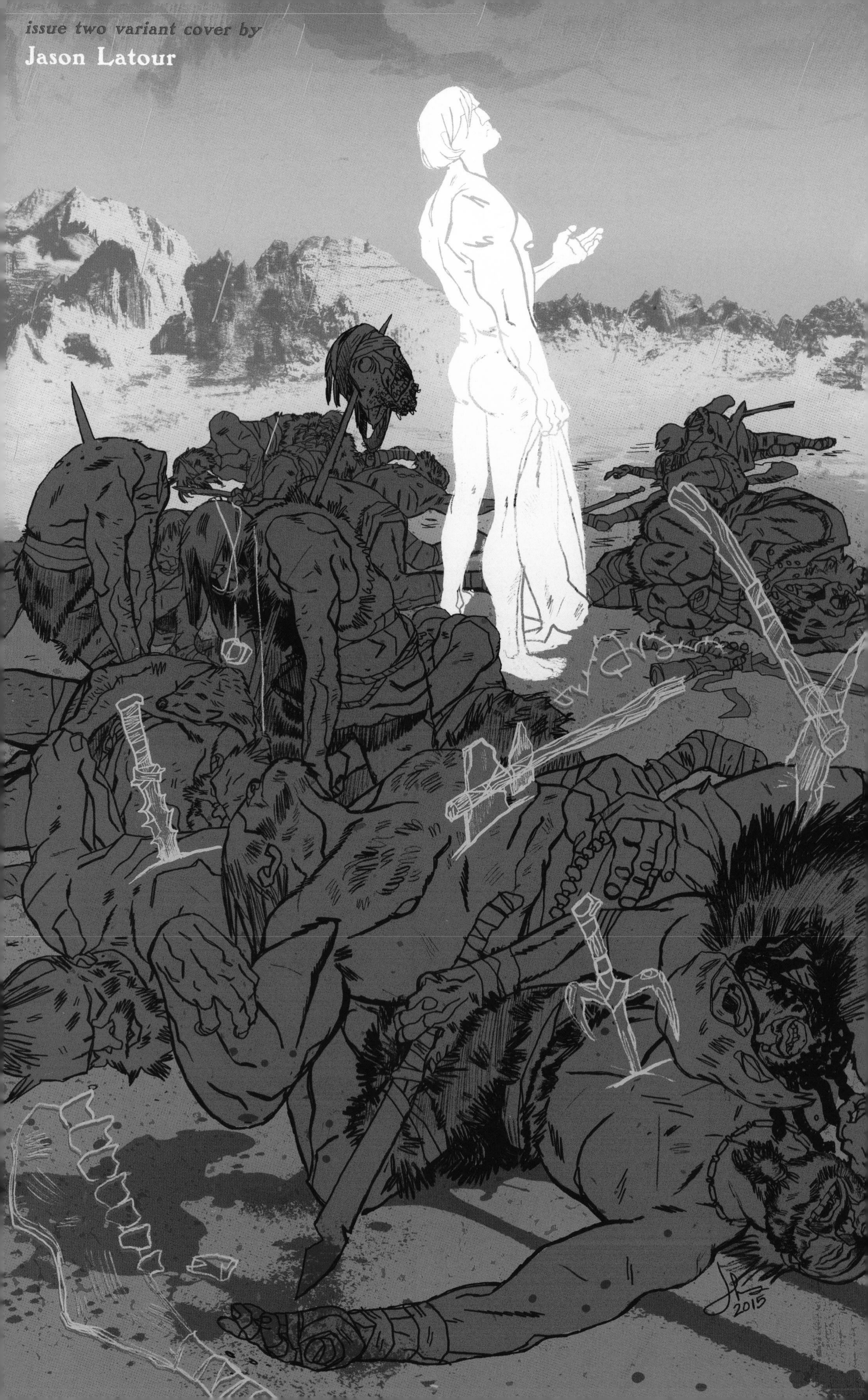

issue two variant cover by

Jason Latour

issue three variant cover by

Esad Ribic

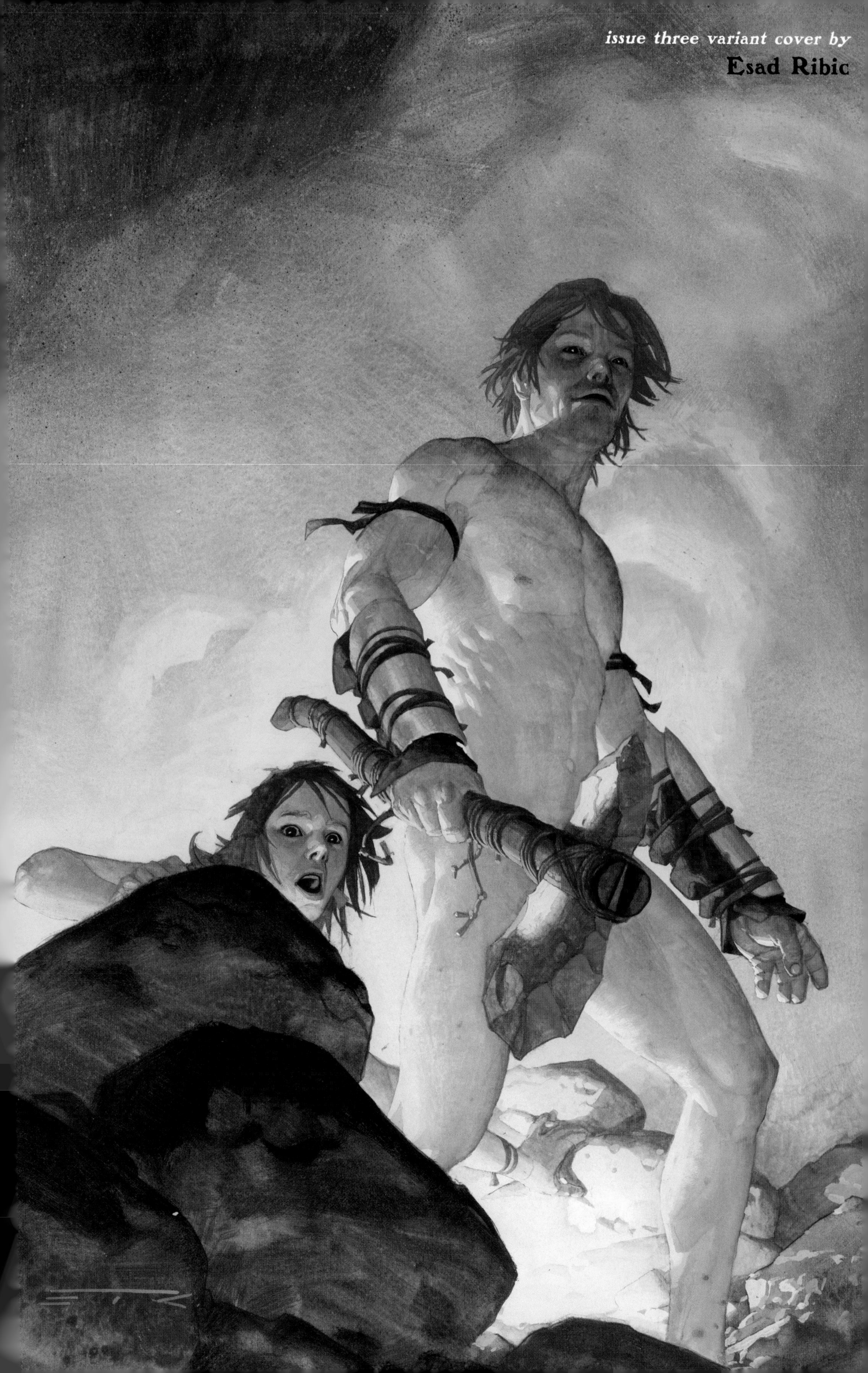

issue four variant cover by

Skottie Young

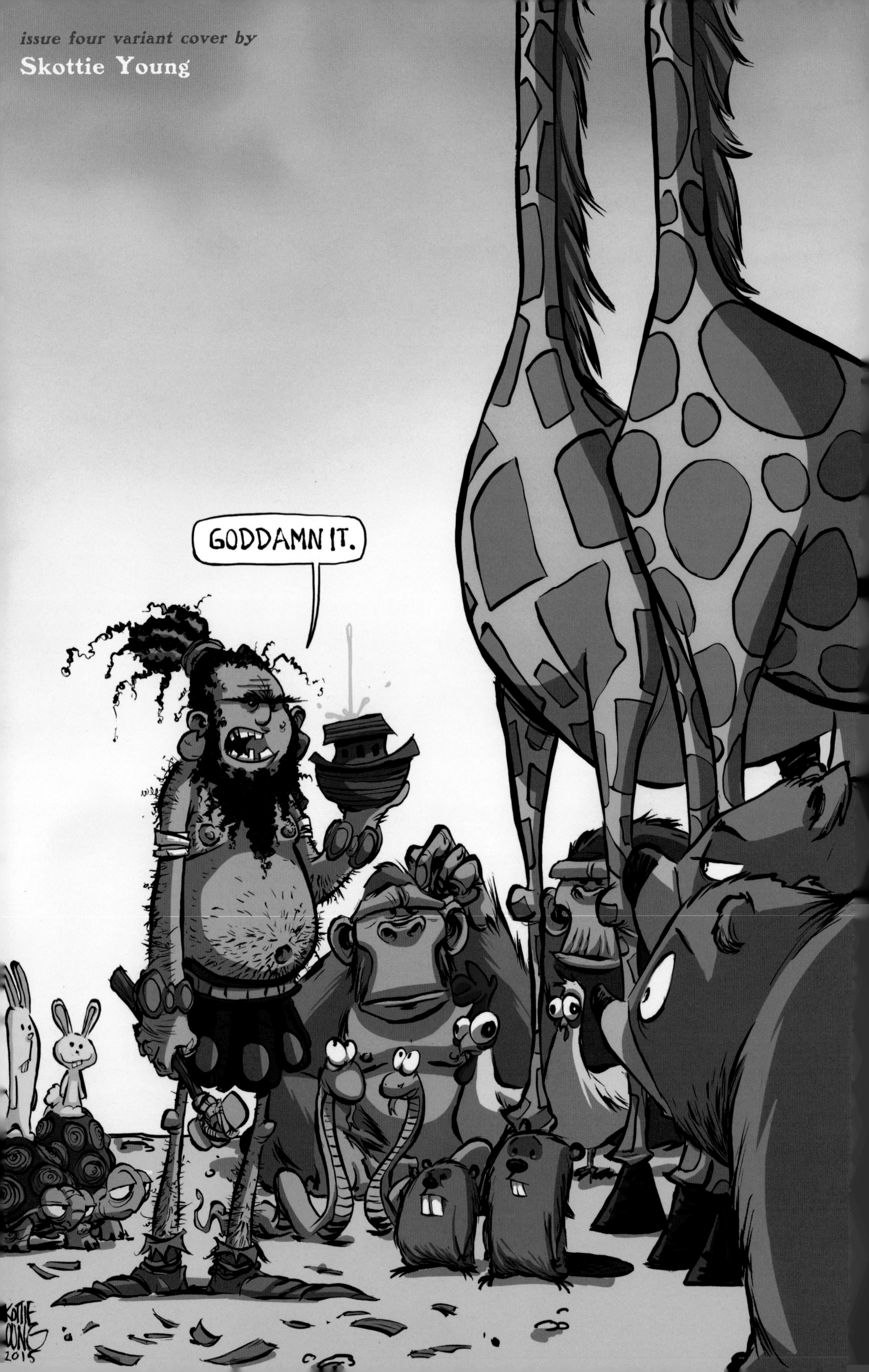
GODDAMN IT.
SKOTTIE YOUNG 2015

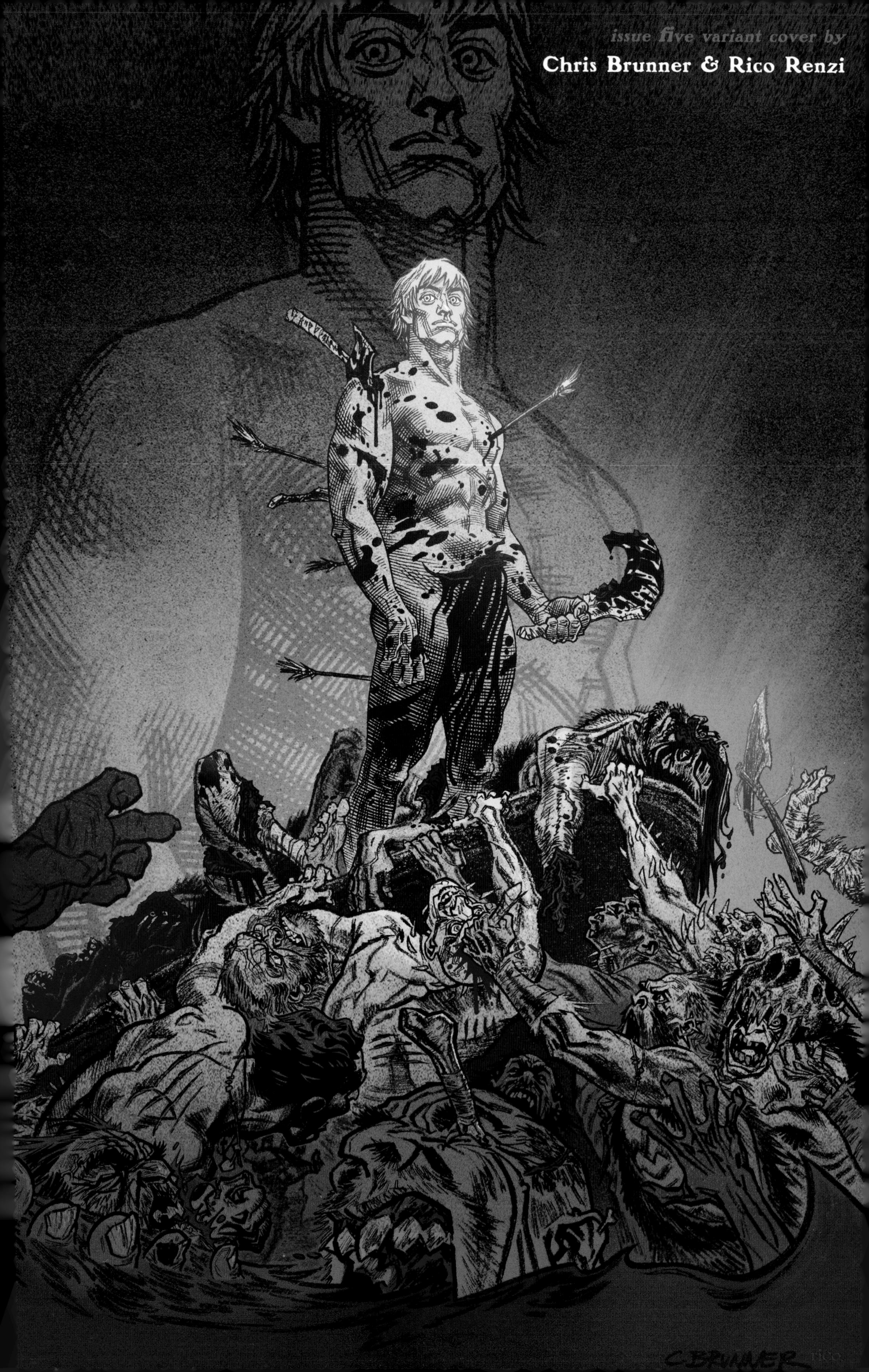

issue five variant cover by
Chris Brunner & Rico Renzi

Issue One Script

Jason Aaron

BEFORE THE FLOOD #1
BOOK ONE: GOD DAMNS
Part One: "The Man Who Invented Murder"
First Draft
By Jason Aaron

Opening Title Page

And God saw that the wickedness of man was great in the earth, and that every imagination of the thoughts of his heart was only evil continually.

And it repented the Lord that he had made man on the earth, and it grieved him at his heart.

And the Lord said, I will destroy man whom I have created from the face of the earth.

Both man, and beast, and the creeping thing, and the fowls of the air.

For it repenteth me that I have made them.

--Genesis 6:5-7

Pages One-Two

Two Page Splash

We open on a pool of filth. With our main character, Cain, lying facedown in it, completely nude. And being pissed on by a young caveboy who stands on the bank. Quite the noble intro for our hero, eh?

It's a huge pool of tainted water. A pond of slime and piss and shit. Once upon a time, this spot was a tranquil oasis on the outskirts of the desert. That's why people first came here. But those people have since turned the oasis into a massive shit hole. Literally.

Everything around the pond is ruined and defiled. There are dead fruit trees, hanging with rotten fruit. And some have rotten bodies hanging from them. There's no grass, no plants. Nothing green or blooming at all. The ground is a thick muck of mud and shit. There are bones and rotting animal carcasses scattered all about the bank and also sticking out of the pond. And rotting heads on pikes. A few vultures (or weird birds that are something like vultures) sit in the dead trees, eyeing the man in the pool. The air is thick with flies.

Beyond that, we can glimpse a village of ramshackle huts and smoke drifting from a fire.

The young boy's who pissing is dressed in crude fur rags and is missing half an arm.

CAPTION:	Somewhere on the edge of the desert.
CAPTION:	1500 years after Eden.

Page Three

Four Panels

3.1) Tight on Cain, still lying facedown in the pool of shit, with a stream of piss hitting the back of his head.

3.2) Same. He's still being pissed on, though the stream of piss is running out. He still hasn't moved.

3.3) Same. The last few squirts of piss hit him. He moans, but doesn't move.
CAIN (weakly):   ngh

3.4) Cain starts to rise from the pool. The kid falls back in shock.
CAIN (weakly):   Ugghh
KID: **Holy fuck!**

Page Four

Five Panels

4.1) Cain is standing in the pool, nude, and dripping with filth. He's looking around, trying to remember what the hell happened to him.

4.2) The kid gawks at him. His face is smeared with dirt and covered with scars and scabs. He's a filthy, ragged mess.
KID: You…
KID: You been face down in that shit pond all fucking day.
KID: How goddamn come you ain't dead?

4.3) Tight on Cain, looking around. His face is smeared with shit and slime and blood.
CAIN: Where am I?

4.4) Cain is still standing in the middle of the pond. The kid is standing on the bank. Cain looks back at him.
KID: Standing in the shit pond.
CAIN: This place. What's it called?
KID: Ain't called nothing. It's just a place where we sleep when we ain't hunting or warring or walking to some other place.

4.5) Cain is trudging out of the shithole.
KID: Used to be good water here. But now there's shit and dead things in it. Most folks don't drink it no more.
KID: I heard you came in outta the desert.

Page Five
Five Panels

5.1)   Cain is walking toward a tree where there's a body hanging. A rotting corpse dressed in furs and swarming with flies.

CAIN: I was drunk.

CAIN: That's the last thing I remember.

5.2)   The kid watches as Cain yanks a chunk of fur off the corpse.

KID: I heard you came in and wanted to buy some fire. Said you had good rocks to trade.

KID: But people didn't like the way you looked. People was scared. Said…

5.3)   Tight on Cain, his face coming into view, as he's wiping the filth off himself with the fur.

KID (from off):   You didn't have no scars.

KID (from off):   What kinda man don't have no scars? Even babies got scars.

5.4)   The poor corpse is now hanging there half-naked, while Cain is still cleaning himself, the air still thick with flies.

KID: So the Bone Boys cut your throat and took everything you had.

KID: Threw your body in the shit pond.

5.5)   Tight on Cain, turning toward us, eyes full of rage and the threat of violence. There's no wound at all on his throat where the kid says it was slit. There are no scars or marks on him at all.

CAIN: Where do I find these Bone Boys?

Page Six
Six Panels

6.1)   The kid looks up at Cain, a bit wary of him, not sure if he's a wizard or a zombie or what.

KID: The fuck huts. Or the fire hole.

KID: You better just leave though. They'll kill you for sure this time.

6.2)   Cain looks toward the village.

CAIN: They got any giants with 'em?

KID: Giants?

CAIN: Really big people. Call themselves the Nephilim.

6.3)   Tight on the kid, eyeing Cain.

KID: Ain't never seen no giants. Saw a leper one time. Me and some of the other boys threw rocks at him until he died.

KID: Are you a magic man or something? How come you ain't got no scars? And how come you ain't dead?

6.4)   Tight on Cain, tossing the fur away, headed toward the village, looking focused and determined and ready to get his stuff back.

CAIN: 'Cause God's a fucking asshole, that's why.

CAIN: Best stay outta the village the next few minutes, kid.

CAIN: Until the screaming stops.

6.5)   The kid watches him go.

KID: Shit… you really gonna…

KID: What should I tell folks you was called, after you're dead? You got a name, magic man?

6.6)   Tight on Cain, stone-faced, intense.

CAIN: Yeah.

Pages Seven-Eight
Two Page Splash

We see Cain from behind, marching butt-naked into the village.

Again, the ground is a thick muck everywhere we see. Just like that town in Corbucci's Django.

There's a baby crawling in that muck. And a few mangy dogs barking at Cain. And maybe a dead rotting cow just lying around, swarming with flies.

The village is a collection of ramshackle huts. Made of sticks and mud. They all look different. It's like people haven't yet figured out the best way to build a house, so they all just build however they want. Most are little more than piles of sticks that you can crawl inside. Some have collapsed. Some are burned.

These are still a nomadic people. So a village like this is only temporary. Like a Plains Indian camp. Though this is a spot that they come to again and again.

A few villagers stand about, gawking at Cain, all dressed in rags and furs. Some armed with clubs.

A fire burns in the distance, in the center of the village. That's where Cain is headed.

CAPTION: Cain.

CAPTION: Son of Adam.

CAPTION: The man who invented murder.

Pages Nine-Ten
Double Page Spread, Five Panels

9.1)   Big panel, all across the top tier of the spread. The Bone Boys are sitting around the fire hole in the center of the village, eating and laughing. These are the warriors of the village. A scary looking group of scarred and filthy cavemen, all dressed in ragged furs and adorned with human and animal bones, all armed with crude weapons like wooden spears and clubs, all gnawing on chunks of meat and drinking from waterskins made of animal bladders. There's some sort of dead animal that's been tossed atop the fire pit. Not skinned or butchered. Just tossed onto the fire haphazardly, so that it's partly burned, partly cooked, partly raw. The Bone Boys have just torn it apart and are eating random chunks of meat and guts. There's not a lot of sophistication to their cooking or dining process. The air is thick with smoke.

SFX: HA HA HAAA AHAA HA HA

9.2)   A Bone Boy comes walking in, just arriving, wondering why everyone is laughing. Another Bone Boy who's sitting around the fire explains.

BONE BOY #1:   What? Why Bone Boys laughing?

BONE BOY #2:   Mudfuck drink strongwater we take from stranger. Fall down drunksleep. Burn off arm in fire.

9.3)   The Bone Boy looks over at Mudfuck and laughs. Mudfuck is lying near the fire, weeping in agony. One of his arms has been burned to a shriveled crisp. The other Bone Boys around him are just eating and laughing, not giving a shit about poor Mudfuck.

BONE BOY #1:   Ha! Sorry I miss that.

9.4)   We focus in on one Bone Boy who has a chunk of meat skewered on some sort of antler weapon and is munching away at it.

9.5) That Bone Boy, Ratbone, is suddenly kicked hard in the back of the head by a bare dirty foot.

  RATBONE: HGGH

Page Eleven
Four Panels

11.1) Ratbone is turning and getting to his feet, seething with anger, antler weapon gripped tight. Cain stands before him, butt ass naked and unarmed. And just standing there, daring Ratbone to kill him, completely unafraid.

  RATBONE: Who kick Ratbone? No fucking fucker fucking kicks Ratbone!

11.2) Ratbone is stabbing Cain like crazy with the antler weapon, stabbing him over and over again in the chest. Cain just stands there, taking it. Ratbone is holding the weapon like one would hold a butcher knife and stabbing downwards with it.

  RATBONE: RRRRRGGGGGHH!!!

11.3) Cain punches Ratbone hard in the throat. Ratbone's eyes go wide as all the breath suddenly goes out of him.

  RATBONE: HUGGH

11.4) Cain is calmly pulling the antler weapon out of his own ruined bloody chest, eyes blazing, glaring at Ratbone.

Page Twelve
Five Panels

12.1) Cain stabs Ratbone in the face with the antler weapon. I picture this weapon as something like a sai, but made of gnarled multi-pronged animal antler. So there's one long crooked knife-life stretch of sharpened antler, with two big prongs coming off the side. All three antler blades stab into Ratbone's face. This can be as bloody and nasty as we want it to be, and since it's our first moment of violence, I think it should be very much "in your face," no pun intended. This antler knife, in Cain's deft hands, tears Ratbone's face to shreds, stabbing in through his nose or mouth and stabbing deep into his brain. Cain isn't holding the weapon like Ratbone did. He's holding it like Raphael from the Teenage Mutant Ninja Turtles holds his sai. Which is totally not the way you're supposed to actually hold a sai, but I think it works for this. Bet you didn't think we'd be getting reference shots from Teenage Mutant Ninja Turtles toys, did you? But here we go:

Except, you know, Cain has five fingers. So there are two fingers on either side of the center blade.

  RATBONE: NNG

12.2) Ratbone falls dead at Cain's feet, his face a bloody tattered mess.

12.3) Tight shot of the antler knife gripped tight in Cain's hand. Just the knife and the hand that's holding it, still with the same grip we talked about in panel 1. We'll be doing shots like this for the next few pages, showing tight shots of Cain's different weapons as he gathers them.

  CAPTION: Antler Knife.

12.4) Everything is still and quiet. The other Bone Boys are all staring at Cain. He stands there, naked, bloody knife in hand, looking around at them. He is surrounded and horribly out-numbered, but he doesn't seem to care.

12.5) Tight on Cain, sneering.

  CAIN: Where's the rest of my shit?

Page Thirteen
Three Panels

13.1) And the fight is on. The Bone Boys swarm at Cain from all sides, swinging their clubs and stabbing with their spears. And one of them is wielding something different: the jawbone of an ass. Like the one Samson wielded in the Bible.

Cain is slashing and stabbing away with his antler knife, cutting the Bone Boys to pieces. These next four pages are one big bloody fight sequence of Cain taking his weapons back, while brutally butchering the Bone Boys. Again, I think we need to go as violent and visceral as we can here. The Bone Boys may be big tough cavemen, but Cain is something different. He's the guy who invented murder, and

since then, he's perfected the act and turned it into an art. He cuts through the Bone Boys with brutal ease.

13.2) Another tight shot of a weapon in Cain's hand. Now it's the jawbone.
       CAPTION: Jawbone of an Ass.

13.3) Cain is swinging the jawbone like a club, caving in a Bone Boy's skull. Teeth and brains go flying. That Bone Boy is holding a big axe with a stone head, which is another one of Cain's stolen weapons.

Page Fourteen
Four Panels

14.1) Tight shot of that stone axe now gripped tight in Cain's hands. It's so big and heavy it requires a two-hand grip.
       CAPTION: Stone Axe.

14.2) Cain fights on, cleaving Bone Boys apart with that heavy stone axe. One of the Bone Boys coming at him is holding two sharpened ribs. Big ribs. Ribs from some large unknown animal. Both sharpened like curved short swords, like scimitars. The Bone Boy holds them awkwardly, not sure how to fight with them.

14.3) Tight on those rib scimitars in Cain's hands.
       CAPTION: Rib Daggers.

14.4) Cain is deftly slicing away with the rib daggers, slicing Bone Boys open. The ground is thick with blood and guts. But more and more Bone Boys keep swarming in at him. One of them is wielding a sword made from the bill of a sawfish. A sword like this:

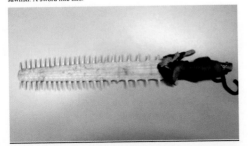

Page Fifteen
Four Panels

15.1) Tight on the sawfish sword in Cain's hand.
       CAPTION: Sawfish Sword.

15.2) Cain is wielding the sawfish sword, whacking a Bone Boy in the neck with it. Blood flies. But there are still more Bone Boys swarming around him. One of them is about to hurl a jagged stone at Cain.

15.3) Tight on some jagged rocks in Cain's hand. Baseball-sized stones that are jagged and edgy.
       CAPTION: Throwing Stones.

15.4) Cain has just hurled one of the stones hard into a Bone Boy's gut, caving his chest in. Other Bone Boys are laid out, with stones stuck in them. One of the Bone Boys who's laid out has tangles of thorns wrapped around his hands.

Page Sixteen
Four Panels

16.1) Tight on Cain's hands wrapped with thorns. Big bloody thorns from some sort of massive gnarly thornbush. Like the crown of thorns that Jesus wore, but wrapped around Cain's fists. Yes, they cut and stab the shit out of him when he wears them. But he doesn't care.

CAPTION: Thorn Fists.

16.2) Cain is punching a Bone Boy right in the face with his thorn covered fist. There aren't many more Bone Boys left standing now. But one of the last ones is swinging a big sword made from a giant animal fang.

16.3) Tight on that sword in Cain's hand, a sword made from the massive tooth of some prehistoric sea monster.

CAPTION: Leviathan Sword.

16.4) Cain is swinging the sword, hacking the last Bone Boy apart.

Pages Seventeen-Eighteen
Two Page Spread, Nine Panels

This is a montage of Cain putting away the various weapons he's just recovered, putting them where they belong inside his fur cloak or belt. He's been carrying this arsenal of weapons for quite a long time, so they all have their own place somewhere on his person. Guera, if it doesn't work to do a small panel for each weapon, you could maybe do three or four panels just showing a few different weapons being put away, with others already in their place.

17.1) Tight on the Leviathan Sword being put away, maybe slid beneath Cain's belt.

17.2) Tight on the Thorn Fists being put away, hanging from his belt or shoulder strap.

17.3) Tight on the Throwing Stones being put away, being dropped into a pouch.

17.4) Tight on the Sawfish Sword being put away, maybe hanging from a loop inside his cloak.

17.5) Tight on the Rib Daggers being put away inside his cloak.

17.6) Tight on the Stone Axe being put away, maybe hanging from his back.

17.7) Tight on the Jawbone being put away inside his cloak.

17.8) Tight on the Antler Knife being put away inside his cloak.

17.9) Big panel. Cain has recovered not only his weapons, but his clothes as well. He's fully dressed now, in furs and animals hides, with all his weapons put away where they belong. He's coming toward us, gnawing on a chunk of roasted meat. The Bone Boys are laid out in heaps all around him, all around the fire. All of them. All dead. And the wounds on Cain's chest that he got back on page 11 are now almost completely healed.

Page Nineteen
Five Panels

19.1) Cain is walking out from the fire hole, tossing the gnawed bone away. The one-armed kid from the opening scene stands there, watching him come out.

19.2) Tight on the kid, staring in shock.

KID: Fuck.

KID: You killed the Bone Boys.

KID: All of 'em.

KID: Fuck.

19.3) Cain stops, looking over at the kid.

CAIN: You should leave this place, kid. Without your warriors, your group will tear itself apart. It won't be safe here.

19.4) Cain and the kid face one another.

KID: Where is it safe?

CAIN: Nowhere. Nowhere I've ever seen. But you still should leave.

19.5) Tight on the kid, full of fear and desperation.

KID: Can I come with you?

Page Twenty
Four Panels

20.1) Tight on Cain, his face hard and emotionless.

CAIN: No.

20.2) Cain turns away, leaving.

20.3) The kid stands there in the village, looking sad, watching Cain go.

20.4) Cain is walking off into the desert, into the sunset.

NARRATION: I had a family once.

NARRATION: It didn't work out.

Page Twenty-One
Four Panels

21.1) Later. Night is coming on. Cain is walking through the middle of nowhere, through the barren desert.

21.2) Cain is walking between piles of human bones. Heaps of them. He doesn't even seem to notice. It's nothing he hasn't seen before, more times than he can count.
NARRATION: My parents were born into paradise.

21.3) He walks on, past wild dogs, who peer out at him from amidst the piles of bones, snarling, eyes glowing.
NARRATION: A place without want. Without death.
NARRATION: A garden they could live in for all eternity.

21.4) He walks on, past vultures feasting on dead men.
NARRATION: It took them about two weeks to get themselves kicked out.

Page Twenty-Two
Four Panels

22.1) He walks on. Tight on him stepping across a ground littered with human skulls.
NARRATION: That's about when my brother and I came along.

22.2) He walks on, past a burned forest full of dead, blackened trees, with fires still burning in places.
NARRATION: Life was hard in those days, but the world was still a tranquil place.
NARRATION: Bountiful.

22.3) He walks on, across a dry river bed, scattered with fish skeletons.
NARRATION: Immaculate.

22.4) Tight on him, walking on, through a harsh desert wind.
NARRATION: And we were a family. We had each other. We had all we needed.
NARRATION: If only I could've been content with that. If only I hadn't gotten so goddamn angry.

Page Twenty-Three
Four Panels

23.1) Pull way back. He walks on through the dark and empty desert. There are no signs of civilization for as far as the eye can see. All we see is more desert and then mountains and an erupting volcano far in the distance.
NARRATION: My brother was always an asshole.
NARRATION: The first two children born into the world and we couldn't fucking stand each other.
NARRATION: That alone ought to tell you how fucked we all are.

23.2) Cain walks on, not seeming to notice that there's a snake right in his path, hissing, about to strike at him.
NARRATION: One day the bastard went and made me so angry, I did something no one had ever done before.

23.3) Cain steps right on the snake.
NARRATION: I killed him.

23.4) Cain walks on. Behind him, the snake is wriggling and writhing, its guts oozing out from where it was stepped on.
NARRATION: Since then, well… things have kind of gone to hell.

Page Twenty-Four
Four Panels

24.1) Cain is climbing up a rocky cliff face.
NARRATION: And I've been here for every last damn second of it.
NARRATION: And unless God suddenly decides to stop being a cunt, I don't expect that to change any time soon.

24.2) He climbs higher. The sky is dark and stormy, like maybe a thunderstorm is coming soon.
NARRATION: My name is Cain. The man who invented murder. The man who cannot die.

24.3) Cain is climbing up to the top of the cliff.
NARRATION: I have walked this wretched pile of shit we call a world for 1500 years.
NARRATION: I have cursed God every way he can be cursed, including to his face.

24.4) He's climbing up onto the ground, as a big shadow falls across him.
NARRATION: I have slain every manner of man or beast that has ever drawn breath.
NARRATION: And I am still searching for something, for anything, that can finally end my curse.

Pages Twenty-Five - Twenty-Six
Two Page Splash

Cain stands his ground, looking up at a giant dinosaur that looms over him, maybe a big roaring T-Rex. Lightning splits the sky.

NARRATION: Searching for something that can kill me.

NARRATION: Something I haven't found yet.

Page Twenty-Seven
Four Panels

27.1)   Cut back to the same shit pond from our opening scene. The one-armed kid is sitting there, poking a dead animal with a stick, looking bored. It's night.

27.2)   The kid looks up with a start.

SON (from off):   What place is this?

27.3)   Three big burly bearded men with iron axes slung over their shoulders and torches in their hands are walking up out of nowhere, tromping through the muck and looking around in disgust at the scenery. These are the Sons of Noah. Shem, Ham and Japheth. The kid stands up, gawking at them.

KID: This is the shit pond. Who the fuck are you?

SON #1:   Are these the only trees around here? They're barely worth the trouble.

SON #2:   You know what father says. We're liable to need them all.

27.4)   The kid is clutching his stick like a weapon, glaring fearfully at the men. But they're walking past, not even seeming to notice him.

KID: You… you better just move along. I'm… I'm the head of the Bone Boys… and we don't want no…

Page Twenty-Eight
Five Panels

28.1)   One of the Sons roughly grabs the kid by the hair.

SON #1:   We'll find a cage for this one at the end of the caravan. He smells of excrement.

SON #2:   The whole world smells of excrement, brother.

28.2)   One of the Sons begins chopping at a tree.

SON #2:   But not for long.

28.3)   One of the Sons is walking toward the village, torch in one hand, axe in the other. The villagers flee from him in fear.

28.4)   One Son is still holding the kid by the hair, as someone else comes walking up. The kid gawks at the figure in terror.

NOAH (from off):   What blessings has the Lord delivered unto us today, my sons?

SON: Not much, father. Another village of heathens and simpletons. They've defiled their own water hole.

28.5)   A beefy hand reaches in to gently touch the boy's face. There are iron rings on the fingers. The kid tries to squirm away, but he can't.

NOAH (from off):   Water would be nice, but wood and flesh are just as necessary.

NOAH (from off):   Tell me, my dear boy…

Pages Twenty-Nine - Thirty
Two Page Splash

Full reveal on Noah, grinning down at us, big axe in hand. Behind him, we see his caravan weaving its way toward us. There are wheeled carts being pulled by strange animals. On the carts are cages filled with other strange animals. All manner of animals. Some we recognize. Some we don't. And people. People in cages and people in chains. Ragged and starving and half-naked people. Chain gangs of enslaved humans staggering along, flanked by guards in crude armor armed with iron swords and carrying torches. And then there are carts loaded with trees. Lots and lots of trees. The caravan extends into the distance, as far as we can see.

NOAH: What **animals** have you here?

CAPTION: **Noah.**

CAPTION: Lumberjack. Trapper. Ship builder.

CAPTION: Man of God.

THE GODDAMNED

next book
The Virgin Brides

> THERE WERE GIANTS IN
> THE EARTH IN THOSE DAYS.
>
> GENESIS 6:4